MALCOLM MUGGERIDGE

A LIFE

MALCOLM MUGGERIDGE
A LIFE

by

IAN HUNTER

Thomas Nelson Publishers
Nashville

Cover photograph courtesy of the Evangelical Broadcasting Company of Holland. Used by permission.

The publisher and author wish to thank Claud Cockburn for permission to quote from his autobiography, *I Claud* (Penguin Books, London).

Library of Congress Cataloging in Publication Data

Hunter, Ian, 1945-
  Malcolm Muggeridge, a life.

  Bibliography: p. 257
  Includes index.
  1. Muggeridge, Malcolm, 1903-   —Biography.
2. Authors, English—20th century—Biography.
3. Christian biography—England. I. Title.
PR6025.U5Z68   070'.92'4   [B]   80-17074
ISBN   0-8407-4084-0

To Alec Vidler
whose company I miss

CONTENTS

INTRODUCTION

Any satisfying biography must have its roots in a deep and varied life. Malcolm Muggeridge's life has been that. He has been at the center of many of the important events of this troubled, fascinating century. He has written about them—and how he has written!—in dispatches, editorials, essays, social history, biography, fiction, and autobiography. He has spoken about them in lecture halls and on radio and television. He has participated in more than a few; some he even has precipitated.

I first conceived this book more as a study of his writing than of his life. However, it quickly became apparent that none of his writings, including the novels, can be separated from his life. So my plan altered, and the book became more overtly biographical. Of course, there is always a danger of falling between two stools; of being inadequately detailed for biography, and inadequately searching to say anything very useful about his writing and thought. Whether or not this danger has been averted is for others to judge. It was recognized.

Even more acutely recognized was the danger of hagiography. I admire Malcolm Muggeridge; I have passed some of the most pleasurable hours of my life in his company; I have learned more from him than from any other human being. Despite this, I can say with total honesty that while writing I was conscious of no inhibition, no obligations of fealty, no loyalty dues. Perhaps in light of his past kindnesses to me I ought to have been, but I was not. If admiration and affection for one's subject disqualified a biographer, the field would be much impoverished. Not only would there be fewer biographies (no bad thing in itself), but many of the best and best-loved classics of the genre, preeminently Boswell's immortal life of Johnson, would be lost.

My profession is the law. I have tried to be suspicious of an exculpatory explanation or a self-serving answer, and instead have attempted to arrive at conclusions after sifting and weighing the evidence. My brief has been to present the evidence, not to make a defense. Whether the verdict be for or against the subject, I have tried to base it on the evidence.

The biographer's art is an exercise in arrogance. It assumes that a man's hidden thoughts and desires, his motives and aspirations, his works and opinions, can be unraveled and critically assessed through an examination of his life and writings. Words, just clumsy, inadequate words laid beside one another on flat paper, attempt to breathe life into their subject and—even more audaciously—to impart a measure of coherence and unity to that welter of chaotic events and emotions that make up the strange adventure of each human life.

Arrogance is compounded with folly when one essays to write of a writer, at least of one so practiced and flexible as Malcolm Muggeridge; as though a vaudeville hoofer should attempt to dance Nureyev, or a man who sings in the shower to serenade Pavarotti, or a keyboard basher to play Rubenstein. Muggeridge is a consummate artisan of words who, through half a century of practicing journalism, has had the opportunity and the inclination to tell his own story. He has expressed his views on practically everything, and in two volumes of autobiography has revealed those aspects of his private life he regards as properly in the public domain. What justification is there then for a raw apprentice to pass judgment on a master craftsman, to take the measure of a skill I admire but cannot emulate, and perhaps cavalierly to recast the boundary between private life and public curiosity?

Beyond pointing out that there has been no assessment of Muggeridge's life and writing except his own and that biography and *auto*biography are two very different things, I concede that I have no wholly satisfactory answer. What I can say is that almost from the first occasion when I became interested in Malcolm Muggeridge and his, to me, startling and illuminating views, I decided at some time I must write about him, even if only for the therapeutic purpose of sorting out why I find him so intriguing. For several years I tracked down his early articles and out-of-print books. A selection of these were published in *Things Past* in 1978, an anthology with a discernibly biographical strain. Even so, I was dissatisfied; all very well to search out what Muggeridge has thought and written about himself, but what do I think of the man and his life?

Motivation and opportunity combined when Muggeridge and I decided to swap houses so that I could spend a sabbatical year at his beloved Park Cottage in Sussex, while he fulfilled a rash commitment to be a teaching visitor in the School of Journalism at Western University in Canada. So, for a year, I sat in his study, surrounded by his books and those few mementoes he keeps—the most treasured, I should guess, a faded picture of Hugh Kingsmill, his arms pumping as he strode along for one of those leisurely afternoons of talk and laughter that Muggeridge once called "half the joy of living." Day after day, I looked out across the yard and garden, away to the rolling Sussex countryside flecked with sheep, or I tramped through the adjacent hop fields over which I had temporarily inherited his special walking rights, and pondered Malcolm Muggeridge, a strange man and his strange, compelling views. This book is the result.

It is customary to conclude by acknowledging that all errors are one's own and all virtues the legacy of those who assisted. The former acknowledgement I readily make—and ask absolution in advance.

I benefited enormously from the advice and assistance of Gordon Blelloch, Christopher Booker, Jeremy Murray-Brown, Peter Chafer, Pat Ferns, Michael Holroyd, Leslie Illingworth, Richard Ingrams, Lord and Lady Longford, and Douglas, Eric, Jack, Leonard, John, and Anne Muggeridge. Dr. Alec Vidler deserves separate mention, for without his encouragement, I would have lacked the courage to begin and the perseverance to complete this book. Joyce Coghill once again prepared a manuscript for me with unfailing skill and dedication.

My greatest debt is to the one who is the subject of these labors.

Ian Hunter
London, Ontario
1979

·1·
STRANGER

The first thing I remember about the world—and I pray it may be the last—is that I was a stranger in it. This feeling, which everyone has in some degree, and which is, at once, the glory and the desolation of homo sapiens, provides the only thread of consistency that I can detect in my life.

Malcolm Muggeridge, *Apologia pro vita sua*, 1968

* * *

"Mr. Muggeridge is a writer of merit, his writing being characterized by a persuasive eloquence, apt quotation, and illuminating bursts of humour."

This would be an apt description of Malcolm Muggeridge. It is, however, a description of his father, Henry Thomas Muggeridge, from the *Croydon Advertiser* of 1930. No other influence, at least in his early years, was half as significant as that of his father. Self-taught, restless, dogmatic, demanding, zealous, resilient—all these qualities of H. T. Muggeridge are reflected in his son.

Henry Thomas Muggeridge was born in Croydon on June 28, 1864, the eldest son in a large family. Malcolm's grandfather, Henry Ambrose Muggeridge, was an undertaker who deserted his family when H. T. was twelve years old. His grandmother supported them from the meager earnings of a second-hand furniture shop on the High Street, Penge. To make ends meet, H. T. was obliged to leave school and go to work. Among his papers is a faded card.

> Penge National Schools: This is to certify that H. Muggeridge has attended the above schools 377 times during the year ending April 30, 1878; and that he passed a satisfactory examination before Her Majesty's Inspector in the VII Standard.
>
> Rev. D. McAnally, Vicar

It was the only diploma H. T. would ever receive. From the age of thirteen, he once told Malcolm, he always had people dependent on him. He seldom complained, though, because he said that a man who becomes conscious of a past injustice is apt to be conscious of little else.

H. T. started work as an office boy at MacIntyre, Hogg, Marsh and Company, a London firm of shirt manufacturers. Unlike Malcolm, who has kicked in the teeth practically every employer with whom he has been associated, his father loyally remained with the shirt firm until his retirement, finishing up with the title of company secretary. His duties consisted of what today would be considered accounting, and these he performed hunched over a rolltop desk covered with a black oilcloth, seated on a tall stool in an office sealed off by glass partitions from the surrounding litter of picked over shirt boxes. His handwriting was small and perfectly formed, and he would write his entries in the ledger so that anyone could read them; when he made a mistake, he would painstakingly eliminate the blot using a specially sharpened penknife to scratch it out. When he had filled one ledger he began another, and the old ledger was stored away in a safe, standing next to other ledgers until, after a prescribed number of years, it was taken out and sold as waste paper or used as wrapping paper for shirt boxes.

Each morning H. T. set out by train for the office on New Basinghall Street. At that time the office was still equipped with a uniformed commissionaire who, like Saint Peter, could grant or deny admission at the gates. In the evening he would return on the 6:05, London Bridge to Croydon East, where young Malcolm would often wait, like any expectant son anxious lest his father not show up, then rushing forward at the first glimpse of the familiar face: "There is no face except Kitty's that I have ever picked out with such joyous relief as his, leading the field up the slope from the arrival platform. . . ."[1]

H. T. was a small man (which he attributed to being undernourished as a child) with a large, bulbous nose (which all his sons have inherited), and a goatee and whiskers, sometimes neatly clipped, at other times tending to be scrubby and unkempt. He was certainly not a handsome man, yet distinctive, with a face of character rather than beauty.

Malcolm's mother, Annie Booler, came from Sheffield, one of the younger children in a large, working-class family. She was two years younger than her husband whom she met on holidays on the Isle of Man. They were married in 1883, and their union was to prove lasting and relatively tranquil. H. T. was not an impulsive man; he studied and weighed alternatives carefully before arriving at a considered decision, and presumably marriage was no exception. Once having committed himself, he exhibited dogged fidelity—to his wife, to his employer, to his principles.

His political activities necessitated frequent evenings away from home, and Annie occasionally harbored dark suspicions as to his whereabouts and doings. There is no evidence to suggest that her suspicions were in any way justified. Certainly, H. T. had a sensual disposition, something he passed on to his sons, and one that may well have craved satisfaction outside of marriage. But since he never forgave his own father for the womanizing that had contributed to the breakup of his parents' marriage, it is most unlikely that he similarly put his own marriage at risk. Also, he was a man of iron self-discipline. What his wife really resented was that he had a fuller life than she—attending meetings, debating, dining out with influential people—while she was housebound.

Nevertheless, her doubts remained and led to bitter recriminations; also, she developed an elaborate belief that a neighbor's maid was habitually disporting herself in an attic window so as to divert H. T.'s attention from his gardening to the more intriguing parts of her anatomy. So real did this notion become that Annie would flit about from window to window, peering out from behind the curtains, trying to catch the seductress *engagé*.

Despite such minor strains, the marriage wore time well. As youthful passions cooled, both found that unconscious familiarity in each other's company that is the key to all enduring unions. Undoubtedly in tribute to Annie, H. T. copied into his diary some words written by a blind German naturalist named Huber who had rejoiced in his blindness because it demonstrated to him the depths of his wife's love: ". . . to me my wife is always young, fresh, and pretty, which is no light matter."

For her part, Annie was just the kind of wife H. T. needed. Her qualities exactly complemented his. She was practical; he was theoretical and idealistic. He would set right social systems and nations; she would solve the problems of a bustling household. She liked to look after him, taking care to see that he wore the right thickness of underwear at different seasons, that his black coat was clean and brushed when he set off for the city, and that his socks and shirts were properly darned. Also, she imparted a measure of order to his life that the demands of political causes would have otherwise precluded.

H. T. occasionally spoke of Annie in a patronizing way, which, in light of her loyalty to him, was unfortunate. In a letter to an acquaintance in 1926, he wrote: "Annie is still living in the world of simple love for those who the Great Father has given her. She has no introspections, no doubts, no ambitions—except perhaps still to look beautiful, and is,

I think, to be envied."[2] When, in his fifties, he took up bowls, she would go along to the recreation ground each Saturday afternoon and there pass the hours knitting until it came time to return. She was with him when he died in 1942. Annie lived on for twelve years but never fully adjusted to life without him. "The bed in which they had slept side by side through so many nights had two hollows in it; with the other unoccupied, my mother lay disconsolately in hers."[3]

From early youth, H. T. was attracted to politics, not, it appears, through any self-serving ambition to exercise power, but because he was genuinely sympathetic to human suffering and anxious to alleviate it. For a brief time he was associated with the Liberal party, typically in a campaign to obtain a free borough library. Libraries meant education, and to him education was man's great hope for the future, a way to civilize base instincts and elevate one's vision. As a young man, H. T. belonged to what was called a Mutual Improvement Society, as well as to a literary and debating club connected with a Baptist chapel. He defined education as "everything that helps to appreciate truth, beauty and goodness," and he labored continuously to educate himself, reading voraciously, and teaching himself French and music. He had little innate musical aptitude; he just bashed away at the piano determinedly, more often than not playing "The Flying Dutchman," which had some unexplained attraction for him, his eyes riveted on the sheet music and his pipe clenched firmly between his teeth. For seventeen years he served on a Labour party adult education committee, and he was involved in the affairs of Ruskin Hall, an adult education center in Croydon. Had he lived, he could well have become one of the Labour peers his son never misses an opportunity to lampoon, appearing on some earnest television panel to advocate "not just more, but *better* education" as the answer to all of society's ills. What, one wonders, would H. T. make of a visit to a burgeoning campus today, with its degree programs in astrology, sport, film, and dance, and its students found not in the library but grouped intently around pinball machines in the recreation center?

By 1882, H. T. had become a Socialist, a member of the Fabian Society and, later, of the International Labour party. From then on so much of his time was devoted to political activities that he would frequently remark how he earned his living in a fit of abstraction of mind. In his diary he noted Ben Franklin's observation that leisure was the time for doing something useful. MacIntyre, Hogg, Marsh, et al, good Tories to a man, would undoubtedly have sacked him had he not proved so conscientious and valuable an employee. As it was, political involvements were later to cost him a seat on the company's board of directors.

H. T. practiced socialism as well as preached it. He was always fair game for a hard luck story, ready to dig into his pocket and help out. This fact alone distinguished him from some of his more affluent Fabian friends whose commitment to melioration stopped short of personal charity. He lived abstemiously and exhibited little interest in acquiring possessions or wealth—not that he could have acquired them had he wanted to since his income never reached £1000 per year. "In a world given over to the worship of money" he would say with a wry smile, "I am an infidel." Still, the family lived adequately on his unlavish but steady income.

H. T. had a strong element of Don Quixote in his makeup, something he passed on to all his sons, but most notably to Malcolm. He always identified with the underdog and was liable to mount a forlorn campaign on behalf of some issue or cause already hopelessly lost. Too shrewd to be a simple do-gooder, not exactly naive (he liked to quote Ignazio Silone's observation that credulity is the only raw material that no country need import), he was a curious mixture of qualities; selfless, loyal, and honest, yet somehow deluded by the vanity of ideas—a vanity even more dangerous than that of the ego. Theories that did not correspond with reality rattled about in his head; facts he had mastered, but not truth; literature he had read, often patiently committed to memory, but not comprehended; good causes and goodness were not distinguished; he was a man who saw with, not through, the eye and, as William Blake said must inevitably happen, thus came to believe in lies.

Debate was one of his favorite activities, and he excelled at it. Remembering H. T. in his prime, a retired vicar wrote: "I used to listen spellbound as the argument went to and fro between Mr. Muggeridge and his tormenting opponents. I did not understand a word of the political theory he enunciated, but I was fascinated by his words."[4] He was uncowed by being unpopular, always ready to mutiny against what John Stuart Mill (one of his favorite authors) called "the tyranny of prevailing opinion," or in contemporary jargon "the consensus." From a soapbox he would declaim unfashionable views, most notably his pro-Boer advocacy that on one occasion at Duppas Hill led to his being physically assaulted by the enraged audience so that he finally had to be rescued by police. Of all the qualities that Malcolm inherited from his father, it was iconoclasm, this willingness to swim against the tide, that was most significant. There were few things in life more intrinsically abhorrent to father or to son than to find themselves in agreement with the majority of their fellow human beings.

It was more as an imparter of ideas, a teacher rather than a father, that H. T. affected his sons. He read to them when they were children, and as they grew older, he encouraged them to read and think and express their thoughts; but he was too preoccupied with campaigns and political stratagems to be a close personal presence in their lives. He kept up a hectic pace of activities and was given to wistfully quoting Matthew Arnold's lines about

> ". . . that lull in the hot race,
> Wherein he doth forever chase
> That flying and elusive shadow, rest."

He was never close enough to his sons, at least to Malcolm, to be looked on as a confidant, someone to be gone to with intimate, personal difficulties. For example, he never discussed with any of his boys what in those days were decorously called the "facts of life"; not that he wouldn't have done so had they asked, but his mind was preoccupied with other matters, his attention otherwise engaged. Those who traffic in universal betterment frequently overlook requirements and concerns of individuals, even of their own offspring. So, while H. T. introduced Malcolm to literature and ideas, and in his disdain for public opinion could be said to have served as an early role model, he had only a minimal effect on Malcolm's developing character and morals. The father shaped the boy's ideas but not his temperament. Malcolm loved his father and respected his integrity, tenacity, and lack of malice—this comes through clearly in his memoirs. But there is scant evidence of much real intimacy or tenderness between them.

It was left largely to his mother to supply sustenance, physical and emotional. Physical sustenance took the form of "good grub" that she believed, with implacable conviction, produced strong, healthy, and decent boys. She ran a frugal household with a firm, fair hand, brooking little interference; and she retained control even after the boys had grown up and left home. On a vacation from Cambridge, Malcolm complained to a friend: "If I put my legs on a chair, I get ticked off by my mater, if I drop tobacco ash, I ditto—I think you lose half the joy of smoking if you use an ash tray, don't you?"[5]

Annie was not a demonstrative woman, nor did she articulate her love. Her sons had to derive emotional sustenance simply from her presence. She was always there, white-haired and benign. The home environment was overwhelmingly masculine, yet she never made the mistake so many women thus situated do of trying to feign masculine interests in order to be closer to her children. Instead she remained aloof, able to praise, reprove, or chastise equally. Actually, because of her husband's frequent absences, physical discipline fell more and more to her eldest son, Douglas, whose lenient disposition ill-suited him to this task.

Thomas Malcolm Muggeridge ("my impossible name") was the third son, born on March 24, 1903. His parents were slightly disappointed that their hopes for a daughter had been dashed again. Malcolm's birth coincided with the appearance of George Bernard Shaw's *Man and Superman*, and H. T. liked to say that he had edited the publication of a superman.

At three months, Malcolm won his first and only beauty prize in a contest sponsored by Mellins' baby foods. The transition from cherub to *enfant terrible* was gradual. Exceptional promise must have been evident early; on September 21, 1905, H. T. wrote to his brother, Percy: "I have now three youngsters. Little Malcolm, who is now two and a half, is the youngest and we think the most promising of them all."

Two more sons followed, and the presence of five brothers ensured a competitive, rambunctious environment; "those dreadful Muggeridge boys" they were called in the neighborhood. Ingenuity and thrift were two qualities Malcolm exhibited early on, both likely to have been derived from his mother. His brother, Stanley, once offered him five shillings to walk on his hands and knees from The Red Lion to The White Horse, two Croydon pubs about a quarter of a mile apart. On all fours, Malcolm crawled along so convincingly pretending to be looking for a lost coin that he not only won the bet but quite failed to excite any curiosity. On another occasion, he accompanied two of his brothers on a boating expedition. After a picnic and a lazy afternoon, he tried to shove off and, in the process, fell in the water soaking his clothes. His brothers undressed him, wrapped him in the picnic blanket, and gave him ten shillings (a great sum to them) to go home by taxi. On arrival at the railway station, they were astonished to find Malcolm waiting—still occasionally dripping under the blanket and perfectly content to incur public stares to make ten shillings. His brothers chose separate seats on the train and exhibited no fraternal ties, but they were sporting enough to allow him to keep the money.

Few things are more tedious and exasperating than biographies that construct elaborate theoretical edifices on trivial childhood foundations. Yet both of these incidents illustrate, in a small way, Malcolm's iconoclasm, his independent mind, and his willingness to look silly in order to attain a desired end. He has always been ready to play the fool. In one of his first published articles, he pleaded for a return to the Feast of Fools that the medieval church celebrated.[6] (It is often forgotten that Shakespeare's fools not only have the best lines but usually exhibit greater wisdom than all other players. It is the clown who brings the curtain down; a Cervantes, not a Rousseau or Marx or Freud, who writes the last chapter.)

Malcolm's earliest childhood memory is of feeling estranged, of being a stranger, a sojourner rather than a citizen in the world. Psychologists might fish about for explanations based on maternal deprivation or peer rejection or whatever, but these strivings for meaning are mostly nonsense. Such a feeling is not uncommon among those of spiritual temperament—those who feel, often from a very early age, that here we have no continuing city.

> Just walking along the road we lived in when I was a child, I would find myself wondering, with a poignancy I find it difficult now to convey, who I was and how I came to be in that place. As though it were a foreign land and I a stranger, knowing no one and unable to speak the language.[7]

There has always been a theatrical side to Muggeridge. He is a ham, sometimes unconsciously. As a boy, he and his brothers enjoyed acting. They frequently staged plays, or important scenes from a play, devising props from whatever a suburban Croydon home would yield. The audience consisted of parents and those neighbors that could be readily dragooned. Malcolm particularly enjoyed playing ghosts, delivering whatever lines ghosts have with considerable conviction and gusto. Once, playing Banquo's ghost, the performance was cut short by his mother's insistence that he immediately return her best white sheet to its proper place. At school he was active in the drama club and is remembered for a spirited performance as Sir Andrew Aguecheek in *Twelfth Night*.

He has written of a recurrent dream in which he is on stage when, to his horror, he realizes that he has learned the lines from a different play. As the audience begins to hiss and shout, he freezes and can think of nothing to do but to go on speaking the only lines he knows. The theatrical motif of this little parable is revealing. Fifty years after his ghost performances, Jonathan Miller cast Muggeridge as the Gryphon in a television version of *Alice in Wonderland*, leading Geoffrey Moorhouse, *The Guardian's* theater critic, to write: "Mr. Muggeridge's whole life has been leading up to the evening when he would dance a dab-toed quadrille before a carefully prepared audience, against a sky of gathering gloom."[8]

His first school, just around the corner from the Muggeridge home, was run by two sisters (fittingly named Monday) who endeavored, without much success except in letters, to inculcate the rudiments of knowledge. At mathematics, he was particularly hopeless. "An inability to apply myself to anything which did not interest me manifested itself at an early stage, and has, alas, never been overcome."

At the age of twelve, he won a scholarship to the Borough Secondary School (later to become Selhurst Grammar School). The examiner was the local inspector of schools, a Scotsman with a large mane of white hair. Malcolm was full of righteous indignation when word began to filter back that his success in the scholarship examination was attributable to the inspector's desire to ingratiate himself with H. T., then a Labour councillor and an active member of the local education committee. "I hope this malignant suggestion was baseless, but honesty compels me to admit that this was the only examination in which I ever achieved any success."[9]

At Selhurst he excelled in English but little else. His extracurricular activities involved drama and the debating club, and he was a Sergeant-Major in the cadet corps. One contemporary recalled him as "a bit of a chump"; another as ". . . an odd fellow . . . an emotional person and frightfully excitable"; yet another as "very verbose and self-assured . . . He certainly loved the limelight."[10] A common memory was of the headmaster wearily repeating, "That will be quite enough from you, Muggeridge. Be *quiet*, Muggeridge. Sit *down*, Muggeridge."

Few families escaped the disruption of 1914. Against their father's wishes, Malcolm's two older brothers joined up. He was too young to participate but old enough to feel keen disappointment at missing out on the grand adventure. As it happened, his chance was still to come. For now, he endured the local elementary and secondary schools with benign indifference. Half a century later, in the course of making a BBC film about his childhood, he visibly disconcerted the headmaster at his old school by telling the students: "School in my day was a place to get away from as soon as possible and for as long as possible. Everything exciting, mysterious, adventurous, happened outside its confines, not within them."[11]

What he learned that mattered came from his father and from his own reading and writing. Words were his passion. "There was nothing else I ever wanted to do except use them, no other accomplishment or achievement I ever had the slightest regard for, or desire to emulate. I have always loved words, and still love them, for their own sake. For the power and beauty of them; for the wonderful things that can be done with them."[12] On his eighth birthday, he had received a toy printing set that he put to immediate use. His very first story is no longer extant, but he has recalled it.

It was a story of a train going along very fast and, to the satisfaction of the passengers, racing through the small stations along the track without stopping. Their satisfaction, however, turned to dismay, and then to panic fury, as it dawned on them that it was not going to stop at *their* station either when it came to them. They raged and shouted and shook their fists, but all to no avail. The train went roaring on. At the time I had no notion what, if anything, the story signified. It just came into my mind, and the rubber letters dropped into place of themselves. Yet, as I came to see it, and see now more clearly than ever, it is the story I have been writing ever since; the story of our time.[13]

Of all his childhood experiences, none made a more vivid or lasting impression than those occasions when he accompanied his father to a market in Surrey Street where H. T. would mount a soapbox and, against a gathering night sky, preach socialism to a shifting, disinterested crowd of passersby. Standing thus alone and isolated, his father seemed a heroic figure; his voice that of a prophet calling the people to cast off the economic chains that held them in servitude to property and capital and to venture forward to a land of milk and honey. Laughing at his jokes ("the government says it is interested in ships; well I am interested in ships, too—*hardships*"), applauding his witty repartee, intoxicated by his oratory, Malcolm could almost glimpse the New Jerusalem which would be ushered in by nationalization, cooperatives, equitable taxation, and local grants for housing, health, and the safety of school children.

The Muggeridge home, at 17 Birdhurst Gardens, was a frequent meeting place for the socialist intelligentsia of the day. Ramsay MacDonald came on occasion, as did Philip Snowden, Hugh Dalton, the ineffable Webbs, and, once, H. G. Wells. There they would gather, the men lighting up pipes, the women smoothing down their skirts or hitching up their trousers, and after clearing their high-pitched, reedy voices, they would proceed self-assuredly to set the world aright. For H. T. these were golden moments, talking things over in a civilized way with what were, to him, the finest flowers of his generation. Even when they occasionally treated H. T. condescendingly (as when, after Malcolm married her niece, Beatrice Webb wrote to her sister that H. T. was "a very worthy person, though of modest means"), well, that was a small price to pay for consorting in such company. To Malcolm it seemed that H. T. lacked a certain dignity, became a bit servile on those occasions; looking back, he attributed this to a kind of "raw sincerity" that prevented H. T., unlike most of the others, from later "selling out to the Establishment."[14]

Curled up on a corner divan that was covered in red damask, Malcolm would remain mute, fearful of being sent off to bed. Immobile, avoiding attention, but what passions seethed within him! Like an impressionable novitiate stumbling upon venerable fathers speaking in tongues, he listened with a kind of reverential awe to the babble of voices, the dialectical logic, the irresistible conclusions, the glorious visions. This was life and learning. He accepted, with unquestioning faith, the picture of a humane, equalitarian society based on communal service rather than individual greed—to be brought about by these very people seated in his own living room and supported by all men of intelligence and goodwill who would hearken to their call. Great names invoked: Plato ("Of course, my dear Jordan, what is the *Republic* but an early socialist blueprint . . ."), Ruskin, Tawney, William Morris, Edward Bellamy; it might even be Jesus, but always as a rebel, a champion of the downtrodden and oppressed, a friend of the poor, and an enemy of the money changers. The talk would go on all evening, often into the early hours of the morning. If H. T. happened to inject a good line, it was a special thrill. When his guests had gone and Malcolm had long since been discovered and sent to bed, H. T. would carefully preserve his contribution in his diary, writing with his fastidious handwriting and carefully dating the entry: "The Conservative is very useful—when you have brought about fundamental reforms, he takes care of them for you. Self. 8.7.26." Through it all Annie would knit, or just doze in her folding chair, now and then jerking awake to make some incongruous remark; as once when H. T. had demonstrated how a new social program would cost only half a crown on taxation, she suddenly came to and blurted out: "Yes, and you owe me half a crown for the greengrocer."

H. T. professed to be an atheist, but really he was a born believer. His creed was socialism. Just beneath the surface, away from public scrutiny, ran currents of religious belief as well. He came from the chapel and believed in God, at least in the sense of an animating spirit behind the universe. His diary contains numerous illustrations of this. One entry, on February 22, 1928, manages to ally God with his resentment at private property; he had been walking at Reigate Hill when he saw a plaque explaining that walkers were indebted to Sir Jeremiah Coleman for permission to walk through these grounds: "Indebted to Jeremiah Coleman, not to God. Had that worthy chosen he could, of course, have put a high wall around it and reserved the beautiful view for himself or for those to whom he chose to sell the land. Sir Jeremiah Coleman thus stands between men and their creator. . . . While I wrote this a robin redbreast, with the utmost assurance, came and sat beside me. He looked out of the corner of his sharp eye at me with curiosity and friendliness as though he would like to talk about the scene. He, at least, had no intermediary between him and the enjoyment of God's work."

As he got older, H. T.'s references to God became more personal. He also appeared to have developed a notion of accountability and judgment for one's earthly activities. Paradoxically, however, he remained skeptical about immortality: "How can I square the idea of personal immortality with my knowledge of myself?" he wrote.

Just how long Malcolm's belief in socialism lasted is difficult to say. In some of his Cambridge letters he calls himself a radical socialist or "temporary Bolshie," but in others there are undertones of skepticism about all political ideology. After his disillusionment in Russia, he wrote articles that appealed strongly to conservatives, and he was frequently labelled a "neo-conservative" (once by as astute a critic as George Orwell). Still, he had not completely discarded the socialist nostrums he had first heard from his father's soapbox. As late as 1958, *The New Statesman* called him "a man without a faith" but added ". . . on occasion he is capable of outlining a revolutionary programme for the British Labour Party with the wistful air of one who, in different circumstances, would not mind helping to foster it."[15]

Father and son shared a love of getting out of the city to the countryside, bicycling or hiking. It was while cycling that Malcolm had his first conscious, mystical experience.

> I can remember the occasion perfectly. . . . The light of the setting sun slashed the trunks of the trees, so that they were half gilded and half in shadow. Suddenly I realized with a tremendous feeling of exultation that this golden light of the sun, this fragrance of a June evening and light rustle of leaves—the whole glorious scene had some special significance in which I participated. That in its all-embracing beauty it conveyed a oneness, and that to identify oneself with this oneness, and with the spirit animating it and giving it meaning, contained the promise of ecstasy. It was a moment of great illumination. . . . I will not pretend that, bicycling with my father and brothers near Chipstead Church, all, or any, of this came into my mind. At the same time, it marked a sort of turning point; thenceforth wherever I have been, and however dismal my situation or prospect, there has been the never-failing solace of feeling earth below my feet and seeing sky above my head.[16]

Whether this illumination was communicated to his father and brothers, and what their reactions to it might have been, is not recorded. His father might not have been unduly surprised, for such excursions were times of particularly sharp and vivid insight for him too. The incident at Reigate Hill has already been mentioned; even more revealing of H. T.'s dark side is this entry written in his diary while hiking near Chelsham Church on February 24, 1928:

> The sun is glorious; the spot secluded, the birds hail spring, and my heart ought to rejoice. But it doesn't—there is a weight of defeat resting upon it. Mortification arising from self-failure has no such solace as

bereavement has. There is a dignity and completeness about the dead that the living can never even try to reach without being ridiculous. Life is too jagged and crude—too littered with half tried out ideals—it shows us to be means ill-adjusted to ends (except the everlasting reproduction of our imperfect selves) to achieve the rounded wholeness of the dead. Their quiet superiority hurts me.

This bout of depression proved temporary; not only did H. T. continue to be active in municipal politics but, within a year, he was elected as Labour member of parliament for Romford, running on the slogan: "Stand for TRUTH and vote for MUGGERIDGE." In four previous attempts, he had always been defeated by Conservative candidates. At last he had a parliamentary platform from which to declaim. Among the many congratulatory telegrams and letters was one from MacIntyre, Hogg and Marsh expressing pleasure that ". . . You have attained your heart's desire and achieved the result you set out to achieve so many years past." There may even have been a faint sigh of relief on New Basinghall Street now that the company's accounts would be tended by someone whose attention was not forever elsewhere. In any case, amicable arrangements for a leave of absence were made. His moment at last.

H. T. cherished his new initials—M. P. He put them after his name on all correspondence. In the House of Commons, he fought for the removal of "unsightly and malodorous" municipal dumps, raising the school leaving age, and electrification of railways to eliminate ". . . the tortures of the damned in steam trains in which commuters are packed like herrings." He also was instrumental in the passing of the Silicosis and Asbestos Act of 1930.

But his glory was short-lived. Two years later, in October 1931, another election was called. H. T. campaigned hard, even printing and circulating a quaint letter addressed "To the Electors" from his wife; since she barely could write, it is likely that this letter was composed by Malcolm, and it does, in fact, bear some stylistic evidence of his hand.

We have been married for over thirty years, and I have four boys, of whom I am, of course, like all mothers, very proud. My husband has always worked hard for the Labour and Socialist movement. Sometimes, like wives of most public men, I have felt it hard that he had to be so much away from his home, but when I have thought of the work he has done or tried to do for those who suffer from our unjust poverty, I have been reconciled to his absence. . . .

I can only tell you that he is a man who believes what he says, and practises what he preaches. I have found out that the moving spirit of his life is sympathy with the poor, whom he looks upon as the victims of a wrong system of society. I am quite sure, after forty years study of him and his ways, that he will never alter in this respect, and that is why I thought I should like to write to you this simple letter, asking you to use your utmost efforts to get him returned at this election.[17]

Despite his and Annie's best efforts, the tide was running against Labour; H. T. lost badly to a Conservative, W.G.D. Hutchinson. He returned to municipal politics, but his spirit was broken, perhaps less from electoral defeat than from seeing measures he had advocated with such conviction turn sour: nationalization, which he used to call "preventative medicine against the ills of capitalism," leading to more inefficiencies and work stoppages; education producing greater and greater illiteracy and gullibility; justice appealed for but injustice enshrined; higher taxation resulting in greater inequality; freedoms demanded, but new servitudes coming to pass; world peace—a complete illusion. Several diary entries from his later years express a kind of baffled frustration. Also, death begins to appear as a theme of his reflections, occasionally as a premonition; he quoted Pascal: "I know I shall die, but I don't believe it." Although he retained a sense of humor and never became morbid ("If ever I suddenly find myself entering the portal of Heaven, I am sure I should feel there is a catch on it"), his election defeat ended his illusions. At the age of seventy-two, three years before his death, he wrote: "I know at last I am what I am, and not what I have always wanted to be." Perhaps there was more solace in such hard-won self-knowledge than in the grander Utopian dreams of his prime.

At the age of seventeen, Malcolm fell in love. From the moment he met Dora Pitman on a municipal tennis court ". . .the whole of existence for me was concentrated on that one face, uniquely beautiful, as it seemed, and distinct from all other faces."[18] Most of his leisure hours were now spent with her, playing tennis, or going to and from her home in Thornton Heath. In July 1921, he wrote to a friend: "Am fearfully in love with a charming little girl named Dora—she has simply wonderful eyes and writes poetry."[19]

His memoirs are reticent about their physical relationship: "There were, of course, quarrels and angry partings; we exasperated one another with the sexual urges we mutually aroused, and then only partially and inadequately, or not at all, satisfied."[20] Emotionally, the relationship was intense and lasted for several years; in a letter from India in 1926, Malcolm talked vaguely of returning to England and marrying Dora.

Dora inspired his first literary efforts that have survived—love poems. Few writers would choose to be judged by posterity on their adolescent love poetry, and Muggeridge is no exception. At the time he had a vain regard for his verse and considered himself a discriminating judge; when his friend, Alec Vidler, showed him some of his own compositions, Malcolm read them over and then gravely suggested that Vidler stick to prose. Good advice, it turned out, for both of them.

Perhaps mercifully, most of the poetry written to Dora has disappeared. One poem has survived, a penance for using it satirically in *Three Flats,* a play he wrote after his intimacy with Dora was over. Miss Edwards, the Dora of the play, says of the poet: "Oh, he's a dear, but little and old and vague. He writes poems to me and he's romantic. That's why I like him. It's something to have poems written to you even if they're bad ones. So I keep them and sometimes read them over just to cheer myself up."

> Come, let us sleep, beloved, and not waste,
> Our time in idle passion;
> There are a thousand star-lit nights to taste
> Our loves in wild flesh fashion.
>
> Tonight we'll lie like children after play—
> Sprawling in careless grace;
> Your nightdress all in ribbon'd disarray
> Hair uncomb'd round your face.
>
> My man arm loosely thrown across your breast
> Your soft one neath my head—
> Abandon'd to the gentle dreamless rest
> Of a pure passionless bed.
>
> But when you lean'd towards me from far away
> I quite forgot all this,
> And all the words that I had thought to say
> Spoke through one single kiss.

Exactly how the romance with Dora ended is not clear. Muggeridge's memoirs say nothing whatever on the subject. By 1924 he had met Kitty Dobbs, whom he was to marry in 1927. Yet she cannot have immediately captured his affections because Dora continues to figure prominently in his correspondence from India (not always favorably—one letter refers to her "slobbering kisses") while Kitty is never once mentioned. Yet he had scarcely returned from India when his engagement to Kitty was announced.

By chance he met Dora once again years later in an underground shelter during the blitz. He was now a father of four (she had been twice married), and they huddled there side by side, through the night ". . . while outside the world in which we had been youthful lovers crashed and shook and burnt about us."

H. T. longed for Malcolm to become an educated, self-assured, debonair Socialist—to be all that he had hoped to be had fate not driven him out to work at thirteen. To achieve this, no sacrifice was too much. So, despite a desultory academic record at Selhurst Grammar School, Malcolm went up to Selwyn College, Cambridge, in October 1920.

·2·
CAMBRIDGE

The great advantage of the sort of education I had was that it made practically no mark upon those subjected to it.

Malcolm Muggeridge, *The Spectator*, May 13, 1960

* * *

Selwyn College was of comparatively recent origin, founded in 1882, and named in honor of a church dignitary, George Augustus Selwyn. In Muggeridge's time, it had more compulsory chapels than the other Cambridge colleges, but there is no record of Malcolm voicing any objection to this. Selwyn's accommodations and amenities were intended to be austere so as to be within the range of less affluent parents.

Malcolm read natural science, a disastrous choice of subject in which he had no interest then or since. To his fellow undergraduates, he liked to explain this curious choice by saying that he believed that the practical and realistic side of his nature needed strengthening, thereby managing to leave the implication that for him to read classics or modern literature would have been superfluous or, at least, too easy. Actually, his real reason for choosing the natural science tripos was that science was the only postmatriculation subject provided at Selhurst, and at first he did not realize that one could take up a different subject at university. By the time he did realize it, he was too embarrassed to switch.

His memoirs portray Cambridge as a place of tedium and melancholy. He claims to have loathed the university's pretentiousness, the subservience of juniors to seniors, and the torpor and vague decadence of the place. "For me the years at Cambridge were the most futile and dismal of my life."

There can be little doubt that this is how he now recalls Cambridge. Equally, there can be no doubt that this is *not* how he felt at the time.

28

His letters prove this. They are full of the bustle and gaiety typical of an undergraduate living away from home for the first time: ". . . I had a very good time at the Varsity sports . . . probably even you don't realize what my stay at Selwyn has done for me . . . the boat race was topping too . . . the teaching is going quite well; I love every bit of it . . . It's so jolly hard when one loves the College and the people in it to be able to do nothing for the College. . . ." All of these quotations are from letters he wrote in his freshman year; letters from later years tend to deal with weightier topics, but they contain little evidence that his enthusiasm had palled, or that Cambridge had become a dreary place.

Why are his memoirs so at variance with his letters from the time? There are two probable explanations. First, Muggeridge disdains pedantic research and scholarship: "Truth, not facts, dear boy" is one of his favorite axioms. In writing his memoirs he ran to form and consulted few letters or documents, even those in his own possession. Nor did he bother to check his recollection against other people's memories. Second, and more important, his memoirs reveal how he *now* thinks of those days, how he wants to remember himself. Reality has occasionally been bent to conform with predisposition. Today he feels disaffected from what he was then, and his disaffection, projected back, has produced a misleading, or at least an incomplete, picture. Was he not a municipal schoolboy? Then he *should* have been uneasy surrounded by the cream of the public schools. Was he not a socialist? Surely his conscience rebelled to hear a Cambridge degree described by the dean in his welcoming address as a kind of insurance policy against the economic ups and downs that beset the working classes. Old traditions should have seemed spurious; juvenile pursuits should have occasioned despair, or at least boredom.

One event that did leave an indelible impression upon him during his Cambridge years was the death of his brother, Stanley. Stanley had been in the Royal Flying Corps during the war and afterwards had continued working at the Croydon airfield. On August 19, 1922, he was struck by a petrol truck while riding his motorcycle to work. Malcolm and his father rushed to Croydon hospital and were with him when he died. Three days later Malcolm wrote to a friend, "My brother Stanley was killed in a motor accident on Saturday, three minutes after leaving home. I rejoice for him—he has left all the baseness and limitations of his body and has found a true and infinite peace. God bless him. The tragedy of death is the mother's and sweetheart's that are left behind. Dearest Alec, I have grown up."[1]

It was this tragedy that prompted him to think about death. Henceforth, death was never to be far from his mind. It became a theme—one might even say a preoccupation—in much of his writing. His first published short story (in *The New Statesman* in 1928) is about Alfred Twisted, an elderly schoolmaster who has just retired after forty years' service. He is free at last; free from chattering, inattentive students; free from doting and inquisitive parents; free from assemblies, chaperoning, and the infinite tedium of repetitive lessons. The story ends:

> Mr. Twisted was in the habit of getting up in the morning to make an early cup of tea. His wife smiled when she noticed that the next morning he did not stir, remembering how unnecessary it was now for him to be up in good time. Then she saw something peculiar in the way he was lying, and touched him and found him cold and began to cry quietly; for he was dead.[2]

When, in 1978, Muggeridge made a television film about his life, he acknowledged: "From my earliest years I have been much given to thinking about death, some would say abnormally, or even morbidly so."[3] The death of a brother in his youth, and of a son in middle age, contributed to this; as an old man, he has needed little external prompting to ruminate on death.

Death is the only transcendent and yet universal experience; some might contend for birth or love, but the mind is too embryonic to be aware of the former and too temporarily deranged to make sense of the latter. It is not surprising that Muggeridge should have thought about death, but it is rare for a writer to use it as a recurrent theme, particularly today when death has replaced sex as our dirty little secret.

When Muggeridge says, with Keats, that he has been for many a year "half in love with easeful death" he is often accused of morbidity. Actually, to be in love with death means to see the limitations of life and to long to break free of them. To love life one must also love death, because death is life's fulfillment. Those who see only life's phenomena cling to life like a miser clings to a debased currency, which in the end is bound to be worthless. Clinging to life's phenomena is not loving life. Loving life is accepting its rhythms and moving in step with them; subordinating one's ambitions and egotistic pursuits to the natural ebb and flow rather than striving, like King Canute, to impose one's own authority.

In his writing, Muggeridge has treated death in two ways: As a young man, it is the joker in the pack, upsetting carefully laid plans and disrupting confident expectations. However, in his later writing, death is seen as a rite of passage and man as a caterpillar who must shuffle off an old worn chrysalis in order to fly away.

A similar transition has occurred with respect to his view of immortality. He never would have denied the possibility of an afterlife, but as a young man he was more skeptical and inclined to agnosticism. At the age of eighteen, he said: "There could never be a Hell because we should all soon get quite used to it."[4] Then he would have taken the position that since it was impossible to know with certainty, it was unavailing to speculate about it. And he would assuredly have dismissed as credulous buffoons those evangelicals and fundamentalists with whom in later years he is often incongruously linked for their sort of tour-guide prospectus to the nether regions of eternity. To the extent that he considered immortality even possible, it was because he could not bring himself to believe that these three score and ten years of eating, sleeping, rutting, and acquiring, "measuring out our life with coffee spoons," as T. S. Eliot put it, could be all there was to it. If it were, it would be too banal, too tedious a game for spectator and participant alike, too witless a drama for so spectacular a set. His later writings, by contrast, take a more orthodox Christian position on death and immortality. Death is now seen as a corridor running between the city of destruction and the city of God; corridors are not places one chooses to linger, neither are they particularly foreboding.

His academic record at Cambridge was undistinguished, and he alternated between making excuses for this (some of which were plausible—obviously he was reading the wrong subject, and his health was uncertain; as a child he had been diagnosed tubercular, and he was experiencing heart troubles that required unpleasant medication) and promises to do better. In October 1921, he wrote that his father had given up on him and now looked on him as "a complete washout." There is no evidence that this was so; in fact, a few years later he wrote at some length thanking his father for never losing faith in him through "all my foolish escapades" at Cambridge.

The academic low point came on June 24, 1922, when he got a letter from his tutor, S. C. Carpenter, saying that he had failed his examinations.

He considered quitting, or in the current phrase "dropping out," but decided it would be too great a disappointment to his father. So he stayed on and solicited Carpenter's help in improving his performance, which he did—at least to a minimal passing standard. Actually, Carpenter was a considerable influence on Muggeridge; it was he who persuaded Muggeridge to be baptized and confirmed, which he was in Queen's College Chapel on March 6, 1921.

By far the most important thing that happened to him at Cambridge was making the acquaintance of Alec Vidler, who was also at Selwyn College. Vidler was four years his senior, reading theology, and destined for a distinguished career as priest, theologian, and don—latterly as dean of King's College. Vidler was a rowing man and, in the

Lent term of 1921, coached a boat in which Muggeridge was an oarsman. It fared disastrously, "going down" four times on four successive days. Despite this inauspicious beginning, they became inseparable friends.

They were both active members of an oratory society. Often they played tennis together and even entered as partners in a doubles tournament. During vacations Vidler visited Malcolm in Croydon and found himself attracted to H. T. Muggeridge, as he has recounted in his autobiography: ". . . I at once fell under the spell of Malcolm's father who was soon to become a Labour M.P. He was one of those devoted idealists with a passionate desire to win justice for the poor and underprivileged, who then abounded in the Labour Party. He had already visited Cambridge in the May term and I had written in my diary: 'Mr. Muggeridge I fell in love with right away—in fact I think I had done so long before I ever saw him', i.e., from what Malcolm had told me about him."[5]

In the summer vacation of 1921 Malcolm repaid the visit by going to stay with Vidler in Rye. On one warm, lazy day they strolled together on the beach in animated conversation. There being no one about, they stripped to the skin and swam out a considerable distance. When they turned back, they were abashed to see a middle-aged Rye matron and her young daughter taking up occupation of the beach right next to their discarded clothing. Since they seemed reluctant to move on, modesty compelled a much longer swim than the young men had anticipated.

It is not difficult to explain the mutual attraction that led to their friendship. In Vidler, Muggeridge recognized one of those rare human beings whose company is at the same time stimulating and soothing, and whose spiritual balance is so acute and finely tuned that an inward serenity is radiated. For his part, Vidler detected in Muggeridge, even from their first meeting, ". . . a kind of genius as a talker and writer, and even as a seer."[6] As a result, Vidler retained all Muggeridge's letters from those far-off years, and these provide a vivid picture of the development of his political and religious views. They reveal a searching, often self-pitying young man, earnest though with a redeeming sense of humor, rather indolent, inclined to priggishness, a person who revealed different facets of his personality to different friends. To Vidler, Muggeridge revealed his spiritual side, raising questions about the meaning of life and faith and God, occasionally revealing doubts—although, on the whole, he was then a remarkably sanguine believer—and always finishing up by requesting Vidler's guidance and prayers.

For most of his four Cambridge years, Muggeridge actively considered becoming a priest. In 1921 he discussed this with a clergyman named

Philips who ran a mission to the destitute and derelict of Croydon: "God prosper him—if he will let me I am going to join him."[7] It was at Vidler's suggestion that Muggeridge went to live for his last Cambridge year at Oratory House on Lady Margaret Road, the home of an Anglican religious order of celibate priests and laymen called The Oratory of the Good Shepherd. At first he fell contentedly into the daily routine, saying the offices, observing the silences, taking the sacraments. Looking back on this period, he later wrote: "I think I was happier there than I have ever been or ever can be. . . ."[8] He came under the influence of Wilfred Knox, of whom he grew very fond, and Knox pressed him strongly to enter the priesthood. So unrelenting did this pressure become that to escape he moved out of Oratory House for his final term, taking rooms at 46 Owlstone Road. The landlady, a Miss Lloyd, had known better times and never tired of telling her boarders that her family had once kept a carriage and pair, each time glaring at her listener as if to say: "And look what I've come to now—taking in the likes of you." So tedious did this repetition become that Malcolm resolved to devote his first earnings to replacing her carriage and pair. It was in this house that he met Leonard Dobbs and his sister, Kitty, whom he was later to marry.

From the beginning of his time at Cambridge, he was imbued with a strong sense of mission, of some unique destiny that he must find and fulfill. At first he identified this with the priesthood, but by late 1922 he was already turning his thoughts more to writing. To Alec Vidler, he wrote: "Sometimes, dearest friend, I long to be in the fray—to be able to stand up and speak all the burning words of which my heart is full—to *Do* something . . . God has some destiny mapped; some work for me to do and it is growing on me. . . ."[9]

Although he continued to attend mass regularly, the seeds of doubt about the institutional church were already taking root. He and Vidler argued about this endlessly. Vidler would defend the church as a necessary evil; Muggeridge, failing to perceive its necessity, scorned or mocked it. To the extent that one had to choose between religious denominations, Muggeridge expressed a preference for a church of "strict principles" where "on Sunday mornings you hear about Hell fire as I regard that as most important." But as time went on, his Cambridge letters reveal growing doubts about the church and the priestly vocation. He described his soul as "groping in the dark, restless and dispirited." In September 1921, he sent Vidler this epitaph: "My Epitaph: Here lieth one whose soul sometimes burned with great longings. To whom sometimes the curtain of the Infinite was opened just a little, but who lacked just the GUTS to make any use of it."

To Stanley Ellams, another Cambridge friend, Muggeridge showed quite a different side of his personality. With Ellams he would relax and go to parties, go on walking or cycling expeditions, and generally lead the dilettantish life that one expects of an undergraduate. In such company, he was an amusing, carefree companion, ready at a moment's notice to put aside books in favor of a lark.

He entertained generously and spent extravagantly (particularly on clothes)—in fact, well beyond his limited means. As a result, he came to know the Cambridge bank well ("the jolliest bank in the world") and its manager, known to undergraduates simply as "the old man." The manager had an austerely bald head and a severe countenance, but actually he was an easy mark for a loan. In Malcolm's final year, a new manager came who refused what would have been his third overdraft that year. "I walked away in a quiet and dignified way, never to apply to him again. If it hadn't been for the fact that I had a small overdraft at the time of my application, I should have threatened to withdraw my account from the bank altogether, but that would have been too much in his favour."[10]

Occasionally the two sides of his personality and their separate friends came together. In September 1923, he found himself twelve pounds in debt through extravagant living and wrote asking Alec Vidler to bail him out. He argued that he could not approach his father because the previous year H. T. had paid fifty-three pounds to clear just such debts, and now ". . . if he knew I still owed this much, it would break his heart." As an impecunious curate of frugal disposition, Vidler was having none of it; he replied suggesting that Malcolm make a clean breast of it to his father. He did. "My pater was very decent about it—didn't rave, just seemed resigned. That was gall to me."[11] As Dr. Johnson once stood contritely in the drizzle of the Uttoxeter market place to atone for his youthful impetuosity, so Muggeridge later wrote to his father apologizing for ". . . the many hours you must have spent at ledgers for me to waste my time extravagantly at Cambridge."[12]

His studies held no attraction, but talking, debating, and reading did. His taste in books was eclectic; varied and casual rather than scholarly. At home, H. T.'s library had been small and confined mostly to political theory, economics, and fabianism, so Cambridge was Malcolm's first encounter with a great and catholic library; he made use of it, though not in ways calculated to earn academic dividends. D. H. Lawrence became his passion and, at Malcolm's urging, Vidler too read all the novels and poems, and they talked endlessly about them. In light of Muggeridge's later criticism of Lawrence, it should be said that even during his most worshipful Lawrence period, he dismissed Lawrence's attitudes on sex—particularly his descriptions of encounters between Lady Chatterly and Mellors—as contrived and ludicrous. At Oratory House he began to read books on religious themes, particularly mysticism, although he shunned formal theology as boring and slightly suspicious.

Politically, Muggeridge was still a naive socialist. There were none of the doubts or fitful despair on political questions that there were on religious matters; at most there was only occasional unease. He vowed to ". . . live utterly with the people and their labour party . . . I am with it as heartily as I would have been with the French revolution."[13] When he returned to Croydon during vacations he would campaign for his father's various causes. His reputation as an orator had already become known, and he was often asked to speak on behalf of Labour party candidates in nearby constituencies. To sharpen his son's oratorical skills, H. T. had given Malcolm a lifetime membership in the Cambridge Union Society. In his memoirs, Muggeridge asserts: "I scarcely ever attended, and never once spoke."[14] Actually, his memory again has played him false. He attended frequently (letters to friends are written on Union letterhead) and, in February 1921, he debated the ex-president of the Loyalist Society on the resolution: "That the twentieth century is a general improvement on the nineteenth." For the first—and no doubt only—time in his life, Muggeridge took the affirmative and won.

He left Cambridge in May 1924, having managed to scrape out a pass degree. Four years at Cambridge had not made a scholar of him. Nor had he emerged as the brilliant socialist set for a dazzling political career, a young Laski or Tawney, as his father had hoped. H. T. had dreamed of editing a socialist superman; in fact, he had subbed only a revised copy of himself. Perhaps the most important aspect of the Cambridge years was that Malcolm had met Alec Vidler, to whom at once he confided a premonition that they would remain intimate friends for the rest of their lives. Like many of his premonitions, this was to be exactly realized.

By the time he graduated, he was convinced that he had a mission in life, a destiny he must discover and fulfill, and increasingly his attention had shifted from the church to writing. His brother's death had forced him to confront mortality, not as an idea but as an inescapable reality of life. He remained politically innocent, but on all other issues he was beginning to practice John Donne's advice, to doubt wisely. For the rest of his years, doubt and skepticism would be companions, mental alarm bells that would go clanging off whenever his beliefs began to congeal into dogma, rousing him to shake the dust from his eyes and move on. The church he had begun to see less as a sanctuary in which to worship than as an institution which, like all institutions, was required to make an accommodation with power and therefore deserved to be mistrusted. The gates of hell might not prevail against it, but they would certainly have their innings, and thenceforth he would not be above joining in to hurl a few bricks of his own. Cambridge may have taught him little natural science, but in bringing this rather impressionable, gauche, and irresolute young man to the verge of maturity it played a significant, albeit inadvertent, role in his life.

Near the end of his final term, Muggeridge met the Reverend W.E.S. Holland and was much impressed by his robust, shining earnestness, which was given a halo effect by a bald pate fringed with a cluster of tight grey curls. To Alec Vidler he called Holland "the leading Indian educationalist." Later, after actually observing Holland in action, he revised his opinion considerably: "Most of his life has been spent in India, labouring to shake Indians into the pattern he knew best and admired most—of a godly, righteous and sober Englishman who had been to a good public school, played games, and delightedly, or, as he would put it, prayerfully, read his Bible."[15] Holland offered him a job teaching English at Union Christian College in Alwaye, southern India. For a time, Muggeridge equivocated; he sought Vidler's advice, stressing the points in favor of accepting Holland's offer: The subject— "English as you know is my pet hobby"; the salary—"practically nothing but that I feel is to the good"; and a religious atmosphere—"he is taking me on as a Catholic and the life I shall live will be a community life. . . ."[16] Vidler was unimpressed by all this and replied somewhat snootily, rejecting all his arguments: "Your justification of the action you propose to take seems to me to be an excuse for doing something which has caught your imagination. Rather than a rational case for doing your duty."[17] His duty, as Vidler still saw it, was to enter the priesthood.

Having sought advice, it was characteristic of Muggeridge to reject it, and he decided to go. He spent the summer and early part of the autumn in Belgium, working as a tour guide for Henry Lunn's travel agency, which allowed him to renew contact with Kitty Dobbs who was staying at her parents' holiday villa at Knocke-le-Zoute.

On December 25, 1924, his father accompanied him to Tilbury to see him off on his passage to India. It was a chilly, misty day, and they walked briskly up and down the pier to keep warm. Malcolm could scarcely converse for excitement. "When the bell rang for visitors to leave the ship and walk away, I was surprised and rather disgusted with myself, to find that I felt a kind of relief at leaving him, too."[18]

·3·
INDIA

India is a place in which it is impossible to avoid thinking.

Malcolm Muggeridge to Alec Vidler, April 6, 1925

* * *

Life aboard the S.S. *Moria* was little to his taste. Like most ships, she was ill-suited to physical exercise but lavishly equipped for eating, and the sea air made him hungry. There was a storm in the Bay of Biscay, and he became seasick. Most of the other passengers were tiresome— "rather dull Empire builders"—and Muggeridge was shunned for sharing a second-class stateroom with an Indian clergyman, the Reverend C. K. Jacob. One passenger, an engineer, was overheard to remark that it ". . . was just not right"; later, C. K. Jacob became a bishop and, presumably, an acceptable shipmate. Despite such unsympathetic company and the sheer tedium of the five-week voyage, Muggeridge was delighted to turn his back on England. From Port Said (where he purchased a topee which he discarded almost as soon as he arrived in India) he wrote to Alec Vidler: "There is a great relief in being away from England. I think you are right when you say that the hope for that country, even in our lives, has got slenderer and slenderer, until now one feels it could easily break any moment. It is all very baffling."[1]

By late January he was settled at Alwaye. It was then little more than a village, with the college itself set in the hills three miles off, across the Perrier River in which he bathed morning and night. He moved into a small, plain room in the student residence, furnished with a bed, a writing table, a chair, and an oil lamp.

Union Christian College had been founded in 1921 by a former lecturer at Madras University, K. C. Charcko. Syrian Christians, assisted by Roman Catholic and Anglican missionaries, provided the college's first teaching staff, although by Muggeridge's time all but three of the fifteen lecturers were Indian. There were then 214 students, most of whom were Christian, the rest divided about equally between Hindus and Muslims. Early in his stay Muggeridge enumerated, in typically categorical fashion, the "special advantages" of Union Christian College: "(1) *It is Indian.* The students wear their national dress. We have a bad name with the government, thank God, because of our nationalist tendencies. (2) *The students see Europeans working under Indians.* A thing, I believe, I am right in saying, absolutely unique through the whole of India. (3) *That the Christianity is Indian or Syrian,* and not imported respectable Anglicanism. (4) *That as a member of the staff one is not a missionary,* and so is free from all societies. (5) *That one lives with Indians,* and so comes to understand their strengths and weaknesses without prejudice."[2]

He arrived fired with enthusiasm. "I am very happy and contented here. The work is interesting, the students are delightful, and the whole thing a tremendous adventure."[3] Muggeridge has never been a man for quarters and halves; he loves ecstatically or loathes bitterly, often sliding so quickly from euphoria to despair that he fails to experience the more moderate sensations in between. It is a quality—or failing—that he recognized early in himself: "I cannot live except completely, being of that nature."[4]

As soon as he was settled, he took over the college dramatic society, rashly promising productions in their first season of *Othello, Julius Caesar,* and "a farce" to be written by himself. *Othello* was staged with Muggeridge playing Iago. Of the fate of the other two productions, there is no record; there was, however, a memorable performance of Oliver Goldsmith's *She Stoops to Conquer* on founder's day (January 22, 1926) in which Muggeridge played Miss Neville.

He also set about establishing a college magazine and became its first editor. It appeared twice yearly.

At first the administration applauded his initiative, but their enthusiasm began to pall when, in the first issue of the magazine, he lampooned faculty and students alike. He mocked the faculty for supposing that their labors, ". . . in the spirit of Mr. Dryasdust, B.A., B.L., author of notes on this, and notes on that and notes on every possible thing except on life,"[5] could possibly make any lasting impact on anyone. They were alien teachers on foreign soil, mouthing the last words of a dying civilization. It was not a point of view likely to ingratiate a new boy. The administration soon came to regard him as a thorn in their side, while his colleagues' reactions ran the gamut from amusement to disapproval. A few teachers would have nothing to do with him. Since he had already come to regard the staff as ". . . low-level liaison officers with the Indians" he paid little heed. His only close friend at the place was not a European but a strict Brahmin, V. S. Venkatranam, who taught mathematics but introduced Muggeridge to Eastern religious thought and mysticism, matters in which he has retained a life long interest.

Of the students he wrote: "The Indian undergraduate is a strange being. He imagines that to be impressive, he must be pompous."[6]

What exactly the students made of this brash, energetic twenty-two-year-old addition to the faculty, with his dogmatic, unorthodox views, argumentative disposition, and charitable personality, it is difficult to know. Shortly after he arrived, he was made warden of the residence, and this proved to be a popular choice. He was benevolent to a fault, winking at the most flagrant violations of the rules, venting his anger only at the interminable parliamentary style proceedings by which they were formulated and amended. "Why waste time over rules which I ignore anyway?" was his attitude.

He particularly encouraged the more nationalist students who appreciated the fact that he made no attempt to set himself apart, either as a *sahib* or as an instructor. He lived with the students, adopted Indian dress and dietary habits, sat cross-legged and meditated with them, and slept without a mattress. He was eager to converse and yet made no effort to convert anyone to anything. Since the students were surrounded by missionaries of one sort or another, this alone must have made him attractive. And, despite the self-denigrating tone of his memoirs, he was an outstanding teacher. Enthusiasm, eloquence, and a touch of ham are the lecturer's trump cards, and he had all three; knowledge is a bonus, a face card in reserve, and he had enough of that to get by. The only direct evidence of the students' attitude is this parody of the Book of Chronicles that was anonymously submitted to the college magazine and gleefully published by its editor.

And there dwelt in the N.E. Hostel a warden by name Malc, the son of Mug, a white man, and one who laughed with all his might: for he was very humorous.

And he said unto himself, I will buy unto myself a machine, for to speak with me: for I am very lonely.

And he bought unto himself a machine, cunningly made, for to speak to him; and behold, it sang him songs.

And Malc, the son of Mug, he bethought unto himself a new device, for to amuse himself and he said: I would make unto myself a garden.

And he digged the ground, and put manure and planted the seeds: and he did this in a privy part of the compound: for he said, lest anyone should see it.

And he fenced it round with wire netting: lest the beasts of the field should tramp on it: for he was a wise man.

And the rest of the doings of Malc, are they not written in the book of the Chronicles of the staff, and in the hearts of the members of the College?

Let us therefore take heed and stop, lest we should bore anyone, and he should say: There is nothing new in this.[7]

During his first term, the poet Rabindranath Tagore came to open a student hostel named in his honor. Muggeridge met Tagore and later went to visit his ashram where he donned a saffron robe and sat on a grass mat at the guru's feet. He was disappointed: "Tagore's discourse delivered in a rich, melodious voice failed to hold my attention—which was no reflection on it. I have always found it almost impossible to maintain interest in any form of oration, lecture or sermon. . . . All I can remember is that Tagore was then concerned with Western materialism, and the great part Asia or, more particularly, India, had to play in turning those who were bogged down in this gross delusion to more spiritual attitudes."[8]

Muggeridge also wrote to Tagore raising questions about celibacy, a topic that dominated his mind and correspondence at this time— ostensibly because he had not yet entirely abandoned the idea of the priesthood. Tagore replied in rather vague terms, indicating that ". . . some check upon procreation is common ground between us," but that they were "diametrically opposed" on acceptable methods to achieve this result. Muggeridge's side of this correspondence is lost, but in all likelihood he was advocating contraception and sterilization— measures he would only later come to regard as anathema.

Muggeridge's concern about celibacy is revealing. Two kinds of people are attracted by celibacy: those for whom sex is, for reasons of temperament or capacity, an incidental, unimportant aspect of life; and those for whom it is so central and relentless a force that celibacy appears to offer the best hope of maintaining one's balance, perhaps even one's sanity. Muggeridge belonged to the second category. He believed that he must learn to control lust or be controlled by it. For him, lust was the devil's ace of trumps, and the devil played it well and often.

In one letter to his father, he described his reaction on unexpectedly discovering a woman bathing during his evening swim.

She came to the river and took off her clothes and stood naked, her brown body just caught by the sun. I suddenly went mad. There came to me that dryness in the back of my throat; that feeling of cruelty and strength and wild unreasonableness which is called passion. I darted with all the force of swimming I had to where she was, and then nearly fainted, for she was old and hideous and her feet were deformed and turned inwards and her skin was wrinkled and, worst of all, she was a leper. You have never seen a leper I suppose; until you have seen one you do not know the worst that human ugliness can be. This creature grinned at me, showing a toothless mask, and the next thing I knew was that I was swimming along in my old way in the middle of the stream—yet trembling. . . .

It was the kind of lesson I needed. When I think of lust now I think of this lecherous woman. Oh, if only I could paint, I'd make a wonderful picture of a passionate boy running after that and call it: "The lusts of the flesh."[9]

From an early age, Muggeridge obviously had sex on his mind which, as he later acknowledged, is an odd place to have it. He had that combination of fascination and fear about women that is common to men who have grown up without sisters. Sex is a recurrent topic, particularly in his early writing, fiction as well as nonfiction. His first play, *Three Flats*, was attacked for its casual approach to sex and adultery. Similarly, his novel *In a Valley of this Restless Mind* was looked at askance for its preoccupation with lust; so much so, in fact, that when it was reissued in 1978, Muggeridge wrote an apologetic introduction in which he admitted that ". . . the obsession with carnality, looked back on across four decades, could not but seem distasteful, especially as I have often criticized other writers for indulging this particular obsession." Today, both books would be regarded as being as tame as a spinster's parrot, pure in outlook and language. But this is a different age, awash in sexual permissiveness.

Muggeridge's attitudes on sex must be assessed by the standards of his own time and generation. This is no easy task, partly because he is one of the few contemporary writers to appreciate and exploit the comic possibilities of sex. Among his notable contributions in this vein was a brilliant send-up of Wayland Young's portentous and ludicrous book, *Eros Denied*, in which Muggeridge suggested that sensibility and language might both be better served if the old four-letter verb for fornication (one which he has never been averse to using) was allowed to lapse and be replaced instead by the more elegant verb "to wayland."

Yet beneath the laughter is strain, perhaps even anguish. The frequency with which he dragged a sexual reference or innuendo, of no particular relevance, into an article or book review suggested a kind of smutty curiosity that ill accords (but frequently accompanies) high-minded piety. It is inflating a valid point to write, as Bernard Levin did, that Muggeridge's latter day campaigns against pornography and the permissive society amount to ". . . begging the world to stop trying to inflame his withered desires, lest the attempt should prove successful."[10] But it is true that there is a connection between these campaigns and his own past; he knows, from personal experience, just how insatiable the sexual urge can be. Lust makes its greatest appeal to imaginative people because it offers the nearest fleshly equivalent to the soul's longing to be submerged in oneness, in unity. In sex the ego's tentacle grip is loosed, and one momentarily forgets self and enters the realm of ecstasy, otherwise reserved for mystics.

Muggeridge also knows what social scientists and others of that ilk take such pains to deny: Namely, that exposure to pornography or other material designed to inflame sexual appetite can have a corroding effect on some people—people like him. Not for nothing is lust ranked last and most deadly of the seven deadly sins.

Also, his journalistic experience has conditioned him to seek out what really interests readers, as opposed to what they purport to be interested in. Sex is interesting. What honest person would not prefer to know who someone sleeps with rather than who they vote for? Muggeridge has taken his turn at churning out juicy gossip paragraphs that are avidly seized upon by eyes unstrained by surrounding high-minded editorials.

The sexual tension that manifests itself in Muggeridge's writing comes, in part, from trying to keep a balance between what he believes, with utmost sincerity, about the effect of unbridled lust, and memories of past temptations in his own life—temptations not always overcome. For most of his life, he has been torn between forswearing lust and yielding to it with a delicious shiver.

Another early visitor to Union Christian College was Mahatma Gandhi, who came there in March 1925, from Vaicom where he had spoken on untouchability. Muggeridge and most of the students waited for hours at the railway station to glimpse his arrival. When his wooden, third-class railway carriage pulled in, Gandhi immediately went over to a group of untouchables who had been specially cordoned off and began singing hymns with them. When he spoke at the college, he received a tumultuous reception. Afterwards, Gandhi planted a mango tree in the college courtyard as a perpetual memorial of his visit.

In the first issue of the college magazine, Muggeridge wrote an adulatory editorial praising the simplicity of Gandhi's address: "Take a wheel and spin and as you spin, sing, and as you sing, love your fellow men and the troubles of the country will be ended." This, he wrote, was the only sensible alternative to the "absurd visionaries and idealists"—politicians, militarists, businessmen, and missionaries—who had "failed utterly" to better the lot of the Indian people and, in the process, had made a botch of world affairs. Muggeridge even praised

Gandhi's impracticality: "It is time that such impractical people were given a chance to try their hand at government."[11]

Muggeridge followed up Gandhi's visit with a letter urging the *Swarajist* movement to adopt a more aggressive and explicitly socialist policy. Gandhi replied and published their correspondence in his newspaper *Young India*.

Several of Gandhi's characteristics were bound to attract Muggeridge. He was an underdog, and Muggeridge is temperamentally suited to be in opposition to any established authority or institution. While Gandhi preached revolution, it was a revolution to be won by each person transforming himself, becoming a new man or new woman imbued with the spirit of *satyagraha,* truth and force, rather than by collective struggle. This approach exactly suited Muggeridge's mistrust of collective action ("Organization carries in itself the destruction of the ideal organized," he wrote) and his fierce individualism. Then, too, Gandhi's asceticism—his peculiar notions about diet, dress, and sexual behaviour—would all appeal to a young Englishman, living an austere, celibate life, and seeking to put as much distance as possible between himself and his fellow Europeans. Even Gandhi's religion which, although nominally Hindu, borrowed eclectically from Buddhism and Christianity, encouraged Muggeridge to expand his own religious horizons and to delve more deeply into the Upanishads and the Bhagavad Gita to which V. S. Venkatranam had recently introduced him. The more he read and pondered, the more tawdry and confined the dogma and practices of the Church of England seemed.

Muggeridge did not share all of Gandhi's views. Nonviolence and pacifism seemed to him unattainable ideals, and he later set out his objections in a long, thoughtful article "Why I am not a Pacifist."[12] He was more nationalistic than either Gandhi or the most ardent students at Alwaye, and he never passed up an opportunity to employ his oratorical skill to stir up trouble. He urged the students to rebel against the Raj and all vestiges of colonialism, including (perhaps especially including) the faculty and staff of Union Christian College. After one such oration a colleague warned him that men had served time for less inflammatory and seditious remarks. "Rather to my disappointment, the authorities either never heard of my vapourings or, if they did, decided, quite rightly, that they were of no importance, requiring no response on their part."[13]

Muggeridge kept a diary and most of it has been preserved, written in his crabbed, nearly illegible handwriting by fountain pen on sheets of yellowed onionskin paper, stuck together, it seems, as much by the oppressive heat and humidity in which it was first written as by the passage of years. His diary and letters provide a detailed picture of his daily routine.

He would rise early and read, usually poetry ("I believe it is good to start one's day to the tune of poetry"), until a manservant named Kuruvella delivered tea at six. Kuruvella was good-hearted but slow-witted. Once Muggeridge was burned by a box of matches that exploded when he was smoking in bed. He shouted to Kuruvella for ointment. Kuruvella first brought brasso, then toothpaste. On another occasion he came upon Kuruvella trying to light the primus stove with communion wine. After tea, Muggeridge would bathe in the river. There followed a light breakfast, more reading and writing until the bells at nine-thirty signaled the beginning of lectures. Muggeridge had a tendency to be late, and once, encountering an Indian colleague in the staff room, he inquired breathlessly if the bells had gone yet. The Indian slowly raised his head, studied him, and gravely replied: "Some bells have gone, some bells are yet to go. . . ." The rest of the morning he would pace back and forth at the front of a classroom with open sides, looking out on paddy fields where rows of brown backs were stooped in the baking sun, brown arms extended picking rice, brown legs treading round huge irrigation wheels. In the cooler shade he would try to make sense of English literature, drawn from an anthology called Little Dowden, with students whose comprehension of tragedy was acute enough but who failed to grasp why King Lear should choose to give away his kingdom to his daughters. After lunch, a siesta, then more of the same—it might be Wordsworth and the Lake poets, or Tennyson's requiem for Arthur Hallam—with Muggeridge becoming ever more "physically anguished" by the bizarre contrast between the reality of life all around him and the fantasies on which he was obliged to discourse. Or the afternoon might be blessedly free of lectures; time for tea and reading and writing. In the evenings, he would invariably walk. Walking has been one of the few constant passions of his life, whether on Croydon back streets, by the Thames or the Cam, between paddy fields under a sweltering sun, in the drizzle of London, the dust of Cairo, in Moscow, Geneva, Washington, and Rome, or now—in old age—through the woods and dales of Sussex. This is Muggeridge at his most typical; pounding along, dueling with his walking stick at offending shrubbery, alone and silent, wrapped in his own thoughts; or with one or two others or a company of people, voluble, laughing, with a stream of mirth, eloquence, and character assassination erupting from him.

At Alwaye, his favorite walk took him along the Parur road to a village about two and a half miles away whose name meant "the fort," although no trace of a fort was then visible. He would set out in late afternoon, turn again in twilight, and complete the walk at dusk when little lights were just beginning to flare up as families gathered here and there for a bite to eat before the darker oblivion of sleep. So often and regularly did he walk this road that he came to know its *habitués* by sight, if not name. He studied their faces and habits. None made a deeper impression on him than a retarded boy who drove geese; Muggeridge wrote about him in *The Calcutta Guardian* on November 4, 1926.

His chest is sunken, his face is vacant and his eyes are dull, yet he drives his geese skillfully; and believe me or not as you like, he speaks to them in the soft, caressing voice a mother uses to a very little baby. He carries no stick to assist him in keeping order amongst them, but only a large leaf, which he waves slowly to and fro; and one might easily imagine that his speech was nothing but the noise of the wind through this, so like is it to the sound of a forest when, in the evening, a light wind blows. With this he keeps his charges as a compact, disciplined company, not stupidly military in their orderliness, yet not by any means a rabble; rather they remind one of a band of pilgrims, or of workers working voluntarily together. They seem to be not so much numbered and uniformed as to make a harmony of which he is the conductor: not so much to march in step as to dance with perfect understanding of each other's movements. I realized how supremely successful he was at his work when, one day when perhaps he was ill, I saw another boy at it. This other boy was a bouncing, bumptious fellow, who carried a switch like a sergeant-major, and who shouted at the geese as *sahibs* shout when they want something. The result was that they spread over the road in a screaming, cackling mob—some getting left behind; some getting run over by a passing motor; all of them lost and bewildered. And the more he shouted and beat them the more hopeless the position got.

There are pretty morals to be drawn from this contrast between the persuasive methods of the idiot boy with the sunken chest, who understands the speech of geese, and those of the sane boy with the broad chest, but moralizing is a thankless task; indeed it is a confession of incoherence, so I shall avoid it. But I must say that I envy the goose boy. I feel that he has found the secret of happiness in that he has done one useful thing which he can do superlatively well, and which he is content to go on doing from day to day until he dies. When his soul leaves the poor, puny body, with its gapingly vacant face, I believe it will be found to be a rare and beautiful soul, pleasing to its maker. Sometimes I wonder about him—whether he will marry; whether he prays or has any kind of religion; whether he ever wonders about the meaning of things. All this is doubtful; what is certain is that he can drive the geese efficiently; and to do that is quite as worthy of praise as to write a book or bleat a lecture or drone a sermon or do any of the things we wretched intelligentsia preen ourselves on.[14]

Leaving behind the goose boy and the fish man and the laborers driving the cattle and the unmistakable smell of dust and jasmine, he would arrive back at the college, bathe again in the last light, and pick his way perilously up the narrow path back to his residence. The college grounds were supposed to be lighted by oil lamps; however, the lamplighter put in only half the oil required, saving the rest for his personal consumption, so walking about at night was hazardous.

It was the experience of being in the Indian police that turned George Orwell against imperialism: "In order to hate imperialism, you have got to be part of it" he wrote in *The Road to Wigan Pier*. Muggeridge's experience in India soured him on both imperialism and, for many years, on Christianity.

Running the college dramatic society, producing Shakespearian tragedies and Restoration comedies with native students got up in wigs and powder to look like knights or rakes, soon proved wearying. And editing what was, in effect, a foreign language magazine for young, mostly apathetic students, whose interest in letters seldom extended beyond the two they wished to add to their own name, seemed even more absurd.

As for the missionaries by whom he was surrounded—with their ersatz piety and vulgar phrases: "spreading the gospel net," "converting heathen," "winning souls," and so on; their colonialist mentality and prostration before the most ridiculous excesses of the Raj; and their churches, in which men not wearing trousers were unwelcome and Indians had specially allotted pews—he soon grew utterly contemptuous of them. Within two months of his arrival he referred to them as "awful tripe" and ridiculed their efforts "to bring a thing, decayed and effete in England, here and expect to see it live under this blue sky where its hypocrisy seems doubly shown."[15]

He spent the long vacation of March 1925 at Ootacamund in the cooler Nilgiri Hills, staying at a bungalow for missionaries run by an evangelical spinster, Miss Edith Hopwood. She was a great lover of Bunyan and called the Nilgiri peaks, visible from her garden, the Delectable Mountains. Although she died in 1944, the bungalow called "Farley" is still there, having been bequeathed by Miss Hopwood to a missionary society. She was a simple, decent sort who went out of her way to be kind to Muggeridge, but he found the missionaries who gathered there intolerable. To escape them he hired a pony and tent and set off alone for several days of solitude and meditation. Just before leaving, he wrote to Alec Vidler: "I feel as though it were a sort of pilgrimage, as though I might find something on it." He did. He found that his estrangement from the missionaries had spread to the church they purported to represent, "its organization, its uniforms and its rule of thumb moralities," and even to Christianity itself. While he had had vagrant doubts at Cambridge, now he set about a wholesale reexamination of his beliefs. It would be going too far to say that he became an agnostic on this expedition, but his beliefs were shaken. "Organized religion kills the living beauty of God," he wrote to Vidler when he got back.

How often it happens that a spiritual straggler turns aside at the church door when he catches sight of those coming out of it! This is an understandable attitude, but not a wholly rational one—as Muggeridge himself was later to realize. No doubt Christ's rather scruffy, ragtag band of followers, with their own power seekers, egomaniacs, and, of course, Judas, upset some of the more sensitive Galileans of His day. But Christ deserves to be judged for Himself, on His own, not on the basis of His twelve hand-picked disciples, still less by His ostensible representatives twenty centuries later. For Muggeridge it would be many years before he could erase from his mind what he had seen of the church and its agents in India and consider Christianity, at least in its organized, institutional dimensions, afresh.

Back at the college, it came his turn to preach the Sunday morning sermon in the chapel. It must have been quite a scene, with Muggeridge delivering himself of just the kind of vaporous, leftist rhetoric then regarded as shockingly inflammatory, but which now has become the church's last remaining orthodoxy. As usual, he was years ahead of his time. Had he delivered this sermon at, say, the 1978 Lambeth Conference of Anglican bishops when the assembled delegates paraded into assembly to the tune of the Groovers rock band and voted to donate their parishioners' offerings to arm the revolutionary terrorists of Zimbabwe, it would all have seemed yawningly familiar and old hat.

Muggeridge began by telling the students that Jesus was "a glorious revolutionary" who cared nothing for creeds and dogmas and religious orthodoxies, "those miserable and pettifogging ideas," but instead preached a gospel of revolution to the downtrodden and oppressed of Jerusalem. If he did not actually say that Jesus was an early Fabian, he might as well have. His text was Christ's great commandment—to love God and one's neighbor as one's self—"the two commandments are virtually the same" and this meant, he said, working for social betterment so that man can "mould the world anew." Even the recently founded League of Nations had a part to play in ushering in the kingdom: "What a new Jerusalem they could create from Geneva!"[16]

What the students made of this sermon is unknown. The more evangelical of his colleagues were unhappy, and he became even more a pariah. It is ironic that in 1925 he was condemned and ostracized by the ecclesiastical establishment, such as it was, of Union Christian College for having the temerity to espouse a particular view of Christianity for which, when he came to denounce the same view forty years later in *Jesus Rediscovered,* he was condemned again by the ecclesiastical establishment.

In July he was back in the Nilgiri Hills, this time on doctor's orders. His recurrent stomach troubles, aggravated by unfamiliar food, dysentery, and a cook named Albert whom Muggeridge discovered straining soup through a cloth that had been used all day to wipe dirty pots, had resulted in some sort of intestinal collapse. He was sent off to the higher, cooler altitude to recuperate. If he did not mend quickly, the doctor said that he must be sent home. He passed the days reading, exercising, and sleeping. He was put on a strict vegetarian diet, which he discovered he enjoyed, and he vowed "to stick to it forever"; he didn't, actually, although in his sixties he reverted again to a vegetarian regime.

Although he recovered quickly and was back at work by the end of August, the prospect of going home was no longer unpleasant. He had been at Alwaye for little more than six months, but already he pined for the "jostly crowds" of London, its clamor and action. He was increasingly restless and dispirited. Every day in the classroom, reciting Little Dowden to students who would commit his words to memory, seemed ". . . an inward Hell, because I am doing nothing." Lecturing was a process by which his notes became the student's notes without passing through the heads of either. He disliked having to sit down with a student and review his, perhaps desultory, performance: " 'Ah, Soolapani Warrier, you must be more serious at your work, you have brains but you are lazy'; what would have been my fate had such a review taken place at Cambridge?"[17]

Perhaps he should return to England but to what? Teach? His heart was not in it. Preach? Yet now he had little left but doubts, and although he still occasionally raised the possibility of a priestly vocation in letters to Vidler, he knew that a catalog of one's doubts scarcely makes a compelling sermon. Politics? "The House of Commons has caught my ambitions and I have seen myself as a member of it," he wrote to his father. But with whom would he cast his lot and would they want him? And where and how should he get himself elected? A successful statesman or a pedantic schoolmaster? A priest or a writer? A celibate or a Don Juan? Anything but *this.*

In October he was ill again, this time with a skin infection with symptoms of extreme itch and weeping, like acute eczema. An English doctor came from Ootacumund and prescribed various ointments, all of which aggravated the itching. By chance an Indian physician, who was visiting another patient at the college, heard of his predicament and looked in. Muggeridge had made inquiries about native medicine and had learned that if an Indian physician made a correct diagnosis the probability of cure was high; the trouble was that few were capable of making correct diagnoses.

> Presently he looked at my hands and my feet and my tongue and then he sat in silence rocking slowly to and fro. I thoughtlessly said something here but I was soon put to silence. For some quarter of an hour he sat like this. He was consulting his books and he carried them in his head. At last he spoke and his words were obviously intended to have the effect of an oracle: "The *Sahib* must put leaches on his hands" he said "to suck away the bad blood. He must eat gee and apply a preparation I shall send him." Then he went. I didn't put the leeches on—the very idea of it is revolting; and I certainly didn't eat gee (which is foully indigestible) but I may put on the curious inky thing he has sent me as a lotion.[18]

He did so, and his skin infection disappeared almost immediately.

He spent a morose Christmas, 1925, at the village of Tinevelly, staying with a Cambridge acquaintance, Stephen Neill, who had just been turned out of the mission he had come to India to serve. Neill's father was a doctor, and Muggeridge accompanied him to several nearby villages that had been struck by a cholera epidemic: "The village headman tells us chattily how many died the day before and how many have sickened that day. A little permanganate in the well would probably have prevented the whole thing. A mudheap of a world this that we live in."[19]

The sky was blue, the temperature hovered around one hundred degrees, and the English newspapers, which arrived weeks late with their pages stiff as boards from salty sea air, promised snow for Christmas. With his season's greetings to his family, he enclosed a poem that concluded:

> Two thousand years have passed of Church and King
> And vast has been the flow of blood and speech,
> But brothers do we know the simplest thing
> He died to teach?

Up until this time, his father's praise for Malcolm's literary efforts had been sparing, no doubt to avoid fanning the flames of unrealistic ambition, but also because he was genuinely out of sympathy with the passionate way in which his son wrote—his ecstasies and despairs, and his frequent references to sex. For some reason, this little poem made a deep impression on H. T.; he copied it into his commonplace book of treasured literary quotations and wrote back to Malcolm that the poem was "brilliant" and the last verse "inspired." Malcolm lapped up such unexpected praise: "I don't think that I had ever been happier in my life than when I read in your letter that you had found something inspiring in my last verse. I imagined you saying it through to yourself and the thought of it was delicious. More and more all ambition and purpose for me crystallizes to this—to inspire by written words of mine. . . ."[20]

All the time at Alwaye he had been writing—poems, essays, short stories, fragments of a play, and a novel (called *Splendid People*). Now he redoubled his efforts. Inevitably he began to collect rejection slips. Discouraged, he remained persistent. On September 19, 1925, he wrote to his father: "How sad these little notices are. One waits and posts and waits; alternating between hope and despair; eternally running over in one's mind what one has written, wondering if it's good, wondering if it's stupid, but always rather leaning towards the former view. Then comes an envelope with the name of the paper on it. 'At any rate they have not returned the MS,' one thinks hopefully. One opens to find the above note. All is over with that then, but alas 'hope springs eternal' and the thing must be repeated again.

"I swear to you solemnly that I would infinitely rather settle down to being a perfectly good schoolmaster and have no more of this scribbling, but I simply can't do it. It's not so much ambition as it is necessity. I am almost sure that I shall never succeed—without any fatuous false modesty I doubt whether I have the ability to do so—and yet I shall go on forever trying."[21]

His first successes were modest enough; editorials and articles in the college magazine which he edited. Then *The Calcutta Guardian* ("A Christian Weekly of Public Affairs," according to its masthead) reprinted an article from the school magazine called "On The Loneliness of Being a Sahib" and invited him to submit more articles at ten rupees a time. He replied that he would write one essay per month for no fee and this he did, most of them unmemorable, on such light topics as "Riding on Trains" and "The Comic Opera Element in Indian Life." Some of these articles were reprinted abroad, and gradually his reputation and self-confidence grew. In September 1926, his father wrote to request an article for the Ruskin Hall magazine whose editor, McLeod, had expressed admiration for Malcolm's work and ". . . tactfully suggested that I am now getting known as the father of Malcolm (a reputation I enjoy better than any other)."

Money was never a motive for writing. In India he lived so frugally that his paltry salary was adequate enough. Any excess he gave away—a lifelong habit. He asked his father to raise the possibility of his contributing a regular column to *The Daily Herald* and stipulated: "Of course, I shouldn't want any pay. I have enough to live on and, praise God, no ambition for more." H. T. did meet with the *Herald's* editor, Fyfe, but nothing came of it.

When he had completed an article or short story, he usually sent it back to his father in the hope that he might be able to find an English publisher. One of the first such stories, called "The Mess of Pottage," H. T. considered so sexually explicit that he refused to send it around. Malcolm was angry: "I feel that you are quite as unbalanced about sex, the other way, as I am," he wrote, and went on to lecture his father on how most of the world's great literature concerned this subject. Years later, however, in a controversy over the Booker Prize, he emulated his father's action by resigning as a judge rather than read through novels he regarded as little better than pornography. In any case, "The Mess of Pottage" was never published. Eventually, *The New Statesman* did publish several of his Indian articles, beginning with an unusually ponderous piece on Indian education that appeared on May 25, 1928, but by then he had left India.

For someone as determined to write as Muggeridge, to actually see one's own words in print is a kind of narcotic. First, the ecstatic high when, riffling anxiously through the pages, one comes upon it: One's own creation. Utter self-absorption as one reads it through. The sting of a misplaced comma; the anguish of a word omitted! Then a short-lived euphoria as one pronounces it good and imagines countless unknown people hurriedly scanning pages, their eyes momentarily arrested by your words, then slowly, attentively moving from side to side, lower and lower, as an appropriate look of acquiescence or awe or delight or enlightenment or hilarity spreads across their face. Like an orgasm, sharp and intense, this excitement soon passes, and one feels vacant and empty, a peculiarly desolate emptiness. The pangs of withdrawal set in, and no anodyne will serve to assuage them. No cold turkey either, for that means oblivion. One takes up pen or sits down before a typewriter with a resigned, almost fearful, knowledge that to get the same high next time, the dose will have to be increased or the product made purer, more refined.

At the beginning of 1926, Muggeridge's spirits temporarily perked up when it appeared that Alec Vidler might come to India. Vidler had been invited to become private chaplain to the Viceroy, Lord Irwin (later Lord Halifax), and to tutor his sons. Vidler considered it seriously but declined because he was then priest in charge of St. Aidans, Birmingham, and in the midst of a protracted, divisive controversy with Bishop E. W. Barnes over one of those small, dull differences that periodically ruffle the placid surface of Anglicanism. Despite personal disappointment that his best friend would not be joining him in India, Muggeridge praised Vidler's decision: ". . . the powers that be are, by their very nature, in my eyes utterly immoral in this country—immoral in the sense that they are killing a people's soul, and I'm glad you aren't to be bound up with them."[22]

As the months dragged on, his resolve to leave Alwaye increased, and he gave notice in April that he would go the following March. He would need some sort of job back in England. "There are three kinds of jobs I should like," he wrote to his father: "(1) To be secretary to an MP—or almost anything connected with politics. (2) Journalism—any job on the staff of a Labour paper. (3) A teacher." He knew the first possibility was remote, even though he professed himself willing to sweep the floor at Labour party headquarters. The second, journalism, was unlikely, at least until his work and name became better known. So teaching, alas, it must be, and in August he enlisted Vidler's help to find a teaching position somewhere near Birmingham so that they might live together. Also, he made inquiries about enrolling for post-graduate studies in, of all things, economics. Having read the wrong subject as an undergraduate, he seemed determined to repeat his error as a postgraduate. Fortunately, like so many of his schemes at this time, nothing came of it, and the dismal science was left to Keynes and his contemporaries to wreak their particular brand of havoc through recessions, deficits, and inflated, worthless currency on an unsuspecting world.

Any lingering doubt he may have had about leaving India was laid to rest after an incident at the Sunday morning chapel service. His preaching turn had come round again. His previous sermons had caused a certain amount of disquiet, but the principal, K. C. Charcko (whose toleration of Muggeridge's disruptiveness can only have derived from genuine affection), had always come to his defense. Now he lost his last defender. The actual sermon he preached has disappeared, and all that exists are these references to it in a letter to his parents on August 6, 1926: "I preached a sermon last Sunday showing the dangers of making divinities of our great teachers—how that leads to fanaticism and divorcement of action from belief. All the great prophets of God have caused war and Hell in the world—Jesus, Mohammed and the others, but Socrates has not—why? Because no one has been foolish enough to regard him as a God, and yet in his words we find all the great moral truths that there are in the New Testament."

His sermon was pronounced "heretical," and Muggeridge was formally barred from ever again preaching in the chapel. He was not upset. In fact, he found the row hilarious, particularly such a ponderous defense of orthodoxy in so unlikely a setting. But it did serve to make the already oppressive atmosphere of the place seem even more stifling.

His last months in India were spent teaching, writing, corresponding with prospective employers, and reading. His usually eclectic reading was now concentrated on books that might assist him in sorting out his religious position. He read *Religion and the Rise of Capitalism*, Plato's dialogues, Marcus Aurelius, Albert Schweitzer, and several books on Eastern religions. He had decided that one must choose between a religion like Hinduism, which provided some logical, reasonable explanation of the universe, or one like Christianity, which gave a motive for good living. Christianity, it seemed, provided no answers; at its heart were unfathomable mysteries. In a world created by a loving God, why is there so much needless suffering? Given man's evil nature, why should God so concern Himself with our sordid affairs as to offer Himself in sacrifice for His own creation? The answers to questions like this, he came to believe, were obscured by the cloud of unknowing that is forever between man and God. Instead of answers, Christianity provided a way of living that related time to eternity, history to truth, a way by which God could appear in the flesh of a man and a man be crucified because He was God. It was less something to be understood—as one understands why two plus two make four—than something to be experienced—and then verified through the actual process of living. "Christianity is to life what Shakespeare is to literature," he wrote. "It envisages the whole. It sees the necessity for a man to have spiritual values and it shows him how to get at those through physical sacraments. . . . Your logical Hindu takes a circle for his divine symbol—a complete and rounded and satisfying thing—but we take an ungainly, unsymmetrical cross—a bare jagged gibbet, as a paradoxical expression of a paradoxical faith."[23]

He was beginning to develop a view of Christianity as remote from the formulas of the evangelical missionaries as it was from the Anglo-Catholicism of Oratory House; it was unique, it was precious, and the rest of his life would be spent fitfully trying to escape it or express it. He would not then, nor perhaps ever, have said that he had a faith; rather he had a way of looking at life and of relating himself to it and to its Creator. He imagines putting his position to God in these terms: "Sire, though I am prepared to help you all I can—to accept the sacrificial way of living; yet because you have not shown me all I cannot do all. My faith is that as I see what is good and true and beautiful, I may find strength to live them, to speak them, to write them, to apply them, to oppose what seems to me to blaspheme them; and, if necessary, to die for them. Beyond this the responsibility is yours; for, if you will pardon my indelicacy in reminding you of such a sad matter, you, either in frolic or madness or in some mood too deep for me to understand, did in fact make this mudheap, and impose on me limitations whereby I do see darkly only."[24]

Originally, he planned an ambitious route home that would have taken him up the Persian Gulf to Baghdad, across the desert to Beirut, on foot through Egypt and the Holy Land, from Alexandria to Italy, and then back to England. Miss Hopwood, the evangelical spinster who had nursed him at Farley, intended to accompany him as far as Alexandria, and he idly wondered if their combined experiences might yield material for a travel book. But a closer check of his finances revealed that he had saved practically nothing in India, so the longer route had to be scrapped. Instead he booked passage on an Orient line, the S.S. *Otranto*, leaving Colombo on March 23, 1927, and docking in Naples on April 8.

Meanwhile, his father asked McIntyre, Hogg and Marsh if he might have a two-week holiday to surprise his son at Naples. This arranged, he wrote to Alec Vidler:

> You will, I think, find Malcolm greatly altered—more of a responsible man and less of the wild youth.
> He is learning how to use his pen. He had quite a lot of his writing published in India. He only wants more and deeper experience of life to make him, I hope, an inspirer of good causes, and a help to struggling souls.
> His verse, I sometimes think, is his best stuff. It has marks in it of sandstorm. His spirit is one that will never be quiet. He has Hell to go through and I could wish for no one to be near him so much as you. His sympathy with the poor and miserable is intense, but he has to learn that he mustn't let it burn his soul and sanity out. He must master his emotions, not be mastered by them, and so fritter away his strength (if I am not mistaken in thinking he has much) in mere protests and declamations.[25]

Muggeridge's final days at Alwaye were clouded by another row, this time over a critical article he wrote on unemployment among university graduates, which seemed to mock Indian education in general and Alwaye college in particular. The anger of the authorities was understandable; not only had he called the teachers "dead" and their lessons "artificial"—"wax hyacinths and pink paper roses imported from the West"—but the article specifically identified its author as a faculty member at Union Christian College, Alwaye. The principal cancelled a planned farewell party (although one wonders why, since, under the circumstances, his departure ought to have been an occasion for rejoicing) but still came and shook him by the hand and said that he had made a unique contribution to the life of the college and would be welcomed back at any time. By the time he went back, four decades had passed; the principal was dead, and the college, India, and the world were vastly changed places.

The journey from Alwaye to Colombo had to be made by foot, boat and train. Muggeridge was delighted to have his friend, Venkatranam, accompany him as far as Allepey. They left the day after term ended with Muggeridge clutching a stack of unmarked examination papers under his arm. As the boat drifted downstream, he graded each paper and then chucked it overboard. As the pile of papers progressively diminished, he threw them with ever greater abandon, as one might fling the last confetti at a departing bride. The papers floated briefly on the backwater and the ink ran, blurring the scribbled words and phrases that he had first spoken in an open-sided classroom; words and phrases dutifully committed to memory and now being carried about in the heads of newly minted graduates, ready, should occasion arise, to be repeated verbatim. As the boat moved on, the papers sank from sight beneath the surface without so much as a bubble rising to mark their descent to the primeval mud of India. In his ebullient mood, no student failed.

·4·
EGYPT and
The GUARDIAN

Always I seem to take up impossible loyalties that break down and then I am stranded. All my enthusiasms seem to have been such failures.

Malcolm Muggeridge to Alec Vidler, August 25, 1925

* * *

It was shorter and pleasanter to come back from India than to go there. On April 8, 1927, Muggeridge met up with his father, to whom (along with Alec Vidler) he had written faithfully every week; the intimacy of their correspondence is more suggestive of brothers than of father and son. In Naples they stayed at a *pension* on the Piazza Amedeo, then journeyed on to Rome and Paris. In Paris they were entertained by a travel agent who was an acquaintance of H.T.'s. The evening's entertainment turned out to be lewd, and the hostess of the establishment, clad only in high heels and a diaphanous scarf, came and perched on H. T.'s lap. More from embarrassment than encouragement, H. T. gave her a pound note that she proceeded to stick in her shoe, that being the only readily available receptacle. Later, as they both trudged back along the Champs Elyseés, Malcolm could hear his father muttering over to himself: " 'Her shoe! She put it in her shoe.'

"I looked sidelong at my father—his head, as ever, a little tilted in defiance, the wings of his city collar whitely protruding, his outsize bowler down on his ears, and felt a pang of deep, anguished affection for him."[1]

Once back in England, Muggeridge went to stay with Alec Vidler, then living in a clergy house at Small Heath in Birmingham. Although one of his last letters had expressed "dread" that ". . . my complete driftage away from Christianity may estrange us,"[2] it did not prove so. The reunion was a happy one, and their friendship only matured and grew deeper.

Vidler had arranged some supply teaching work for Muggeridge with the Birmingham Education Authority. Initially, he had little heart for such temporary stop-gap employment. Yet gradually, perhaps because of the unpredictable nature of the work, never knowing when a sickness, death, resignation, or pregnancy would lead to his being dispatched, he came to enjoy it. It had a certain, nomadic quality that suited him. He was usually at a school just long enough to appreciate the students and too briefly to antagonize the masters.

On July 2, 1927, he was sent to what was then the worst school in the heart of industrial Birmingham. Its little asphalt courtyard was surrounded by belching chimneys that obscured the sun; the walls were gritty and black with the accumulated filth of generations. He wrote:

The children were puny and, in feature, curiously aged. There was a weariness about some of their eyes, and lines in some of their faces, which one usually associates only with a world-weary middle age. They seemed to have plunged into tragedy when most of us know only days of careless freedom in the forest of Arden. Winter, with them, had set in desperately early.

But with all this the school was full of happiness. There was something real about it; a flavour of the sacredness that comes only when things are being made. It was as though human life felt itself, in such conditions, put upon its metal, and determined therefore to show us all what it was capable of. For these children who were herded together at night—four, five, six in one room; many of whom came breakfastless to school, and had, for mid-day meal, only a hunk of bread; who had been bullied and harassed from earliest recollections; who, instead of a sky—and how may we know God if we are prevented from seeing his eyes?—looked up to a smoky pall, and instead of trees and grass and all the infinite sweetness of nature found around them blackened bricks shutting them in like a prison; these were good at their work, good at their play and good in themselves. There was a boy there, with a face like an angel, who was one of seventeen living in four rooms. He showed me a composition he had written about a brook; and, in all his life he had never seen one. There was another who recited, with passionate fervour, a poem about gold dust—a gold dust that, dropped in a man's eye, made all this mudheap radiant. And he had six brothers, and his father sold matches in the streets, and had, two days before, been put in jail for begging; while his mother had lost some wretched casual job she had by attending at the police court.

. . . Just as I left three urchins from the top standard—louts of Punch's vicious drawings—brought in a sparrow in a hat. It was injured and they were afraid that it might die. I fear I wept at this, for their kindness to the little bird made the world's unkindness to them seem the more cruel. "Strange" said the head "that a creature with wings should come here."

I would advise anyone who still believes that there is a difference in kind between the cultured and the uncultured; between the neat coated and the ragged coated, to visit one of these slum elementary schools, for there even the most dense cannot fail to see clearly that God, like the birds, never sings out of tune.[3]

There was more to this incident than a mere rekindling of the socialist ideals to which his father had devoted his life. It had this effect, and he did take up the possibility of a political career with influential Labour party stalwarts to whom H. T. introduced him. But of more lasting importance is what it reveals of his attitude toward deprivation and suffering, an attitude that has changed little throughout his life.

For many people suffering is the major stumbling block on the road to Christian faith. It has never been so for Muggeridge. Although his family circumstances were comfortable enough, he is no stranger to poverty or affliction; in fact he has been surrounded by both for most of his life—in childhood by the indigents of Croydon who sought his father's assistance; in India and in Egypt; in Russia at the height of the famine; during wartime; in later years through his association with one of the few saints of this sordid century, Mother Teresa of Calcutta.

Muggeridge sees suffering as something basic and integral to human life, like sharps and flats are to music. Take away sharps and flats, and there is no music; take away suffering, and there is no life. The point is not to single out individual notes and debate their whys and where-fores, but rather to catch the melody of the whole composition. Life is, to use his friend Anthony Powell's evocative phrase, a dance to the music of time in which he who strains may hear secret harmonies.

The key to Muggeridge's attitude is that he envisages life not as a *scientific*, but as an *artistic* creation; God's action in making us and our world and our universe was, as it were, comparable to Shakespeare's writing *King Lear*. As one cannot fully understand drama apart from the dramatist, so one cannot understand life, in all its vicissitudes, apart from God. This is not to suggest that we can now, or perhaps ever, fully grasp our Creator's mysterious purposes, any more than one sees the dénouement of a play midway through the third act. But from the first moment when King Lear's folly leads him to mistake Regan's and Goneril's humbug for Cordelia's genuine love, the discerning eye senses rather than sees the outlines of a dark, foreboding future. So one may sense or, as Saint Paul put it—"see through a glass darkly," how contemporary man who turns his back on a drama in which suffering is an essential part and harkens instead to the sedulous voices of doctors and eugenicists who promise to eliminate suffering, perhaps even death itself, is fashioning a tragedy by his own hand. Hence Muggeridge's opposition to all those who would presume to decide who shall live and who shall die in the womb; also his scorn for heart transplants and the various bizarre proposals to sort out and rearrange our genes so that everyone will become superman and wonderwoman One can no more eliminate suffering from life, Muggeridge believes, than one can eliminate suffering from *King Lear* and still have a play. For this he is often accused of incorrigible pessimism, although no view of life could actually be more clearheaded and sanguine. It is those who imagine that life can be bent to conform with their own vain hopes and aspirations, and whose disillusionment when this fails, as fail it must, knows no bounds, who are the rankest pessimists. Nor has Muggeridge's view been shaken either by personal tragedy in his own life (such as the death of his son Charles at the age of twenty), nor by close association with the most wretched of humanity, at least in material terms, such as the flotsam and jetsam of Calcutta to whom Mother Teresa ministers daily.

In 1963 Muggeridge appeared on a BBC program on which he discussed his view of suffering. This brought in many letters, some from people who had triumphed over apalling adversity, others from those who had lost their religious faith by the experience of observing or attending a suffering loved one. One particularly poignant letter came from a mother whose twenty-two-year-old son had died during an operation to close a heart perforation. "Where is your God," she wrote, "and why does he allow such things to happen?" He replied: "Where is my God? Dear Mrs. ---, he is everywhere; even in the hole in your son's heart or nowhere.

"No one who has been spared—certainly not I—dare say to the afflicted that they are blessed in their affliction, or offer comfort in universal terms for particular griefs. Yet one can dimly see and humbly say that suffering is an integral and essential part of our human drama. That it falls upon one and all in differing degrees and forms whose comparison lies beyond our competence. That it belongs to God's purpose for us here on earth, so that in the end, all the experience of living has to teach us is to say: Thy will be done. To say it standing before a cross; itself signifying the suffering of God in the person of a man, and the redemption of man in the person of God. The greatest sorrow and the greatest joy co-existing on Golgotha."[4]

Whether or not this answer served to assuage the bereaved mother, it does verge on ". . . offering comfort in universal terms for particular griefs." This is inevitable. Words carry no anaesthetizing power; they cannot lessen the physical pain of the sufferer. At most, if they are good words and true, they help one to comprehend suffering, to put it into an understandable perspective that makes its ravages bearable. Like his mentor, William Blake, Muggeridge believes that "man was made for joy and woe" and that, once grasped, "through the world we safely go."

It must be added that he practices what he preaches: From tiny eccentricities, like refusing anaesthetic for dental fillings or extractions, to being resolute and undeflected by deaths of loved ones, personal tragedy, criticism, or scorn, he is a man who has resolutely made his way through a troubled, dangerous world.

When he was not teaching or writing in Birmingham, he was pacing aimlessly about the streets intent on watching the passing faces. If it was morning he observed the bustle of, in those days, mostly men as they made their way to work, newspapers folded under their arms, piling into trams, with occasional traces of breakfast—it might be a patch of egg white or a sliver of marmalade—still clinging to their lips. In the evening they returned, funneling out of the trams to drift off in every direction, like an ocean emptying its waters into innumerable rivers and tributaries. Then they looked tired and grubby, but relieved by a certain air of complacency that another day in their lives was finished. At night, other passersby, young men in tailored suits arm-in-arm with women in short skirts who walked up and down the pavements past the closed shops, sometimes turning into one of the two garishly illuminated cinemas, sometimes into noisy pubs, a few couples searching out dark alleyways or unlit street corners to pummel and claw and coax a little relief of that same lust that burned intensely in him.

He had seen Dora once or twice since returning from India, but there was no spark of romance left. This is hardly surprising. Although very attractive, she now seemed to Malcolm a shallow and immature girl whose ambition, judging from her letters to him, was to marry, acquire a suburban home with a little, symmetrical garden, and raise three children who would be expected to do the same. Her values were "petty bourgeois," as scornful a term of abuse as his vocabulary then contained. He broke off the relationship by the indirect but final expedient of marrying someone else. Nearly fifty years later he learned that Dora was in severe financial trouble because of protracted litigation with a former landlord; with characteristic generosity, he paid all her legal bills. Shortly after, Dora died.

In August 1927, he went to Belgium to visit the Dobbs family whom he had met when working as a tour guide there. His memoirs imply that there was no forethought to this trip: "On an impulse, I decided to go over to the Belgium coast again . . . ."[5] It seems more probable that he went with the explicit and carefully considered purpose of raising his stock among the influential socialists he was then, with one eye on the political horizon, assiduously courting. In fact, looking back on this time, a diary entry in 1936 says: "The family's aristocratic connections obsessed me somewhat. I liked to think about them." One of Mrs.

Dobbs's sisters was Lady Courtney whose husband had been a member of parliament, a *Times* leader writer and, after 1906, a peer. Another sister, Beatrice Webb, was to the socialist "movement," as it was then still called, roughly speaking what Jefferson was to the American framers of the Declaration of Independence. Although less influential in socialist circles, Kitty's mother, Mrs. Dobbs, was a weird, lovable woman who had met her husband, George Dobbs, while wandering aimlessly about Europe and settled down to live with him in what Kitty once described as "not unreasonable strife." Muggeridge has drawn an unforgettable portrait of Mrs. Dobbs in his memoirs.

Malcolm had originally met Kitty Dobbs when he shared rooms with her brother Leonard in his last year at Cambridge. He had seen her only once or twice since then. Suddenly it was announced that they would be married within a month. Everyone was astonished, not least Kitty's father who considered Malcolm an unworthy match and tried his best to dissuade Kitty. Alec Vidler, who was away from Birmingham on vacation, received a terse note on August 11: "I'm going to be married on September 10. I know it sounds ridiculous but there it is."

Actually, it was not out of character. In contrast to the way his father acted, Malcolm rarely deliberates over personal decisions. He is inclined to rash, precipitate action on those matters that most people regard as critical, on which they take advice, agonize, resolve in a qualified way, and then fret over. On the other hand, on issues that many people regard as self-evident, progress, say, or universal suffrage or censorship, he broods interminably, without ever formulating a fixed, clear position. In a sense, he had predicted how his marriage would come about two years before when he wrote to Vidler: "I fear I shall marry one day in a burst of enthusiasm—for when I am in love I am convinced of its sincerity—and make some poor female unhappy. I might catch a Tartar in which case we should make each other unhappy."[6]

His memoirs are not particularly revealing about the exact circumstances of their engagement:

> It somehow became understood that Kitty and I would get married and quite soon. I cannot recall ever "proposing" to her—something we should both have regarded as very bourgeois and conventional; terms of abuse in our vocabulary. Nor can I remember any moment of decision; or, for that matter, of indecision. Free will, in my experience, is tactical rather than strategic; in all the larger shaping of a life, there is a plan already, into which one has no choice but to fit, or contract out of living altogether. So, it was borne in upon me that Kitty and I belonged together; that somehow, to me, the shape and sense and sound of her existence in the universe would always be appreciable in every corner of it, and through all eternity.

To this essential proposition all sorts of other hopes, desires, appetites, egotistic aspirations, corporeal needs and mental strivings, were attached, like subordinate clauses; sex being one of these.[7]

On the day appointed, their union was solemnized at the Birmingham Registry office. Only one guest was invited, she to serve as the essential witness; however, Mr. Dobbs turned up uninvited and reluctantly gave the bride away: "When, in the course of the ceremony, the Registrar put the crucial question, he intervened sharply, telling her in a loud voice that there was still time for her to withdraw."[8] As soon as the formal ceremony was concluded, Malcolm inquired of the registrar how one went about getting a divorce. Happily, this information proved unnecessary; despite the squalls and tempests that lay ahead, their marriage was to be enduring. After lunch they returned briefly to Small Heath where they found a check for fifteen guineas, intended as a wedding present from Mr. Dobbs's employer, Sir Henry Lunn. To Malcolm's horror, Kitty ripped it up on the grounds that Sir Henry was a despicable character. After they had gone, the other residents managed to collect and piece it together, but the check was never cashed.

They stayed five days in Croydon (no doubt to atone for Malcolm's callousness in not inviting his parents to the wedding), then a week in Paris, and a few days with the Dobbs's at Montreux in the Swiss Alps near Lake Geneva. At the beginning of October, they were back in Birmingham in a two-room flat near the outskirts, for which they paid one pound a week rent. "It was an impermanent household, with coloured lampshades, and sincere conversation, and hired, untidy furniture."[9] Neighbors looked askance when, in the early morning, Malcolm and Kitty were to be seen dancing barefoot in the recreation ground opposite.

They had hardly settled in before Mr. Dobbs, by now reconciled to the marriage, drew Malcolm's attention to a newspaper advertisement for teachers in Egypt. It meant steady employment and a dependable income. He applied and was accepted. They packed up what few belongings they possessed, mostly books, and set off for Minia in upper Egypt, by way of Paris, Genoa, Alexandria, and Cairo. To Vidler, he wrote: "It seems strange to be at large again after so short a stay in England. But there it is. When I move about I feel that my one desire in life is to be quiet in one place; and when I'm quiet in one place I only want to get away from it. That's what comes of having no religion."[10]

In Cairo they waited at the station for the train to Minia. It was late afternoon, early in November 1927, and the glancing rays of the sun bathed the vaulted glass roof and steel girders and platforms in a gentle, soft light. Porters squatted nonchalantly, only stirring themselves when a train arrived. Hawkers were everywhere, pleading, flattering, cajoling travelers to buy trinkets, sticky circular cakes, cigarettes, and nuts. The newlyweds strolled up and down the platform, happy with each other and content with whatever fate awaited them. Malcolm wrote in his ever present notebook: "The trains come out of the sunset, and their carriages, as they pass slowly by, are like the years of one's life: seemingly endless, yet inevitably and at last coming to an end."

Teaching in a government secondary school in Minia, he might almost have been back at Alwaye. Here the classroom had walls, but one could still look away over the cultivated fields to the Nile and beyond to the yellow desert that turned a sullen brown when the sun dipped behind the hills. The voices of men singing in the fields drifted in through the open windows. Again, a gavotte with English literature before another lot of blank faces and inert minds.

"Sir, what is meant by 'I see a lily on thy brow/With anguish moist and fever dew'?"

"His forehead is pale—white like a lily you know; and he is hot with fever and pain, so he perspires, and the perspiration is like dew."

"But, sir, what is perspiration?"

"Sweat."

"Ah, yes."

Instead of Little Dowden, he read from *Man and His Work*, a presentation of human achievement in the form of facts, set out in statistical tables and dry, arid prose. The bell for lunch promised momentary relief, only to be followed, too soon, by another bell calling for the afternoon performance. If a sudden plague should kill off all the masters and students, he reflected, the bells would continue to ring automatically. The heat of the afternoon made thought heavy and speech forced and movement painful. Some of the boys would fall asleep, their heads lolling forward, occasionally emitting a croak or snore. At three o'clock, more bells, these as welcome as the trumpets that sounded for Bunyan's pilgrim when at last he crossed over.

In the evenings he walked by the Nile, or sat at his typewriter, or he and Kitty took turns reading aloud. It is a fundamental article of faith to him that the ultimate test of a book is how well it reads aloud; *Madame Bovary* stood up so well that he proclaimed it ". . . easily the most wonderful novel I have ever read." He and Kitty were happy—at least ". . . as happy as people like us ever can be."[11] Marriage suited him, and in its first charms, he wrote: "It is as though all my days were suddenly flooded with a golden light, making them rich and beautiful."[12]

His general contentment was bolstered by increasing literary success. His articles were finding more receptive and prestigious publishers, particularly *The New Statesman*, which in socialist circles was accorded canonical status. He was beginning to synthesize what he had seen and experienced in India and Egypt and was forming a mature, more comprehensive view of imperialism, power, and world affairs. His writing had become self-assured and was already taking on a distinctive prophetic quality; in a truly astonishing number of cases, his prophecies would be borne out by events.

In October 1928, his article "Subject Peoples" appeared. The British Empire, and with it the whole concept of imperialism, collapsed so quickly and irretrievably that it is difficult now to remember that in 1928 it appeared omnipotent and impregnable and was confidently spoken of by many as divinely ordained to continue forever. Muggeridge wrote:

> We have to face the fact that there is today a stirring of subject peoples all over the world. They are demanding the right to govern their own destinies in their own way. Egypt for the Egyptians, they say; and India for the Indians; and China for the Chinese.
>
> . . . There can be no doubt that the subject peoples will go on demanding concession after concession, and that the Powers will be forced to give way to them. The only thing is that the more graciously they give way the better it will be for all concerned. And the half-way houses will be dangerous and uncomfortable. They always are. There is that amount of truth in the contention of the die-hard as against that of the sentimental liberal—it must be a steel frame or nothing: wooden scaffolding is useless. And nothing it will, of course, be in the end; in much the same way that in the end the labouring classes in England had to be given the right to vote, not because it was particularly good for them or for England that they should have it, but because it was in their souls to demand it; and what is in a man's soul is invariably achieved.
>
> Reaching this end, however, would seem to be a weary, wrangling process, full of hartals and strikes and wars and bloody revolutions.[13]

In the spring of 1928, two events changed the Muggeridges', by now, rather placid lives. First, Kitty became pregnant, an apparently unanticipated event: "The real joke, Alec, about birth control is that there is no such thing. And I'm rather glad."[14] Then Malcolm was invited to join the English faculty of the Egyptian University in Cairo, at that time headed by Bonamy Dobrée.

At three months;
winner of Mellin's Baby Food Prize

Malcolm at five; brother Eric,
Stanley and Malcolm (left to
right) outside Croydon home

Harry Muggeridge, Malcolm Muggeridge's father in his sixties (about 1927)

Dora Pitman; first love, 1920

They spent the summer vacation in Vienna where Kitty fell over a washtub and had to be rushed to a hospital. Initially, a miscarriage was feared. After three days rest in bed, she was pronounced fit and released. In September they made their way back to Cairo, first to a flat on the Avenue Ramses in Heliopolis from which Malcolm took a tram into the city each day. Egyptian University was then quartered in the Zaffarian palace, and he held forth in a classroom that had formerly accommodated a harem. "There were still odd traces of the previous usage. Little frivolous twists and turns in the masonry and woodwork, fragments of marble frescoes; up in the ceilings, coloured designs and figures, now faded, and in the neglected garden a rusty, disused fountain in the middle of what had once been obviously an ornamental pool. It added an extra dimension of fantasy to our disquisitions on *Antony and Cleopatra* chosen for its topicality "[15]

French and English were the languages of the university, and teachers were required to lecture in both. His actual teaching duties were not particularly exacting; the students were often stupefied with hashish or occasionally missing altogether, being on strike against something or other.

Most of the students were fervent supporters of the nationalist movement, the *Wafd,* and eagerly seized upon any presumed slight from a European. Of course, Muggeridge encouraged nationalism, occasionally to his own detriment—as once when he recited Keats's line: "Black as Egypt's night" and a student leaped to his feet protesting: "Always you insult us, Sir."

It should be said that Muggeridge's nationalistic sympathies did not arise from any naive or romantic belief that self-government would mean any objective improvement in the life of the average Egyptian. Life, he knew, would be no easier, no less cruel or more dignified, and no less corrupt. The peasant would drudge on as before, working no less and eating no more. His identification with the nationalist cause came about because he instinctively identified with an underdog, with the oppressed against the oppressor, and because the arrogance of an imperialist ruling class was repugnant to him.

In addition to lecturing, essays had to be read through and graded. One student, dealing with the hackneyed topic of what one would do after graduation, wrote that he wanted to be a doctor because ". . . a doctor carries his secrets in his bottom." Muggeridge happened to mention this curious turn of phrase to a school inspector, Gilbart Smith, who replied: "Yes, and from what I know of this country, a very unsafe place to carry them."[16]

Drama was an occasional diversion. There was a production of one of Yeats's plays, *The Countess Kathleen,* in which Kitty played Kathleen and he played an angel. Since this was to be one of his last stage forays, his thespian career could be said to have run the gamut from ghosts to angels, with Iago and Miss Neville intervening.

Their first son, Leonard (named after Kitty's rather forlorn brother whom Hugh Kingsmill once called "more loveable than likeable"), was born in October. Six weeks later, Muggeridge wrote to Vidler: "My son is well but giving unmistakeable signs of a natural perversity of temperament which can, I fear, only be inherited from his mother. To give you an example—from time to time we hold him over a toilet, but his bowels remain stubbornly intact; then we fit him with a new nappie, and immediately a mighty flood. Again, through the whole day he sleeps like the dead only, I must think, to conserve his energies for an amazing and painful outburst from 3:00 a.m. onwards. Such, old boy, are the cares of parenthood."[17]

Shortly after Leonard's birth, they began taking Russian lessons from an ex-cavalry officer in the white army, now down on his luck and living precariously in Cairo. In his letters from India, Malcolm had occasionally expressed a desire to see at firsthand the results of the Russian Revolution. Kitty agreed, but how? It seemed improbable, but even so they decided to prepare themselves.

Malcolm was now sending short stories off to T. S. Eliot who had written a note praising his work. And he had completed one play and was working on a second.

Expense of Spirit is a rather tepid play about a newly elected Labour M.P. Muggeridge had, of course, followed his father's successful campaign in Romford in the 1929 election, and his protagonist, John Ramsden, is a rather cruel caricature of H. T. The play was never performed.

Three Flats, on the other hand, is a curious play that allows the audience to look into the lives of the occupants of three high-rise flats. On the bottom floor live two spinster schoolteachers quietly desperate to get married; one sublimates her yearning into her work and is miserable; the other yields to it in promiscuity and is content. Then a middle-aged couple, Mr. and Mrs. Mason, whose marriage of twenty years has become a worn husk in which the seed has shriveled; finally, on the top floor, Maeve Scott, a naive young woman of what today would be called liberated views, unmarried and living with a "struggling, unsuccessful litterateur" named Dennis Rhys who, undoubtedly speaking for Muggeridge, wonders to himself: "Why does one write?—a silly trade. Why isn't it enough to live; to feel things—why must one always be grinding them out in words? And yet it seems the only thing to do."

Mr. Mason is discovered by his wife directing affectionate remarks towards one of the schoolteachers, Miss Edwards. Dennis, happening on the scene, takes up Miss Edwards's defense and becomes smitten with her too. Maeve, his mistress, then takes poison and dies. What is the unity, the play asks, in these three lives? What is it that makes such people, and countless others like them living in flats everywhere, carry on from day to day? Muggeridge was sensible enough to realize that a play provides insufficient scope to answer such questions; he is content just to raise them and to imply somehow that behind the harlequinade of life—now tragedy, now melodrama, now farce—one may glimpse some overall purpose. There is a point to it all, he seems to be saying, but I am not yet sure I know what it is.

The play was first performed at the Prince of Wales Theatre on February 15, 1931. Its frankness offended his family and some critics. His father came to opening night, but still voiced disapproval of what he considered a preoccupation with sex. Kitty's aunt, Beatrice Webb, disliked it intensely; she said she was "shocked," not so much for herself, but for those in the audience whose sensibilities she presumed to be less robust than her own (actually, this was a rather improbable assumption).

Even this early and insignificant play has a weirdly prophetic quality about it; in one sense it is an examination of the effects of high-rise living, then comparatively rare, on individual morality. This was to become a subject much speculated upon by sociologists, urban planners, psychologists, and so on, though seldom with such insouciance.

The play attracted extensive notices, most of them favorable. Closest to the mark was Ivor Brown who said in *Weekend Review*: "There was plenty of truth in the offing, but the bane of the contemporary theatre, Dr. Freud, would keep breaking in."

By now Muggeridge's innate restlessness was gnawing at him. "Egypt is a dreary place, and I wish the time would come quickly when I could live by writing," he wrote to his father at the beginning of 1929. The added responsibilities of a wife and child had made it more difficult to kick over the traces and make off for a new place. He was twenty-six years old, his accomplishments were slight, and the prospect of drifting along teaching had become a nightmare. He kept writing and hoping.

One of the many newspapers to which he dispatched his efforts was *The Manchester Guardian*, then still edited by an aging C. P. Scott whom Muggeridge had met through Kitty's aunt, Lady Courtney. In July 1929, Scott nominally retired, but actually he stayed in office until his death, superintending the staff of obsequious journalists who filled the paper's columns with platitudes designed to appeal to his high-minded vanity. His son, Ted, succeeded him in the chair, and Ted had been favorably impressed by some of Muggeridge's efforts, particularly those dealing with the Egyptian political scene. Muggeridge's obvious sympathy for the nationalists and his acquaintance with some of their leaders (particularly Makrami Bey whose brother had been a Cambridge friend) gave an added trenchancy to his analysis. Ted Scott cabled for more, which Muggeridge gladly provided, "feeling mighty proud about it," he told his father. Then Arthur Ransome, a longtime *Guardian* correspondent, turned up in Cairo on one of his periodic foreign excursions and made a point of looking up this promising young writer. They took an immediate liking to one another and henceforth passed many hours together. Muggeridge was awed by Ransome's experience: "His great glamour in my eyes was that he had witnessed the Russian Revolution, and had known and talked with Lenin, Trotsky and the other leaders in the flesh. It all made him, to me, more remarkable than if he had actually been present at the Crucifixion, or accompanied Moses when he received the Ten Commandments carved on stone at God's hands. When he told me that he had actually played chess with Lenin, who proved to be rather a poor player, and with Litvinov, a much better one, I inwardly genuflected."[18] Ransome, too, was impressed, and he advised Scott to take Muggeridge on. Scott wrote offering him a three-month probationary job on the editorial staff. "I believe I have never received a letter which gave me so much delight; waving it triumphantly in the air I rushed to tell Kitty, and then to the post office to telegraph my acceptance of the offer. Whatever feelings I may have subsequently had about the high proportion of my time and energy given to journalism, I cannot claim that harsh necessity drove me into the trade. No one could have embarked upon it more hopefully or thankfully or joyously."[19] Only later did he think to inquire about the salary, which turned out to be five pounds a week. Later on, when he got to know some of the old hands on the *Guardian*, he heard one reporter grumble that the paper had always dispensed a great deal more uplift than cash.

Muggeridge completed the university year and arrived in Manchester in August 1930 (not 1932 as his autobiography mistakenly asserts). In one important respect, it was a different England to which he returned: now ensconced in the corridors of power was a Labour government, something for which his father had toiled so long and faithfully; and H. T. was himself a member of it. "They had advanced, not very formidably against the Kingdom of Mammon, and now found themselves its forlorn garrison."[20]

From the moment Muggeridge acquired a perch on the editorial corridor (one lately vacated by Kingsley Martin who moved over to the chair at *The New Statesman*), he knew that he had found his element. In journalism, if anywhere, he would make his mark. The very pace and rhythm of it suited him; as though in addition to blood his heart pumped ink to be dribbled out on paper. The last feverish moments, with a deadline looming, his words came best; when the paper was set, beyond changing or amending, he was languid and dissipated and would usually make for the Stock Exchange bar handily located beneath the offices. "Pulp to pulp—this was my line."

Kitty and Leonard (called Pan by the family) joined him, and they found a house next to Kingsley Martin's in Didsbury. According to Martin, as soon as she settled in, Kitty "hung her pajamas out of the window as a flag of defiance."[21]

Malcolm asserted his defiance in the *Guardian's* editorial columns. In the beginning, clashes arose less over the paper's high-minded liberalism, which he could still then with some gagging swallow, but over the savage and unconventional way he expressed himself in print. He was still a disciple of D. H. Lawrence (in Egypt he had wept on hearing the news of Lawrence's death), and a practitioner of what Lawrence called "thinking with the blood." In one editorial, on the cult of sunbathing in Europe, he managed to slip a quotation from Lawrence about "the genitals of space" by the usually omniscient eye of C. P. Scott. It caused embarrassment. Then, on July 29, 1931, he took after Winston Churchill: "The cost is too great—in money, in blood, and in shame—and even if we were less squeamish about investing in murder, massacre and demoralization we should like a better guarantee than Mr. Churchill's for the profits to be derived from his sanguinary speculations." But the worst row came over his review of Catherine Carswell's biography of D. H. Lawrence, *The Savage Pilgrimage*. His critique began: "Inevitably birds of prey hover over the corpse of a genius, and by far the most rapacious of these are his women admirers"; it concluded: "How sick one gets of Don and John and Patrick! How sick one gets of Lawrence himself! How sick, how unutterably sick, of Mrs. Carswell." Mrs. Carswell turned out to be a valued contributor to the paper and took understandable objection to such treatment. Ted Scott admired Muggeridge's passion, still more his ability to write, but begrudged the time spent mollifying the *Guardian's* irate readers.

Whenever Muggeridge got to London, he would look in on his father at Westminster and sit in the government gallery to hear him speak. Once, H. T. took a Conservative M.P., O. Locker-Hampson, to task for calling the Soviet government "bounders and crooks"; words, said H. T., of a man "bitten by the mad dog of Russian hate." Even as the Stalinist trials of the old Bolsheviks were getting underway and the boxcars were disgorging their human baggage throughout the far-flung camps of the Gulag Archipelago, H. T. was declaiming: "It is time that we dropped this perpetual nagging at everything that is Russian. Why should honourable members opposite go out of their way to discover everything in the shape of a stone to cast at the Russian government? . . . We should approach them not by an epithet, but by friendly gesture. If we set a good example, very likely they will follow . . . and our relations with Russia will be newly cemented."[22] Such sentiments might well have come from a *Guardian* leader.

An election was called for October 27, 1931, and Malcolm spent all his spare time campaigning in Romford. Polling day was foggy and bitter, and he prowled the suburban streets like a sheep dog, rounding up recalcitrant stragglers and shepherding them to the polls to "Stand for truth and vote for Muggeridge." In the evening, he accompanied his father to the committee rooms to await the returns. On the way they passed a pub with a little knot of people hanging about outside; even at this eleventh hour, H. T. could not resist an audience, and somebody brought a chair and he clambered up onto it and began to speak: "I heard his harsh voice, watched him gesticulating, almost crying with I don't know what feelings. He was so brave and so pathetic and so preposterous."[23] By the time they reached their committee rooms the first returns had already served notice of a crushing Conservative landslide. For H. T. it was a humiliating defeat in the last election he would ever contest; for his son ". . . the end of that road to the promised land I had so often rejoiced in on Saturday nights, securely tucked away in the tall, red cosy corner in our South Croydon sitting room."[24]

It was in Manchester that Muggeridge met Hugh Kingsmill. Hugh Kingsmill Lunn (he dropped the surname for writing) was the second son of Sir Henry Lunn, founder and impresario of Lunn's Travel Agency, for which Muggeridge had briefly worked as a tour guide in Belgium in the summer of 1924. Kingsmill was then a struggling writer and literary critic, and Muggeridge hoped to use his influence on the *Guardian* to land him some book reviewing. He later recalled their first meeting.

> He arrived quite late on a Friday night and we went to the station to meet him. You know that curious feeling one has of meeting someone with whom one is going to be intimate. You feel as though you know them already. Features, tone of voice, gestures, are all at once familiar. Thus I remember, in the barrier, picking out Hughie without the slightest difficulty and greeting him as though we were old friends instead of strangers . . . I have never had so strongly this feeling of recognizing, as distinct from making the acquaintance of, someone as I had it with Hughie. He came rolling into my life with that characteristic gait of his, with that

always cheerful, friendly voice, and I knew that he had been there all the time.

On Sunday morning, Kingsmill had the idea that his friend, Hesketh Pearson, was bound to pass through Manchester on his return from an acting engagement in Newcastle, and he proposed that they go down to the station to meet him. "This expectation seemed, as far as I could gather, to be based on very faint premises, but we went along to the station all the same. It had about it that air of desolation which only a railway station in the north of England on a Sunday morning can produce. There were no trains and no expectation of any trains, then, or, it seemed, ever. We walked up and down the long platform, still talking, with a vague notion that Pearson would somehow appear, though by what means was not apparent." Finally, Kingsmill ". . . reached the conclusion that what he imagined to be a carefully arranged rendezvous was not as definite as he had supposed." Muggeridge later wrote to Pearson: "We went off, however, feeling quite satisfied. If we had not met you, we had gone to meet you; and anyway, in his company I discovered, for the first time, that Stockport Station was full of interest."[25]

The book reviewing assignment, the ostensible purpose of Kingsmill's visit, was attended to last and failed to materialize. Kingsmill, it seems, struck a discordant note with Alan Monkhouse, the *Guardian's* literary editor. Afterwards, they repaired to Muggeridge's room on the corridor while he tapped out a fulsome leader for the next day's paper. "At that time I was still very young," Muggeridge recalled, "and inclined to over-seriousness. For instance, I was very serious about politics and even about the *Manchester Guardian*." It was Kingsmill who first made him see the absurd humbug of the *Guardian's* pompous editorial style: "The people of this country . . . it is greatly to be hoped . . . surely wiser counsels will prevail . . . ," all the unspeakable cant of liberal Utopianism. That night one leader began: "One is sometimes tempted to believe that the Greeks do not want a stable government . . . ," and it concluded by expressing the hope that "moderate men of all shades of opinion" would rally together. Henceforth, moderate men of all shades of opinion were to figure frequently in their conversations.

Meanwhile, an American publisher, Putnams, had published *Three Flats* and encouraged Muggeridge to submit a novel. In India and in Egypt he had tried his hand at fiction without completing anything. Now, with this encouragement, he set to it in earnest. In November 1931, *Autumnal Face* was published; the title came from John Donne's exquisite couplet:

"No spring nor summer beauty hath such grace
As I have seen in one autumnal face."

To the extent that the novel can be said to have a plot, it is (to put it mildly) improbable. A Croydon family, forebodingly named the Pills, are blighted by tragedy piled upon tragedy, all arising from their daughter Minnie's inconsequential flirting with a young suitor named Fred. First, Granny discovers them spooning on the stairwell, has a stroke and collapses, and remains a sinister, gurgling, comatose presence until late in the story when she is accidently burned to death. Then Minnie dies of the flu, contracted after an innocent dalliance with Fred at the Sunday school picnic. Minnie's vacant room is taken over by Mr. Pill's crippled brother, George, who is soon run over and killed in his wheelchair by a careening lorry. Mr. Pill then loses his job (as an accountant with a shirt manufacturer) and becomes a salesman of folding lamps; he dies, brokenhearted and mad, in a village in Hampshire where no one wants his useless product. Since Minnie died as chaste as the day she was born, all this cannot be seen as a wages-of-sin parable. So what is the point?

The point is Mum, in whose autumnal face the tragedy is etched. As the house progressively empties of living creatures, she comes to understand the emptiness of her own existence. If this seems a heavy casualty toll for such meager self-knowledge, well, this is to take the plot seriously, which was obviously not intended.

What was intended, and is achieved though in a flawed way, is a novel of character—the Pills are exact, albeit very cruel, portraits of his parents—and of atmosphere. The characters are drawn in the minutest detail, like a pencil sketch; the plot, by contrast, is slopped on in broad, unheeding brush strokes. This is true of all Muggeridge's novels. He lacks the creative imagination necessary to be a first-class novelist; for imagination he substitutes the journalist's practiced eye for telling detail. On the other hand, he has too much imagination to write prosaic, or what is called "straight," journalism, and so infuses his journalism with imaginative insight. It would not be inaccurate to say that as a novelist he is a good reporter, and as a reporter he is a good novelist. As a result, his novels contain some of his best journalism: for example, *In a Valley of This Restless Mind* which is a profound essay, in the form of a novel, on the subtleties of religious belief and unbelief. Similarly, his journalism is often a kind of imaginative fiction, as in *The Thirties*.

Autumnal Face is also a novel about love and growing old. It contrasts the young, Minnie and Fred, whose love is shimmering, tender, and in the spring, with the old, Mum and Dad, whose love is wan, repetitive, enfeebled, yet somehow enduring, like a blackened ember still giving off a tiny shard of warmth.

Certainly, no one could accuse Muggeridge of making his fictional debut with sentimental, escapist literature. The surroundings are somber, the characters are barren (not to say misanthropic), tragedies are heaped on one another thick and fast, and in the end all is darkness and waste. Of all his writing *Autumnal Face* is the bleakest. Yet even here the final passages suggest a stoical acceptance of life, rather than rejection or despair. Mum finishes up in an almshouse, the last Pill survivor, ignored by former friends and acquaintances, passing her days walking aimlessly about in a courtyard full of ghosts whose presence she refuses to acknowledge lest the authorities think her mad.

> What had it been worth?—all the years she had lived. Were they so many? Were they so long? What had it been worth that she should have lived? What was the significance of the pain and love and doubt and hate that had shaken her body and then left it a gray, tired, worn body? Their significance? Mum smiled. They had happened. She had lived. She was glad to have done so. Soon she would die, be no more. Soon her body would be laid on a bed and wrapped in sheets and nailed in a coffin and dropped into the earth. That, too, would happen. She had lived a life and the life would come to an end. How exquisite the life had been. How exquisite her white, adolescent skin; how exquisite the life that had bound her in close union with others; how exquisite the work she had done—the cleaning, the preparing of food, the hot water on cloths and the froth of soap; how exquisite the shopping and the walk through the park, the quiet warm evenings at home; how exquisite the discontent she had felt and the afternoons she had spent in the garden with George. Mum was exhilarated as she walked around the courtyard in the hard, frost air.

The reviews of *Autumnal Face* could not but have delighted him. Despite its bleak tone (in *Weekend Review* H. P. Hartley called it "the most depressing book I have ever read"), it was widely acclaimed. The *Morning Post* hailed it as "the first novel of a genuine artist"; Gerald Bullet said it "rose to dignity and tragic beauty" and was the work of "a young and acute intelligence"; and the *Sunday Referee* ran a banner headline: "A Young Novelist To Watch." In retrospect, however, the most perceptive comment came from the anonymous reviewer in the *Evening Standard* who wrote: "*Autumnal Face* is, in a sense, a horrid book. I could wish that I had not read it. But this will not prevent me from seizing eagerly on anything Mr. Muggeridge writes hereafter. The man has force . . . He has something to say."[26]

What he had to say could not be said in the pages of *The Manchester Guardian* whose sanctimonious posturing had come to seem ever more confining to him. His enthusiasm for moderate men of all shades of opinion drawing together so that wiser counsels might prevail was finished. There were, he had discovered, only immoderate men drawing forever apart, so that conflict and strife prevailed as usual. Yet the charade had to be maintained, not because it bore any relation to reality, but because at the end of the editorial corridor sat C. P. Scott, ailing, no longer robust, but still implacably determined to shape the world, or at least the *Guardian's* version of it, closer to his heart's desire: "Wars which threatened, all to be averted; wrongs which the downtrodden and oppressed suffered, all to be righted; conflicts all to be honourably resolved, and injustices all to be honourably corrected. The people of this country will never for one moment countenance, we sternly proclaimed; ourselves, the people of this country, and C. P., momentarily identified; one in three and three in one, another Holy Trinity."[27]

Even more than C. P. (whom Muggeridge actually got along with well under the circumstances), he abominated and had frequent rows with W. P. Crozier, the news editor. Crozier was an able journalist, but his austere, circumspect ways in life and print rankled Muggeridge's extravagant, bumptious temperament. By the summer of 1931 Malcolm was sufficiently exasperated to consider resigning, and he discussed this possibility with one or two other disgruntled colleagues. Word of this got back to Ted Scott who, on August 5 wrote to J. L. Hammond, another staffer and close friend: "I am afraid we may not be able to keep Muggeridge very long, and even P. J. Monkhouse may find it difficult to associate himself permanently with a paper that will remain bourgeois to the last. I wonder on which side of the barricades these clever young men will eventually find themselves."[28]

In the early hours of New Year's Day, January 1, 1932, C. P. Scott died. Ted became editor, in fact as well as title. Muggeridge was elated. He had grown fond of Ted Scott who, in turn, had come to depend heavily on him. He put aside all thought of resigning. With Ted in control, the wheezing, ponderous old dirigible might yet be deflated and transformed into a sleek fighting craft. He threw himself into his writing with zest.

It took a while for Ted Scott to make the transition; first, there was his father's obituary to arrange; then C. P.'s unfinished business to be cleared away. By April the transition was completed, Ted was in harness and ready for a brief holiday. On a Friday evening, Muggeridge drove him and his eldest son, Richard, to the Lake district, and he dined with them at Windermere the following evening. On Sunday morning, Muggeridge returned to Manchester leaving them behind to sail. At about five o'clock that afternoon, while sitting in his office puzzling over a leader on Indian self-government, the telephone rang. The message was short. Ted Scott was dead, drowned after a freak squall had capsized their boat. His son was alive. Muggeridge went straight to the office of his nemesis, W. P. Crozier (in Scott's absence, acting editor) and said simply, "Ted's dead." He went back to his room and prepared his friend's obituary. It was one of the last *Guardian* articles he wrote in Manchester.

He was finished with the *Guardian*, full of "dead words, dead hopes, dead principles which no longer bore any relation to what was happening in the world."[29] He was finished with patient Fabianism and parliamentary elections in which, as he considered, decent men like his father were defeated by money and class. He was finished with moderate men of all shades of opinion.

A continent to the east, immoderate men of one opinion had seized power decisively and were boldly fashioning a just society based on need not privilege, on equality not class, on the dictatorship of the proletariat and the withering away of the state. There he would go and cast his lot with a future that would work.

The opportunity arose when William Henry Chamberlin, who had covered Russian affairs for both the *Guardian* and the *Christian Science Monitor*, left Moscow to return to America. Muggeridge was eager to replace him, and Crozier, who had become editor, was only too happy to facilitate his departure. Leonard was settled at a school in England. Kitty was again pregnant, so their next child would be born a Soviet citizen. They discarded their marriage certificate, degrees, and all other documentary intimations of the dying bourgeois society on which their backs were turned.

Their last weekend in England was spent at Passfield where they had journeyed to receive a benediction from Beatrice and Sidney Webb to whose New Civilization they were journeying. "Sidney and I," Mrs. Webb said, "have become icons in the Soviet Union."

In early September 1932, they set sail from Tilbury, aboard the Soviet ship *Kooperatsia*, bound for Leningrad and a last flirtation with utopias.

·5·

MOSCOW

The trouble with kingdoms of heaven on earth is that they are liable to come to pass, and then their fraudulence is apparent for all to see.

Malcolm Muggeridge, *Jesus Rediscovered*, 1968

* * *

Their voyage was uneventful. The crew entertained the passengers by singing revolutionary songs, and the passengers reciprocated by putting on a play. A slight quandary arose over gratuities. The mostly fellow-traveling passengers considered tipping to be a manifestation of bourgeois capitalism and resolved instead to take up a collection to purchase progressive literature for the ship's library. This plan was communicated to the chief steward who, Muggeridge noted, "failed to kindle."

He and Kitty arrived in Moscow on September 16, 1932, and they checked into the Nova Moskovkaya Hotel. Muggeridge went immediately to see Lenin's tomb in Red Square. He was fascinated by the endless procession of people shuffling past the embalmed corpse under the watchful eye of grey, impassive sentries. A few people touched their caps; one old woman made the sign of the cross. What were they thinking? What were they hoping? Their faces were expressionless; their movements mechanical; their voices, when they spoke, hushed. They were pilgrims, he decided, pilgrims worshiping at a shrine to power. "I didn't quite like it. The whole thing was tawdry."[1] Even so, the place exercised a hold on him. He would often visit it two or three times in a single day, shivering in the dank interior with its stale smell of humanity, peering in at the shriveled body in a glass cage, and at the bearded head, raised slightly, and resting on a red cushion.

His initial dispatches from Moscow inevitably consisted of warmed-over offerings from *Pravda*, that being the only source of information available. *Pravda* meant truth, and the foreign correspondent's greatest problem was reconciling truth and *Pravda*, with truth invariably the casualty. To lighten the sheer weight of tendentious assertions and dubious statistics, Muggeridge fell into the habit of injecting a light touch but soon discovered, to his chagrin, that the *Guardian*'s sub-editors took *Pravda*'s claims more seriously than the Russian censors did. With luck, he might occasionally manage to slip a witty aside past Oumansky, the censor, only to find it taken out back in Manchester. When he wrote that Stalin's threat to overcome agricultural disorganization by using party men "of iron discipline" was comparable to "sending Jesuit fathers to strengthen local missionaries," it was omitted. The result was similar when he added this sentence to a dispatch on Russian fury at German anticommunism: "The spectacle of one oppressive regime waxing indignant over another is always entertaining." But no such problem arose when he quoted *Pravda*'s condemnation of the British press that included a specific exception for ". . . honest, truthful newspapers like *The Manchester Guardian* and *News Chronicle* which recognize integrity of Soviet justice and the humanity of OGPU methods."[2]

He and Kitty moved into a *dacha* at Kliasma, loaned to them by a German businessman named Herr Schmidt. It was an old house with a Russian wood-burning stove on the top of which, in the old days, servants would have slept. Since all dispatches required official clearance, he frequently went into Moscow on an electric train jammed with passengers; their faces, he noted, were "gloomy, hungry, full of despair." Whenever possible he stayed at Kliasma, walking through the pine forest, and writing articles that reflected a growing disenchantment with this strange New Civilization.

In mid-October Kitty fell ill with a fever. A German doctor was summoned who diagnosed paratyphus. When Malcolm suggested that Kitty go to a hospital, the doctor involuntarily shuddered and crossed himself. Some time afterwards, turning over the pages of an effusive report by visiting Western doctors who claimed that Soviet hospitals were second to none, he thought of the German doctor's reaction. As Kitty's condition worsened, he feared for her life. With her temperature standing at 104 degrees, his diary records: "I think of the possibility of her dying with unutterable dread. We are alone here in this gloomy country, amongst alien people . . . I know that whatever happens, whatever mess I make of things, whatever follies I commit, I can count on her sympathy and forbearance. This is the single redeeming fact of my life."[3]

For several weeks he stayed at Kliasma, nursing Kitty, sleeping on the floor beside her bed and constantly taking her temperature, elated by any slight sign of improvement, and once smashing the thermometer in pieces because it recorded no drop. Then a bedpan had to be procured, and he set off to Moscow in search of one. He settled eventually for an old porcelain sink obtained, with considerable difficulty, from a pawn shop. On the way home he stopped at Red Square where a parade to commemorate the fifteenth anniversary of the Bolshevik Revolution was underway. It was a grey November day, and bleak winds blew across the open square.

> The Red Square was densely packed; there, the Proletariat, and up on the Mausoleum, the Dictatorship. How were the two connected? As Lenin so succinctly posed the question: Who Whom? The scene seemed pure fantasy; I couldn't believe in it. Not even as the mighty procession rolled past; the gymnasts, the troops, the bands, the armoured vehicles, the dashing cavalry. I wanted to raise my bedpan in the air in a special salute of my own; particularly when I noticed a little group of vaguely familiar faces behind a banner emblazoned C.P.G.B.; they, too, paying their tribute to the great Dictatorship of the Proletariat. We who are nothing shall be all; he hath put down the mighty from their seats, and hath exalted the humble and meek—it was the everlasting theme of revolution here exemplified in all its majesty and fatuity.[4]

Back in Kliasma, a Russian woman doctor prescribed a bizarre treatment called *banki*, which consisted of attaching warm suction cups to bare flesh so that, as the cups cooled, the infection would be sucked out of the pores. It was extremely painful but must have had some therapeutic benefit, for Kitty soon began to mend. Even so, this illness and her advancing pregnancy made it unwise for her to stay much longer in Russia. On December 17, 1932, she left Moscow by train to return to England, leaving Malcolm "desolate and melancholy" behind.

He now moved into the city, to a flat at Borisoglebsky Pereulak, and spent most of his time in the company of A. T. Cholerton, a correspondent for *The News Telegraph*. Cholerton was a gregarious man whose cynical mind and dry, ironic humor were an antidote to the granitic dullness of life around them. When inebriated, he would mutter incoherently into his beard, but even his incoherence seemed a bastion of clarity compared to the logical lies and propaganda of the regime. Cholerton often lay on a sofa all day long, mocking the regime, its bosses, its monstrous cruelty and stupidity to anyone who would listen. Muggeridge once asked a censor, Podolsky (who was later shot), why the Russians tolerated Cholerton when he took so few pains to conceal his loathing of the Soviet regime. "We find him irresistible," Podolsky replied; "He reminds us of the old days. He's just like a Russian intellectual."[5] It was Cholerton who delivered what may be the most illuminating remark ever made of the Soviet Union; it happened when a group of Western lawyers were being shown the courts in which the show trials of the Old Bolsheviks were staged. "But are their confessions true?" one inquirer earnestly persisted. Before the Intourist guide could reply, Cholerton interjected: "In Russia, everything is true except the facts."

Muggeridge and Cholerton devised a contest among the press corps to see who could get the most nonsensical story accepted among touring Western intelligentsia. Muggeridge's best effort was to persuade Lord Marley that queues outside stores were not a result of food shortages, but rather a cunning device by which the authorities induced workers to rest—their zeal to complete the five-year plan otherwise being all-consuming. A French correspondent put about the story that the cause of the milk shortage was due to excess allotments to nursing mothers. But Cholerton took first prize for reassuring a group of visiting British jurists that while the system of *habeas corpus* might be unknown in Russia, the system of *habeas cadaver* was punctiliously observed.

To his delight, Muggeridge discovered that whatever havoc the Communist revolution had wrought on Russian cultural and spiritual values, the people managed to retain their native sense of humor. Once he overheard a boy in Red Square ask his father about Lenin's mausoleum:

"Daddy, what's that?"
"It's Lenin's grave."
"And what is Lenin?"
"Lenin is our grave."

Jokes, doggerel, and satire circulated widely but, of course, anonymously; anti-Soviet thought was a serious crime. Humor provided a more accurate indication of what ordinary people thought about the regime than any official publication. As for the outpourings of the regime's sycophantic Western admirers who wrote glowing accounts of bursting granaries, apple-cheeked dairy maids, and Stalin himself getting up early to go down to the rail yards to help the workers unload (the latter gem from Julian Huxley), well, these Muggeridge regarded as beneath contempt. They belonged to the world of fantasy; humor, on the other hand, was real. He was once asked by a Russian acquaintance, "Do you know why Lenin's coffin is put in a glass case?" He did not. "You see, after issuing each decree, Comrade Stalin goes along to see if Lenin has turned over in his grave." He was also told (although the story itself may be apocryphal) that at Frunze's funeral the Kremlin leaders carried a banner with the legend "Frunze, the Pride of the Revolution is dead" followed closely by another banner "Let us follow his example." But in light of what we now know, thanks to the witness of Alexander Solzhenitsyn, about the inconceivable scale of the Stalinist horror, the most poignant joke he heard was about a peasant to whom an engineer was explaining a new village radio:

> " 'You see this small thing,' says the engineer pointing to the microphone: 'If you speak into it your every word will be heard through the whole world.'
> 'Are you sure everyone will hear me? You are not pulling my leg?' says the incredulous peasant.
> 'Yes, it's the truth.'
> 'May I say something?'
> 'Go ahead. Speak.'
> "The peasant runs to the microphone and shouts: 'Help! Murder!' "

In his memoirs, Muggeridge calls his eight months in Moscow ". . . a total reversal, in light of what I had seen and understood in the U.S.S.R., of everything I had hitherto hoped for and believed in." But what exactly had he "hitherto hoped for and believed in"? Not very much. India and Egypt had soured him on all forms of imperial authority. He had few illusions left to shatter about the nature of power. He had already seen through the humbug of *Guardian* liberalism and the futility of Fabian socialism.

Even at the time, he wrote of intense disillusionment. Shortly after leaving Moscow, he described himself, in a letter to the editor of *The Daily Telegraph*, as ". . . one who went to Russia eight months ago full of enthusiasm for the Soviet regime, absolutely taken in by untruthful and deliberately misleading propaganda, and who has now left that country bitterly and painfully disillusioned. . . ."[6] Yet there is evidence, convincing evidence, which establishes that he was not nearly so naive and optimistic as this account suggests.

The very first mention of the possibility of going to Russia is in a letter to his father written in 1926 from India: "I should like to see Russia and taste a communist despotism."[7] This suggests that he had some inkling of the authoritarian nature of the government awaiting him. Alec Vidler visited the Muggeridges in Manchester shortly before they left for Russia, and he recalls that Malcolm was already skeptical of all ideologies, communist or capitalist, and had ". . . few, if any, illusions. We had both pretty much given up on all forms of earthly authority. At most, he regarded Russia as one last hope worth exploring."[8] On the very eve of his departure, Muggeridge told A.J.P. Taylor: "I am going to see Utopia, and I am sure I shall hate it."[9] Wraithby, the central figure in his autobiographical novel *Winter in Moscow*, recalls his reasons for going to Russia as follows: ". . . he had observed from afar the Dictatorship of the Proletariat, and had felt it to be substantial. He knew that it was brutal and intolerant and ruthless. He had no illusions about its consequences to individuals and classes. Only, he thought, it offered a way of escape from himself."[10] His first diary entry, the day he arrived in Moscow, bespeaks doubt: "Already I have made up my mind to call this the diary of a journalist and not the diary of a communist." He visited Lenin's tomb and, instead of being uplifted, found it "tawdry and depressing."

Disillusionment tends to be a gradual, painful process—growing doubts coupled with a slow erosion of faith. This did not occur. He experienced no dark night of the soul over communism. William Henry Chamberlin, his *Guardian* predecessor in Moscow, wrote that Muggeridge, of all the people he met in Russia in the thirties, ". . . made the biggest leap in the shortest time."[11] Consequently, it seems more probable that he was never a true believer; at most, as Alec Vidler says, he saw communism as a last, unlikely hope.

Why the disparity between the evidence and his own account, then and now? Perhaps because he was subconsciously attempting to impose a pattern on his Moscow period, to relate it to the later development of his views, and to see in it a symmetry: the enormity of his hopes matched by the intensity of his rejection. His rejection of communism certainly was intense and for very good reasons. But human experience seldom presents itself in symmetrical equations; it is more random and diffuse, and the evidence establishes that his initial expectations about Soviet communism were never so naive or sanguine as his autobiography suggests.

It is scarcely surprising that he soon found life in the Soviet Union uncongenial. His anarchical temperament is ill-suited to support any form of established authority—and what authority was ever less likely to win his allegiance than the rapacious, stifling dictatorship of Joseph Stalin? He had to deal almost daily with the obtuse arrogance of official press censorship that, apart from the issue of principle involved (and notwithstanding his association with Lord Longford's pornography inquiry, Muggeridge has always been an opponent of censorship), could not fail to breed frustration and resentment. The hypocrisy of the regime grated on him. In his journal there is a long description of the disgust he felt the first time a Russian waiter sidled up to him for a tip, and another when, at a foreign office reception, he was given cold stares for wearing grey flannel trousers instead of evening dress. After all, he thought, he ought not to have dispensed with bourgeois habits and clothes; he had never had such need of them as now. Then, too, Cholerton's company fed his growing contempt for the regime and its functionaries. With Kitty gone, his life was rootless. Moscow offered few diversions, and idleness has always made him liverish. There was no real news to report, only official lies. Life was drab, dull, and lethargic. Most of the time he spent padding about the streets, one of a grey, drifting, anonymous stream of human beings ". . . acrid smelling for lack of soap, their flesh grey or greenish from undernourishment, felt booted, muffled and muted, aloof and inscrutable."[12] He developed a kind of splenetic aversion to everything around him that, at the early stages, was based as much on aesthetic as on ideological grounds.

In an unpublished short story, "The Emperor's Son," he wrote of an expatriate in Russia in terms which explain, more accurately than his autobiography, the source of his initial disgruntlement.

> The people moving noiselessly along the streets were remote, like ghosts. He was not of them—shabby, hungry, gloomy people; though shabby and hungry himself, he belonged to a warmer and more orderly and more balanced civilization. Absurd slogans printed on the outside of buildings only filled him with contempt, and he suddenly realized how dreary his life was in Moscow, how empty of everything he most valued, how stale, flat and unprofitable. He hated even the fantastic golden domes and delicate irrelevant towers of the Kremlin because they too, like the slogans, were abstractions, dreams of a separate mind and not the consequences of a traditional mode of life. Too fabulous, he thought, to be satisfying. Too fabulous.

This vague discontent was transformed into a searing hatred of the regime and everything it stood for by one single experience. In order to gain firsthand material for a series of articles on Soviet agriculture, he took a train trip to the Ukraine and Caucasus to assess the results of the policy of collectivization, then just getting under way. Even forty years later, his journey to Rostov ". . . remains in my mind as a nightmare memory."[13]

He saw the richest wheatlands of Europe turned into a wilderness. He saw famine—"planned and deliberate; not due to any natural catastrophe like failure of rain or cyclone or flooding. An administrative famine brought about by the forced collectivization of agriculture . . . abandoned villages, the absence of livestock, neglected fields: everywhere, famished, frightened people."[14] In a German settlement, a little oasis of prosperity in the collectivized wilderness, he watched peasants kneeling down in the snow, weeping, and asking for bread. He made a vow to himself: "Whatever else I may do or think in the future, I must never pretend that I haven't seen this. Ideas will come and go; but this is more than an idea. It is peasants kneeling down in the snow and asking for bread. Something that I have seen and understood."[15] And he saw the dim outlines of what we now know as the Gulag Archipelago; at a railway station in the grey, early morning light, he glimpsed a line of *kulaks*, or rich peasants, ". . . with their hands tied behind them being herded into cattle trucks at gunpoint . . . all so silent and mysterious and horrible in the half light, like some macabre ballet."[16]

When he got back to Moscow, he wrote of what he had seen—honestly, simply, and without regard to the consequences. If, as he now claims, these articles seem "very inadequate," it is only because the sheer horror and magnitude defied expression even by so adept a communicator as he. In January 1933, he wrote of ". . . a virtual breakdown of agriculture" and of ". . . ruthless campaigns against the *kulaks*."[17] In February, he documented instances of ". . . widespread religious persecution," despite the guarantees of religious freedom in the Soviet constitution: ". . . the religious orders have been disbanded; the church's wealth is gone; a large number of priests have been shot or exiled."[18] And ". . . to say that there is famine in some of the most fertile parts of Russia is to say much less than the truth; there is not only famine . . . but a state of war, a military occupation. In both the Ukraine and the North Caucasus the grain collection has been carried out with such thoroughness and brutality that the peasants are now quite without bread. Thousands of them have been exiled; in certain cases whole villages have been sent north for forced labour; even now it is common to see parties of wretched men and women, labelled *Kulaks*, being marched away under an armed guard. The fields are neglected and full of weeds; no cattle are to be seen anywhere, and few horses; only the military and the G.P.U. are well fed, and the rest of the population obviously starving, obviously terrorized."[19] Then, in March, he wrote an overall assessment in a three-part *Guardian* series that concluded: "The Dictatorship of the Proletariat has come to mean the Dictatorship of the Communist Party; and the Dictatorship of the Communist Party has come to mean the Dictatorship of Stalin; and the Dictatorship of Stalin has come to mean the Dictatorship of the General Idea with which he is obsessed. If the General Idea is fulfilled it can only be by bringing into existence a slave state."[20]

It took courage, as well as prescience, to write this. In the Soviet Union people had, to use Beatrice Webb's gentle phrase, "disappeared" for hinting at less. The three-part series was smuggled out in a diplomatic pouch and appeared in *The Manchester Guardian* on March 25, 27, and 28, 1933. In response *Pravda* ran a special leader denouncing

Muggeridge as a liar. He knew his time in Moscow was coming to an end.

What he did not foresee was the reaction in England. For telling the truth about what he had seen, Muggeridge was vilified, slandered, and abused in the pages of the *Guardian* and elsewhere. Some correspondents, such as Mr. E. H. Benson of the National Committee of Friends of the Soviet Union, took their cue from *Pravda* and accused him of being hysterically unbalanced and a liar; others took a more restrained approach, such as Miss Jean Beauchamp, who demonstrated to her own satisfaction how agricultural production required oil and there could not, therefore, be a famine since Soviet oil production was ample (so ample, in fact, that based on her figures exports alone were five times greater than actual total production). In *The New Statesman*, Sir John and Lady Maynard refuted Muggeridge's reports of famine from personal observation: ". . . it is exceptional to see the urban worker and his dependents looking otherwise than well-fed and well-clothed."

To comprehend this reaction, one must recall how totally deluded the cream of English and American intellectuals were by Soviet communism. The Very Reverend Hewlett Johnson, Dean of Canterbury, from his pulpit praised Stalin's "steady purpose and kindly generosity"; Harold Laski commended the scrupulous fairness of political trials; Lincoln "I have seen the future and it works" Steffens was widely acclaimed; George Bernard Shaw assured everyone who would listen that Stalin was ". . . subject to dismissal at ten minutes notice if he does not give satisfaction"; Sir Bernard Pares proclaimed the Soviet Union "the most interesting sixth of the world and the most charming"; Sidney Webb "hotly repudiated" the suggestion that there was forced labor, while the indestructible Webb partnership dropped the question mark from the reissue of their *Soviet Communism: A New Civilization?* One could easily multiply such examples until they filled a book, but happily it is unnecessary since David Caute did just that in *The Fellow Travellers* (Macmillan, 1973), and what a trove of fatuous imbecility it is—all issuing from the mouths and pens of those who ostensibly possessed the finest minds of their generation.

The fact that Muggeridge, almost alone among correspondents, dared to tell the truth about what was happening in the Soviet Union was held against him for years to come. He was fashionably dismissed as a reactionary, a cold warrior, an opponent of detente—the nomenclature adjusting to each change in cant, but the message remaining the same. Long after Nikita Khrushchev had admitted the truth of what Muggeridge had reported in the early thirties, and Alexander Solzhenitsyn had expanded and documented it in meticulous detail, few of

Muggeridge's detractors came forward to acknowledge their error, or even let up much in their denigration.

By now Muggeridge had understood that people believe lies not because they are plausible, but because they want to believe them. One honorable exception to all this was Max Beloff, who wrote in *Encounter*: "Muggeridge was censored editorially as well as censured, and he resigned. The difficulty is that on the substance of what was going on in Russia, Muggeridge was right and the *Guardian* was wrong."[21]

On March 11, 1933, Alan Monkhouse (cousin to the *Guardian's* Paddy Monkhouse) was arrested along with several other British engineers working in the USSR. At some personal risk, Muggeridge managed to telephone an account of this back to Manchester. When the *Guardian* drastically cut and downplayed the story, he had had enough. He wrote to the editor, W. P. Crozier: "From the way you have cut my messages about this Metrovick affair, I realize that you don't want to know what is going on in Russia or to let your readers know. If it had been an oppressed minority, or subject people valiantly struggling to be free, that would have been another matter. Then any amount of outspokenness, any amount of honesty."[22]

His last hope had turned to ashes in his mouth, and he spat it out. He was alone in Moscow, without a job, without prospects. He should have been depressed, but in fact he was gripped by a curious exultation. He was certain he had reached a turning point in his life; like a mountain climber, he had scrambled up the rock face, through cuts and fissures, along gorges, and now he had reached a juncture: One path twisted up towards a peak; the other sloped away, broader, and more inviting. In *Winter in Moscow* he puts his choice before Wraithby.

> The future seemed empty to Wraithby. It was easy to burn up the past, but not so easy to face a future lacking everything that had given the past substance. Even for him—a person of no importance, a nobody—the patterns he'd made and unmade in his mind had meant something. They'd at least given him an occupation. Now, he thought, my occupation's gone . . . There were two alternatives, clearly marked, unmistakeable; and he had to choose between them. At that moment everything fitted into place. Every tendency in himself, in societies in the past and the future; all he had ever seen or thought or felt or believed, sorted itself out. It was a vision of good and evil, heaven and hell. Life and death. There were two alternatives and he had to choose.[23]

Kitty telegraphed to say that they had been offered temporary residence in Switzerland at Rossinière, running a guesthouse owned by the Workers' Travel Association, a tourist organization with Labour party affiliation of which H. T. was a director. He left Moscow immediately, stopping in Berlin, where, on April 2, ". . . I watched the Nazis march along the *Unter den Linden* and realized, of course, they're Comsomols, the same people, the same faces. It's the same show."[24]

Settled in the mountains at Rossinière, he poured out his hostility for the Soviet Union in five articles published by *The Morning Post* in June. One of the articles included this observation: "The particular horror of their [Bolshevik] rule is what they have done to the villages. This, I am convinced, is one of the most monstrous crimes in history, so terrible that people in the future will scarcely be able to believe it ever happened."[25]

These articles touched off another barrage of criticism, this time including a salvo from Passfield Corner launched by Aunt Beatrice. She called the articles "an hysterical tirade" and, to Kingsley Martin, accused Muggeridge of "suffering from a neurotic joy in libelling persons and institutions." He ought, she said, to "go off and join the R.C. church and confess and be absolved every five months."[26] To Malcolm she wrote more circumspectly, expressing bewilderment at his anger and bitterness. He replied: "Angry and bitter, Aunt Bo, because something I believed in has turned out to be a fraud, . . . not a fraud, though, because of its deplorable economic consequences, but because of what it is trying to do . . . . The most encouraging thing about the Soviet regime was its failure. If it had succeeded I think I should have committed suicide because then I should have known that there were no limits to the extent to which human beings could be terrorized and enslaved."[27]

Beatrice Webb's only comment on his reply was that he was ". . . an artist, anarchistic and aristocratic by temperament" (which is undoubtedly true) who "ought to have smelt a rat . . . and carefully avoided its stinking body." Why his nostrils should have detected a stench that she continued to proclaim the rarest perfume, she did not explain.

The scale of what he had seen defied expression in occasional articles in the daily press. He decided to write a novel about it, partly because he had already proved to himself that he could write fiction. But the danger of a novel was that it might encourage readers to deny the reality of what he described. In the result, he combined novel and documentary, in his introduction calling it "truth imaginatively expressed," and thus defending his unusual method: "Whatever others may think of this procedure, it has enabled me to present a faithful picture of what I saw in Russia; and by no other procedure could I have presented as faithful a picture."

Winter in Moscow is not one of his better books, although it retains a kind of early-fathers-of-the-church interest as one of the first books to expose the ravages of Stalinism. It is a bit awkward in conception and execution but written in righteous indignation and with apocalyptic certainty. One reviewer called it "a satiric poem—a lyric of hate,"[28] which is slightly, but not much, overstated. Essentially it is his diary, in the form of a novel, with actual characters so thinly disguised that, according to William Henry Chamberlin, the Moscow press corps regaled themselves identifying each and every one. The former American ambassador to Moscow, Chip Bohlen, is said to have carried about with him a key to all the characters. Perhaps the most amazing thing is that Muggeridge was not buried under an avalanche of libel writs.

Three themes run through *Winter in Moscow* and much of his subsequent writing about the Soviet Union. First, the tyranny of a General Idea; second, the credulity of the Intelligentsia amounting to a death wish; finally, the futility of Utopianism. Each of these points is worthy of some elaboration.

Muggeridge went to Russia seeking an alternative to the platitudinous liberalism of the *Guardian* and his father's tired socialism. The alternative was to be the Dictatorship of the Proletariat; government not by property, wealth, and class but by workers. From each according to his ability, to each according to his need; the mighty put down from their seats, and the humble and meek exalted. What he found was the enshrinement of ideology, rule by a General Idea, the most tyrannical of all despotisms. Individual tyrants have their moods and must at last die; the tyranny of the General Idea is inflexible and immortal. "Nothing is more dangerous," wrote Taine, "than a general idea in a narrow and vacant mind. Being vacant, they are incapable of questioning it; being narrow, before long it becomes an obsession." Karl Marx provided the General Idea; the Dictatorship of the Proletariat provided the narrow minds. With his own eyes Muggeridge saw the consequences and shuddered: "It destroys everything and everyone; is the essence of destruction—in towns, a darkness; a paralysis; in the country, a blight, sterility; shouting monotonously its empty formula—a classless, socialist society—it attacks with methodical barbarity, not only men and classes and institutions, but the soul of a society. It tears a society up by the roots and leaves it dead. 'If we go,' Lenin said, 'we shall slam the door on an empty house.' "[29]

Once the General Idea had been enshrined, terror was inevitable. One cannot sow new seed without overturning old soil; the bourgeois past had to be uprooted, and that included the people whose beliefs and values had been formed in and belonged to that past. To wage class war required the destruction of whole classes. It was no place for the squeamish. Walter Duranty, *The New York Times* correspondent in

Moscow and one of Stalin's most unswerving defenders, had a favorite saying: "You can't make an omelette without breaking eggs." And lest the class war someday peter out, even through exhaustion of victims, an elaborate secret police network was created whose business it was to keep it going by, on the one hand, making class enemies, and, on the other hand, exterminating them.

In the face of all this, how does one account for the behavior of Western intellectuals, who in their own country would have fought such tyranny or at any rate have raised their voices to condemn it, but who now flocked to the Soviet Union to fawn and abase themselves before Stalin? Even those who voiced an occasional criticism of the regime were doing more to entrench its legitimacy and to raise its prestige than the subsidized propaganda or any number of paid agitators. By being sympathetic, Western fellow-travelers had accepted the regime's premises and, once the premises were accepted, criticism on details became irrelevant.

Muggeridge brooded interminably on this *trahison de clercs*, never hitting upon an entirely satisfactory explanation. They were supposed to be the wisest, most humane minds of the age, intellectual *samurai*—Shaw, Sartre, Laski, Huxley, Gide, Mann, Dreiser, Sinclair—all singing the praises of the most relentless tyranny on earth. Surely the explanation was more than just gullibility; no astrologer or teacup reader, no African witch doctor, would dare push gullibility to such limits. A few buffoons perhaps; one or two true believers who allowed faith to blind vision, yes—that was possible, but a whole class and generation? It must be something more, he decided. A death wish. Incidentally, Muggeridge considered his death wish theory borne out when, on the death of Mao Tse-tung, the latest vintage of fellow-travelers uncorked a crop of obituaries even more sycophantic and excessive than their predecessors of the thirties. The same lies believed; the same obeisance before totalitarianism. It must be saying something. This is how civilization ends, he came to believe: not with a bang or a whimper, but with a death wish. The barbarians lay siege from within, from university chairs and editorial offices and television studios. The trumpets give forth with a blast, the walls collapse, and amidst the rubble are found the trumpeters—the Very Reverend X, Professor Y, Lord and Lady Z. Henceforth such prophets as these were forever discredited in his eyes: "As I came to grasp their almost inconceivable credulity and naivety, their readiness to believe anything however absurd that fitted in with their preconceived notions, I developed a contempt for them and their like which has stayed with me ever since."[30]

If they could be so easily gulled over something as obvious and repellent as Stalin's tyranny, then why pay attention to their pronouncements on subtler questions? He would not, in future, find himself particularly welcome in universities; fine—what did he care for brain boxes capable of such imbecilic credulity? He would find his own answers, without regard to fads and trends and fashions, still less to dons, clerics, and the motley crew that pass as intellectual heavyweights. His line would be his own, idiosyncratic and against the grain; and it would cost him many of the perks and honors that await those who play within the established rules.

What did it all signify? he asked himself over and over. How did the Dictatorship of the Proletariat become the tyranny of the General Idea? Why did the humane laud and magnify the inhumane, the well-intentioned spread the most monstrous lies, the most enlightened prove the most credulous? Why did the quest for a kingdom of heaven on earth end in a Gulag Archipelago? The more he thought about this, the more he found himself thrown back to the fall of man . . . That man, a fallen creature, cannot achieve perfection. Being man, he may apprehend it; being fallen, he cannot reach it, at least not within the bounds of time and mortality. "My disillusionment with the notion of a predestined progress towards a kingdom of heaven on earth led me inexorably back to the kingdom not of this world proclaimed in the Christian revelation . . . ."[31]

It is indeed ironic. As a believer Muggeridge went to India, one of the most religious countries on earth, and returned with his faith in tatters; as a hopeful communist he went to Russia, an avowedly atheist state, and returned with his religious beliefs revived. As between religion and ideology, he knew that he would henceforth choose religion; as between Heaven and Utopia, heaven. He had discovered that Utopias were only places where a different set of people were important, while in heaven all were children of the same Father and so all equally important.

His resurgent attraction to religion should not be overstated. It was, after all, a reaction—a retreat into religion rather than a joyous advance to it. His attitude became apparent to Alec Vidler when he visited the Muggeridges at Rossinière in September of 1933. Malcolm was in the midst of writing *Winter in Moscow* and talked a lot about his experiences in Russia. Suddenly, he asked Vidler to baptize his sons, Leonard and John, then and there. Vidler, who had been waging something of a one-man campaign against indiscriminate baptism, agreed, but only on the condition that Malcolm would undertake to bring them up in the church. Malcolm refused. Neither man would budge, and the matter was dropped. Vidler believed that he wanted his children baptized as a way of showing contempt for communism; another way, said Vidler, "of thumbing his nose at Stalin."

Winter in Moscow is too impassioned and polemical to be great literature. There is virtually no plot, and the narrative is ragged and uneven. Even so, it is very powerful; so powerful, in fact, that the effect of the book lingers in one's mind long after the last page has been turned. It enjoyed some favorable reviews and had a certain vogue among old Moscow press hands. What most delighted Muggeridge was to discover, years later, that it had circulated through the Russian underground in *samizdhat* translation. Oddly enough, it contains several passages that suggest he still had not completely made up his mind about the ultimate significance of the Russian Revolution; for example, in one exchange between Wraithby (Muggeridge) and Blythe (in real life, D. N. Mirsky, a Tsarist prince who returned to Russia from England after the revolution), Blythe says: "To me the thing's justified because of its beginnings. Because for a little while the masses stirred, became coherent, dominant. What had to happen, happened; and nothing can ever alter the fact that it happened, or that, in happening, it made the world different." And two years later, looking back on his time in Moscow, Muggeridge wrote in his diary: "Sometimes I get a pang of regret at having left my soul in Russia; and yet I'd have had to have left it somewhere. There's no keeping a soul for one who was, with all my faults, incapable of sustained insincerity . . . what's the matter with me is that I'm on no side."[32]

He had come to believe that the machinations of power, how it was organized and wielded, who governed whom and by what methods, all this was less important than a nation's soul; its character; its religion; its humor and art and music and literature. In Russia there was darkness, but darkness must inevitably yield to light. Even amidst the gloom, who knew what pens were surreptitiously scratching, what scores being carried about in the heads of unknown composers, what canvasses being daubed with paint? In a remarkably prescient article in 1937, when Solzhenitsyn was still a teen-ager and most of the dissident Russian writers were not yet born, Muggeridge wrote: "Perhaps a new literature will come to pass in Russia, as one did in the darkest days of Tsarist repression. If so, it will be a literature of revolt and so anathema to the Soviet Establishment. Perhaps it is being furtively scribbled even now in concentration camps and other dark corners . . . . Not even Dialectical Materialism, not even that, can put out the light of genius."[33]

He would never waver in his opposition to the Soviet regime. Years later he was instrumental in organizing opposition, ineffective in the result, against the visits of Khruschev and Bulganin to England. He never minimized the suffering of the Russian people nor did he conceal, for expedience or what the *Guardian* used to call "Anglo-Soviet amity," the unrelenting tyranny and chicanery of the Kremlin rulers. But he did point out that some things were beyond the reach even of tyrants; eternal, unchanging things from which, at all times and in all circumstances, men might draw solace and strength. There were the people, with their ineradicable humor and their literature: the literature of Gogol and Tolstoy and Chekov and Dostoevski. And there was Russia itself, the vast land and its never-to-be-forgotten beauty, conveying for those with eyes to see the image of another paradise beyond the machinations of men and power and ideology. A paradise far away and yet within the palm of one's hand. *Winter in Moscow* ends with Wraithby turning to this other paradise.

... Wraithby continued walking round the Red Square by himself. Two peasants and a child were huddled under a doorway. Soldiers with fixed bayonets were on guard outside Lenin's tomb. Suddenly he noticed a change in the wind that was blowing against his face. It was touched with warmth. It was fragrant. Suddenly spring had begun. The frozen river would thaw, and the sun would make the earth bare; then green. Thus it had happened a million times before. Thus it would happen a million times again. Nothing could prevent this process taking place—the sudden, unexpected coming of spring. Wraithby took in great breaths of the warm fragrant air.

·6·

DISCARDED PRODUCTS

I see myself as a discarded product of a diseased civilization, believing nothing, hoping for nothing, fearing nothing except the consciousness of my own melancholy.

Malcolm Muggeridge, Diary, November 23, 1934

* * *

His six months at Rossinière should have been an idyllic interlude; indeed this is how his memoirs recall it. The family (including his new son, John) were together, their surroundings were tranquil and pleasant, and the duties at the hostel were unexacting. Occasionally, he and Kitty climbed up to a mountain hut where they would spend the night and come down again as the first intimations of dawn lit the sky. He established a regular, austere routine: "Each morning before breakfast I have a long walk; then work steadily until lunch; then read Proust in the afternoon; work a little in the evenings and to bed absurdly early." According to a diary entry on August 13, 1933, he was "very happy."

This was the sunny side that his memoirs recall; there was a dark side as well: a spiritual torpor, or *accidie*, always about to assert itself. Like a coin balanced precariously on its edge, he could be tipped to one side or the other by tiny, insignificant events. A chance remark would lead to a row with Kitty; having the children close by was a mixed blessing. A few days later his diary records, "Today I thought quite cooly that I might run away from my family to write. I know I love my children; and yet I sense, too, that I don't take much notice of them unless screams abound. Then I play up to the loving, tender father role. Life is not very nice."[1]

To an extent readily masked by his mirth and amiability, Muggeridge has always been a tormented man. Only his eyes give him away; he has recessed, piercing eyes, wary as a fugitive's. This is due less to external

92

circumstances, however haphazard they might be at any particular time, than to an inner imbalance, an unresolved conflict between his appetites and imagination that has often resulted in a disparity between his beliefs and practices; what Saint Paul called the flesh waging war with the spirit and the spirit with the flesh "so that we cannot do the things that we would." Even at Rossinière, the only thing that really mattered to him was to write. How to communicate his individual vision? He wrote and revised and honed and polished, and still he considered the result paltry and inadequate—a betrayal. "I've set myself this task of writing well. I mean to succeed. If a thunderbolt came along and put an end to me, I shouldn't complain, or feel that anything of very great importance had happened. As long, however, as I exist, I must try to write well; herd all my energies to that purpose. Happiness in the day to day continuous sense is a silly illusion."[2]

Less illusory was the need for steady income, and this meant a job. By mid-September he had found one, working on a study of cooperatives for the International Labour Organization in Geneva. The ILO was an offshoot of the League of Nations set up to promote social justice through fair wages and improved working conditions. For him, it was an unlikely refuge, a flimsy breakwater constructed hurriedly at Woodrow Wilson's urging. As a young man, Muggeridge had admired Wilson; indeed he had once called him "my hero," and had written: "His face alone made me class him differently from all the other statesmen at Versailles. Between the bombast and vulgarity of Lloyd George, Poincare and company, he stood in my mind somehow for culture, refinement, high-mindedness and real idealism."[3] Such illusions had not survived a stint on the *Guardian* dispensing Wilsonian-style bromides to an unheeding and increasingly cantankerous world. As for the League of Nations, his feelings towards it had always stopped well short of idolatry. In India he had composed a poem called "The Ballad of the League of Nations," which began:

> "The place was set, the nations met
> They were a League of Nations;
> From yellow Chink to saxon pink
> All met for disputations."

After several verses in the same vein, the poem concluded:

> "The place was set, the nations met,
> They were a League of Nations;
> But a League that seems, except in dreams,
> To be little but orations."

Now he was himself the League's paid, and thoroughly bored, servant. His function was to obtain, sort out, and collate data about cooperatives supplied by each of the League's member states. Since the information came exclusively from government sources and was beyond verification, its authenticity could not but be suspect and in some cases it was patently absurd. When Muggeridge ventured to raise this point with his supervisor, a Frenchman named Prosper, he ". . . rather crossly remarked that it was not our business to question the genuineness of the data . . . our business was to present it as clearly and cogently as possible." So, in a desultory way, he labored at it, combing through submissions, extracting relevant information, correlating statistics, pruning and compacting and comparing until, at last, the definitive study of worldwide cooperatives emerged under the distinguished imprimatur of the League of Nations. A study punctiliously cross-referenced and indexed, each assertion documented and accounted for, available to politicians with policies to formulate, to debaters with points to make, to journalists with columns to fill, and to scholars with footnotes to drop. The truth about cooperatives, the whole truth, and nothing but the truth, all resting on a foundation of lies. The whole enterprise was little to his taste: "I hate the ILO . . . it's not that I do anything much, but somehow the atmosphere is exhausting. Like living in a vacuum."[4]

They found a flat ". . . which cost us, literally, our last penny"[5] close by the ILO office. Geneva was cold and dull, full of prattling diplomats who hurried to and fro, puffed up with a sense of their own importance and looking "fashionable and unhappy."[6] He was depressed. He quarreled with Kitty's parents over life insurance, which they argued he had a duty to his family to buy and which he, for reasons of obstinancy as well as principle, refused to buy. Marital relations fluctuated between overt hostilities and short-lived truces. In their liberated way, he and Kitty had resolved that marriage must impose no fetters on each other's conduct; the idea of fidelity was dismissed as bourgeois impedimenta. They discovered, however, that jealousy was not so easily discarded: "Their feelings ebbed and flowed with the moon, sometimes love, sometimes hate, sometimes this, sometimes that. If they continued to live together, how many different variations of love and hate lay before them! How many moods, each one passing and leaving nothing behind! Now envy, now jealousy, now tenderness, now contempt—one after the other, unconnected, fitful."[7]

His favorite haunt in Geneva was the Cafe Bavaria, a watering hole for journalists stopping off to see if one more story might be wrung out of the League of Nations or its interminable disarmament talks. It was there, over a late afternoon drink, that he heard a free-lance journalist named P. Beaumont-Wadsworth remark: "I sometimes wonder if I'm licking the right boots." It was said casually and ruminatively, apropos of nothing, yet this remark pierced Muggeridge's mind like an arrow and has lodged there ever since. Amidst the vapid resolutions, debates, proposals and counterproposals, pacts and treaties going on all around him, here was the nub of power, licking the right boots. It was one of those rare, pellucid moments when reality suddenly and unexpectedly breaks in on fantasy.

Muggeridge was anxious to get back into journalism, but he had blotted his copybook by the Russian articles and by the circumstances in which he had quit the *Guardian*. Applications to *The Times, The Morning Post, Weekend Review, The News Chronicle,* and the BBC all met with refusals or polite evasions. Even some articles offered on a freelance basis were turned down; one in particular, called "Red Imperialism" in which he pointed out the territorial ambitions of the Soviet Union, was considered "too extreme" even by the right-wing *Morning Post. The Spectator* rejected a book review in which he predicted the demise of liberalism as a moral and political force, while *The Times* (which he was later to call "that most faithful follower of public taste, belatedly endorsing all reputations and making none"[8]) returned an article explaining how Western journalists in Moscow were induced to toe the party line. In his diary, he wrote: "There is nothing before me but failure . . . failure eating away like a disease."[9]

To compound misery his old stomach ailment flared up again. Some days in October he was too ill to go to work; when he did go he had little to do except to brood on his troubles. They were broke, unable even to pay the rent. He tried to arrange a bank loan of £20 and was turned down. He worried that they would be evicted and their few remaining possessions ("specifically, the baby's pram") seized by creditors. In mid-October, he wrote: "I should like very much to die."[10]

In November, after frequent rows over those twin reefs of marital grief—money and sex—Kitty and the children packed up and returned to London. He stayed on in Geneva to finish out the year. Away from his family, living in someone else's house, hating his job, his spirit sank ever lower. He was trying to write a humorous novel about *The Manchester Guardian*, but his humor was at a low ebb and little was accomplished. "A million regrets and fears torture me now. I am ashen and afraid. What will be the end? God knows; but I feel—I've always felt—it will be tragic, senseless, bitter."[11] Suicide is mentioned again and again in his diary.

At the end of 1933, his job with the ILO was completed. His total assets amounted to forty pounds. He had a wife, who was again pregnant, and two children to support. He had no job and no prospect of one. His last diary entry in Geneva reads: "Reason is nothing; intellect is nothing (at least to me); faith alone gives to a human being salvation and stability. I have, and can have no faith. I believe in nothing, except death; the older I get, the more lovely, desirable that seems. To die. *Chronicles of Wasted Time*—the title of my diary."[12]

In this entry, as in many others, Muggeridge tended to see himself and to write as an old man at an age when most people consider themselves in their prime. He was, after all, only thirty years old. Yet there is a world-weariness about what he wrote during this period that is frequently expressed in a longing to die; sometimes in the smug imperturbability of the man who believes that these old eyes have seen everything there is to see and there is nothing new under the sun. In part, this may have been attributable to his straightened circumstances; in part, to affectation; but not wholly. Throughout the 1930s, his diary was gloomy, sensual, and suicidal. It was as a young man that his writing evinced satiety and a restless yearning for death; the older he got, the more stoical and benign his outlook grew. To Hesketh Pearson, he once offered this explanation.

> It is a favourite proposition of mine . . . that highly imaginative people are invariably miserable when they are young, and on the whole grow progressively happier. . . . It seems to me that the general rule is that the imagination makes for unhappiness when young and can produce serenity when old. Its first struggles with appetite are painful and leave many bruises, and its first realization that the world of time is irretrievably imperfect, whereas delight is only in perfection, cannot but create much anguish. Once this period is passed, the imagination becomes an ever greater solace, until now, in middle age, I feel that it alone makes life worth living, and that to be deprived of it, whatever compensations there might be, would drain life of its delights.[13]

He returned to London in January 1934, and tried to survive on earnings from free-lance writing, which soon proved impossible. One article that was published in this period contained this remarkably prophetic observation: "It would be safe to say that, unless something very unexpected happens, if no vent is found for the pressure accumulating in Germany, another large-scale European war must break out within the next few years whose consequences will be even more ruinous than the last. The structure of post-war Europe is crazy, but not elastic. It will not bend into a more reasonable shape and attempts to make it secure—notably the League of Nations— have only served to increase its dangerous rigidity. So rigid a structure cracks explosively. Who dare to prophesy the possibility of its continuing to withstand the strain of an arming and soon armed Germany? It must crack sometime.

Malcolm Muggeridge,
Cambridge undergraduate

Selwyn College boat, 1921.
Muggeridge standing
second from right; Alec Vidler
seated with megaphone

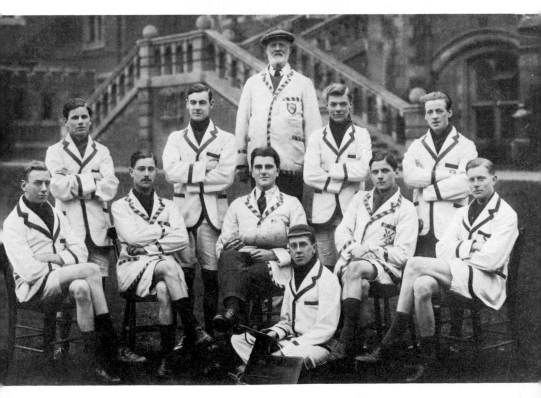

In the grounds of Union Christian College, Alwaye, India, 1925

The question is, where? If in the West then we shall all have to fight again, and, in fighting, destroy what remains of European civilization, leaving its debris, as they have always calculated, to the Bolsheviks."[14]

He obtained a commission from Jonathan Cape to translate Maurice Bede's *New Arcadia*, at twelve shillings per thousand words; working at it eight or nine hours a day, he just could make ends meet. Also, Cape commissioned a biography of Samuel Butler to be published on the centenary of Butler's birth. Neither assignment appealed to him much, but it was a case of indigence over inclination. For the first and only time in his life, money became an obsession, and the topic even crops up in his diary: "I badly need some money, and feel cynical enough to do nearly anything to get it."[15]

In such a mood he responded in the summer of 1934 to an advertisement for an assistant editor on *The Calcutta Statesman*. When, to his surprise, he was offered the position he felt torn: A regular salary was tempting; the prospect of leaving his family and returning again to India was unpleasant. He accepted. In late September he sailed on the *Viceroy of India*, ". . . full of foreboding, as though somehow I'd sold my soul."[16] On board he wrote to Alec Vidler: "Do let me hear from you sometimes. I'll be very lonely in Calcutta—far, far lonelier than the last time I was in India. Then, I'd got all sorts of half-baked loyalties and enthusiasms; now, nothing."[17]

The most crippling blow awaited him. In London he had worked hard to finish his *Manchester Guardian* novel, which he called *Time of Life*, but which his publishers, Eyre and Spottiswoode, decided to call *Picture Palace*. An early version had been rejected in 1932 by Putnam's in America because of concern about possible libel proceedings. Eyre and Spottiswoode had been fully informed of this and had asked for revisions, which had been made. When he sailed for India, the book had appeared on their autumn list, copies had actually been printed and bound, and a few advances had been sent out to reviewers. He arrived in India to find a letter from Eyre and Spottiswoode saying that, unless he put up several thousand pounds to contest a libel action threatened by the *Guardian*, the book must be withdrawn. "As I had no money at all, only an overdraft, and no possibility of laying hands on any, the publisher's proposal was purely a formality, as he, I am sure, knew. . . . This was the heaviest blow I ever received as a writer, and it came just when I was least equipped, financially or in any other way, to withstand it."[18]

It was a heavy blow, and it did come at an inopportune time; even so, he took it remarkably in stride. The day he learned that all copies of the book had been recalled and destroyed and that the publishers had entered into an agreement never to publish it in the future, he wrote: "I think my state of mind must be like a woman who has just had a child aborted that she got by a man she was not very much in love with. It would shake her up and agitate her deep in the instinctive part of her being, but leave the rest untouched . . . so that's the end of *Picture Palace,* also, as I say to myself, untruthfully and self-pityingly, of a year's work."[19]

In retrospect, it was a shabby, peculiar business matter. Rereading the novel today (Muggeridge saved his own copy), it is difficult to imagine that *The Manchester Guardian* had any legal basis for contemplating a libel action. Even if the novel, or parts of it, could be said to have met the test of libel—lowering a person's reputation in the eyes of right-thinking members of the community—which is highly doubtful, the only two people to whom the test could conceivably have applied were C. P. Scott and his son, Ted, by then both dead. Libel is a personal action that does not survive death; no right of action accrues to next-of-kin. So, even accepting that Muggeridge's portrait of C. P. Scott was unlikely to enhance his memory, any libel action on his account would undoubtedly have failed. In the case of Ted Scott (in the novel, Arthur Savoury), Muggeridge's portrait is affectionate not hostile, and could not, by any flight of fancy, be said to have been libelous. What the *Guardian's* proprietors really objected to (as their Statement of Claim confirms) was that *Picture Palace* revealed the financial connection between the lofty, high-principled *Guardian* and its sister paper, *The Manchester Evening News,* in whose pages those sleazy and sensational items that the *Guardian* declined to print got a full and very profitable airing. Had a statement of defense been filed, it is almost certain that the *Guardian* would have quietly and quickly abandoned its threat of proceedings. Had they not done so, the suit could have been successfully defended and the costs attendant on unsuccessful libel actions, while notoriously unpredictable, are invariably high. It would be naive to suppose that the *Guardian* had not received professional advice to this effect. Their threat to sue could only have been intended to capitalize on Muggeridge's insolvency and Eyre and Spottiswoode's timidity. There is no point in waxing indignant over the threat of legal proceedings used to get one's way; it happens every day. But it was rather hypocritical coming from a newspaper that led the liberal pack in howling against censorship and for freedom of expression. "Why do the loudest whelps for liberty," Dr. Johnson asked, "come from the mouths of slave drivers?" However questionable, the *Guardian's* tactics were successful, and *Picture Palace* was never published, although in 1973 *The New Statesman* serialized parts of it without repercussion.

Actually, the novel is diffuse and uneven. Those parts dealing with the death of Old Savoury and his son, and the effect of their deaths on the newspaper they ran, are memorable and, at points, extremely funny. Also, the sections dealing with the protagonist's marital strife have an unmistakable verisimilitude. But irrelevant characters (some, like Mrs. Angel on the Embankment, destined to appear in later novels) are dragged into the narrative for no evident purpose, cluttering it up, and leaving the overall impression that Muggeridge knew exactly what he wanted to write about—and how to begin—but was stumped about how to end it. As in his other novels, *Picture Palace* presents a bleak, foreboding vision: rootless lives, broken relationships, senseless deaths and killings, and despair all around. Again, like his other novels, it finishes up on a note of qualified optimism. Pettygrew, Malcolm's alter ego in the book, returns to nurse his wife through a near-fatal illness and, when her fever begins to subside he reflects: "The struggle was over; and she was alive, and he was alive. Their love was alive. They had triumphed over death. A great joy filled his heart. Whatever the future might be, whatever might happen to them or to the world, the life they had won was worth having. In no circumstances could it be otherwise. He needed no faith in the possibility of perfecting human nature or human society to make him want to live; no guarantee that he would be able to cash out his egotism in any sort of success, no guarantee even of food and drink. Let it all go on as now, he thought. Let it get worse, much worse. Still we are alive." This passage foreshadows a reconciliation in his own life and marriage that was still to come; in the meantime, more storms and strife lay ahead.

The Calcutta Statesman occupied a rather palatial building on Chowringee Street, with white pillars at the front and an elaborate open portico. With appropriate modifications for the change of venue, its editorial slant was much the same as the *Guardian's*, and the same recycled phrases and sentiments suited the purpose: "Men of all colours and shades of opinion . . . it is greatly to be hoped that something or other will abate and moderate voices make themselves heard . . . on this historic moment when . . ." and so on. Something must be hoped, some voice be heard, some moment be historic—what was it? Alas, his wits were frequently too dull to decide. Calcutta was founded on a swamp, and its dank air seeped into his pores leaving him stagnant. "Each morning after breakfast, a mist rises within me; clouding my thoughts, obscuring my soul, distorting my sight. . . ."[20] Still, words must be typed, the paper must be filled; the hopes and voices and plans of moderate men plodded their path across his keyboard while above his befuddled head a roof fan remorselessly turned, blowing the paper in his typewriter back on itself. Like Sisyphus, he felt condemned to labor without respite and without purpose.

He lived above the *Statesman's* office, in a flat he shared with a man named Wordsworth—"a funny, dissatisfied little man with an inferiority complex"[21] who claimed to be a direct descendant of the poet, far removed from his native Lake District. From a balcony, Muggeridge surveyed the ebb and flow of humanity in the street below. How different India seemed from when he had been at Alwaye: Then it was mysterious, jasmine scented, tender, with a dignified, inscrutable rhythm of its own. Now Calcutta seemed raucous, malignant, teeming with people who shouted and cursed and smelled of dust and excrement and impacted sweat. Vehicles jammed down narrow streets with their horns blaring at the pedestrians, cyclists, rickshaws, and animals in their path. Above the city, like a cloud, hung the stench of death, in all the world uniquely pungent in Calcutta, where street sweepers dragged the night's harvest of corpses to the side of the road, there to be stacked up like packing crates and carted off. At Alwaye, Muggeridge had bathed morning and night in the cool waters of the Perrier River; here, the Hooghley River held no similar attraction. At Alwaye he had believed in something: in Indian self-government, the *swarajist* movement, in socialism, love, civilization, and life. What did he believe in now? Had India really changed so malevolently in less than seven years, or had he?

His daily routine was unpleasant: empty work; periodic visits to an American dentist who pronounced his teeth "deplorable" and proceeded "to pound into them like a navvy using an electric drill on a road";[22] recurrent bouts of stomach trouble, no doubt, in part, hypochondriacal—the severity of his symptoms usually corresponded to the level of his depression—but even so it kept him from working (". . . one day I'll write a short story called dyspepsia showing how someone can be tortured by a bad stomach"[23]); for recreation only tedious conversation with tedious people at clubs where the *sahibs* congregated: "I am bored, unutterably bored, as I have been since I came from England."[24]

In desperation he took up riding, usually in the early morning on the Maidan or at the Jodhpur Club, aboard a horse "who doesn't like me and I don't like her and our rides are one long battle."[25] For company, he generally rode with a few acquaintances "who have that queer likeness to an animal that those who spend most of their time in company with an animal have."[26] One morning his horse ran away with him; pounding along, totally out of control, he flew past a sedate and compact group of riders, one of whom detached himself and, on finally overtaking Muggeridge, angrily remonstrated with him for insulting His Excellency the Governor (then Sir John Anderson) by whistling past him in such an unruly manner. "I said I hadn't realized it, but even if I had I shouldn't have been able to do anything because my horse had run away with me. Whereupon he muttered something about how riders as incompetent as I obviously was ought not to be allowed to use the Maidan; and anyway not to let it happen again."[27] Years later, when Sir John Anderson had become Viscount Waverly, their paths crossed again, this time in the more placid setting of a cocktail party; Muggeridge related this incident on the Maidan to Lord Waverly who failed to find it amusing.

Work on the Samuel Butler biography was dull and slow. He solaced himself by planning another novel; it would be about the English *sahib* in India, "the decadence of the West transplanted and absorbed here."[28] The English in Calcutta, he had observed, had two common characteristics: their "essential shabbiness"[29] and their complacent enjoyment of such fleeting distinction and social superiority as their status conferred. This attitude he found depressing and puzzling. Was he deluded in supposing that the pomp and ceremony of colonialism, these marionettes who stiffened to attention when a band played "God Save the King," this vast imperial structure, was on its way out and must soon topple over and they with it? "The British Raj seems to me to be nearing its end; these arrogant, ruthless, vulgar fellow countrymen, half aware that their day is done and stretching out to its utmost limits the delights of being a *sahib*. Other people don't seem to be aware that the whole thing is falling to pieces; perhaps it isn't, and only my morbidity which makes me think so."[30]

As weeks dragged by, he became less and less inclined to write, except in his diary, which received meticulous, daily attention; its tone is melancholy and self-pitying—"the whimperings of a man of sorrows meekly apologizing for having passed the age of thirty without having been crucified."[31] Late in November, he wrote to Kitty: "I'm very melancholic. The world to me is an inhospitable place. I don't think I really care about its present chaos, even like it, since it reflects my own state of mind. What I feel all the time is the sense of being an alien, a stranger in a strange land. I don't think that I've known five minutes of real happiness for years and years. Now I'm in India I watch boats sailing down the Hooghley with deep longing; when I'm in London I watch boats sailing down the Thames in the same way. All of my waking time here is spent wishing I was with you and the children; when I was with you, and might, after all, have stayed with you, I chose to go away."

Such pleasant moments as he had were spent with four Indian acquaintances; one was a professor of fine arts at Calcutta University, another a civil servant, another a rich businessman and Congress party politician, and, finally, Suhindranath Datta, a Bengali poet. The five met weekly for conversation over dinner, usually at the Nanking

101

restaurant. At their first dinner, Muggeridge had casually inquired whether there was anything to the reports of a renaissance in Bengali literature. "The renaissance," the professor replied pointing at Datta, "is seated in front of you."[32] Judging from his powerful but incomplete autobiography, and his brilliant essays in *The World at Twilight* (London: Oxford University Press, 1970), the claim was not so exaggerated. The theme of many of Datta's essays is that the worst consequence of the British Raj was that it created a brown ghost of itself that would continue to stalk India after its demise. This was a favorite theme of Muggeridge's, and he and Datta discussed it often.

Muggeridge grew very fond of all four men, but particularly of Datta whose elegance, sardonic wit, and perfect manners attracted him. There was, also, an underlying sadness about him that Muggeridge found sympathetic. After Datta's death in 1960, he wrote a tribute to his friend in which he said that Datta's melancholy ". . . was not the melancholy of defeat or self-pity; rather of the mystic who senses the imperfection of all human beings, of the artist who knows that he will never be able to convey, except, at best, partially and inadequately, what his soul understands."[33]

Like newspaper offices everywhere, the *Statesman* collected its share of weird people who unaccountably washed up at random, like driftwood. One such, a "raw and ruddy" man, came in late at night while Muggeridge was sitting about waiting for an edition to come back from the printers, and the stranger confided in a conspiratorial whisper that he had made a great discovery: Namely, that the old adage "Laugh and the world laughs with you, weep and you weep alone" was untrue; rather, it was: "Laugh and the world laughs with you, weep and the world laughs at you." This said, he slunk off as mysteriously as he had come.

Another bit of driftwood was a "lean and shiny and lugubrious" alcoholic, originally from Newscastle, who would get drunk and lie about for thirty-six hours or so and then turn up at the *Statesman*. His wife would be summoned to take him home or, if she was not available, Muggeridge took the man back to his flat. "His flat was full of furniture and rugs; all along the verandah birds in cages, and a glass cage full of ivory figures. He sees himself, I think, as a bit of a connoisseur. As he is, in his way. He showed me his fiddle, explaining that it had cost £250. Certainly it has a mellow tone. He played a bar or so of a sentimental tune. Somehow seeing him do this—a raw man from Newcastle, swollen jaws set, a little suffering around the eyes—touched me. I like him better than anyone I've met here.

"He told me to pick up a jade figure and wish, betting me a thousand rupees to one that my wish would come true. I've got a routine wish.

Not to be happy . . . I wish only to be a great writer. A reckless wish—if it comes true it would bring unhappiness instead of happiness . . . All the same it is my wish. It's the only thing I really care about. So I hope it does come true whatever price has to be paid, and however long its fulfillment has to be waited for."[34]

Muggeridge spent the last day of 1934 at Bhugadpur where he stayed with a wealthy landowner named Singh. The New Year's Eve festivities, he reflected, were not dissimilar to what would be happening in Croydon sitting rooms, Manchester flats, and even Russian dachas. The guests laughed and drank and made jokes and pulled exploding crackers; and Muggeridge was asked to lead a chorus of "For He's a Jolly Good Fellow" in honor of the host. Since he didn't know the words, the guests had to settle for his tuneless rendition of "Auld Lang Syne." "As the New Year began a terrible fit of melancholy oppressed me, a feeling that the year ahead was going to be the worst in my life, that awful things would happen."[35]

On January 19, 1935, Kitty arrived in Calcutta for a visit. The next three weeks were to prove to be the nadir of their marriage. They wrangled and fought and neither gave way. All old wounds were reopened and fresh salt poured in. Malcolm had become involved with an Indian woman, named Khouchaid, and Kitty, who met her, somehow immediately sensed this. Each flung accusations and recriminations at the other until at last, exhausted, they reached a reconciliation of sorts. On her last night in Calcutta, Kitty told him: "You'd better stick to me. No one will love you as I do."[36]

After Kitty had gone, Malcolm went on impulse to an astrologer to have his horoscope done. Tucked into his diary, smudgy and dog-eared, is the actual horoscope dated February 20, 1935. In part, it is accurate: "versatile, sensitive, restless disposition; strong imagination; quick marriage; good memory; assumed to be cheerful, but at heart wretched; tendency to live in hot climates; occupation involves travelling"; yet on more objective details, not deducible from the circumstances and personality of the subject, it turned out to be quite wrong: "Chance of becoming a drunkard between twenty-four and thirty-six" (not a bad guess, actually, perhaps foiled by Muggeridge's own injunction, written in immediately following: "Avoid this!"); "marriage biggest mistake committed; two sons and one daughter by second wife; increasing kidney and bladder trouble" (in fact, his health steadily improved as he got older). At the time, he purported to regard astrology as "obviously bogus" but, even so, confided that he was ". . . enormously disturbed by what he said which somehow opened up a new vein of thought and suffering in me."[37]

The spring months were aimless and melancholy. He and Kitty

continued their quarreling by post. He had insomnia and, when he did sleep, had nightmares; in one recurrent nightmare he discovered his children outside their door at 19 Grove Terrace in London, ringing the doorbell and waiting and waiting: "My heart sank. I knew what had happened, went into the house, and found Kit dead. She'd written me a note before she died. It began: 'It doesn't often happen to a human being to want nothing; I want nothing now—not even you.' Marvelling at the beauty of this sentence, I woke up, feeling afraid. I am afraid still."[38]

Writing for the *Statesman* was increasingly farcical, and he now neglected his Butler book for weeks at a time. His liaisons petered out, although poignantly and with no bitterness. In her last letter to him, Khouchaid wrote: "I shall remember you always for the exquisite sensitiveness and charm of your nature. I don't think I shall ever know anyone quite like you again." Only the weekly dinner with his four Indian friends and their occasional outings together (such as to hear Galli-Curci sing: "an amazing hag with an atrocious voice"[39]) made life bearable.

On March 17, 1935, the news came that, despite the Treaty of Versailles, Germany would maintain a standing army of six hundred thousand men. Muggeridge wrote in his diary: "It means war, sooner or later. If this is war, I shall fly home at once and learn to fly. This thought made me quite happy. I realized how utterly desperate I was, how little hold on life. I want to die. Quite genuinely, I want to die. I have no appetite to live because I know what, for us, the future will be like. There must be many like me, and that is why war will come."

In April he left for Simla, the remote mountain eyrie where the whole of the Imperial government decamped for the summer. His four Indian friends saw him off at Calcutta station. They were never to be together again.

In Simla, he stayed at the Cecil Hotel, along with some garrulous Indian army officers. Inevitably, the talk was of war and women. To Muggeridge's surprise, the officers dreaded the possibility of war, a prospect he increasingly expected and, in a way, hoped for. They appreciated the occasional border skirmish to keep their skills and equipment in fighting trim, but feared all-out war. On the subject of women, Muggeridge was taken aside at breakfast one morning by an army officer who sought his opinion as to whether or not artists and photographers who did nude pictures of women "occasionally have a dip"? Muggeridge was delighted by this turn of phrase and allowed that he supposed they occasionally dipped.

Ostensibly he was in Simla to gather news, but since nothing much happened, there was little pressure to write anything. If a story had to be done, it was simply a matter of trekking round the various government departments (all housed side by side in identical wooden structures) looking for a handout or someone to interview.

> Mooning about in these departments, waiting to see someone I didn't want to see in order to ask him questions I didn't want answered, I used to sometimes think of India as I knew it. The dusty roads, the teeming bazaars, the lurid paddy fields, the sluggish rivers, the women carrying water from the well in pitchers on their heads, the brown bodies sweating in the sun as they followed behind the lumbering oxen and steered their wooden ploughs; the innumerable villages and feet endlessly padding—little processions, a man leading, then a woman with a baby on her back, and a child barely able to walk, clutching her hand, other children trailing behind. Everywhere people; washing, sleeping, chanting, buying, selling, giving birth, suckling, living, dying. Where was the connection between them and this typewriter fusillade, these dozing peons, the clerks, the sahibs, the Members of the Viceroy's Council?[40]

His dispatches became fewer and fewer. Such reports as he did make scarcely mattered since he had a falling out with Wordsworth who usually cut them back in Calcutta.

On impulse one Sunday morning he went to mass; later he wrote: "I saw the strength of the church, the appeal it can continue to make to all manner of people in all manner of circumstances. And for my own part, I felt I prefer it, say, to an assembly of Comsomols or Marxists, just as I prefer the *Iliad* to *Kapital*. Maybe the future is with Comsomols and Marxists. Let it be so. Nothing will alter the fact that without having any sentimental illusions about paganism vs. catholicism, my spirit more easily harmonizes with theirs, responds more to them, than to this new conception of totalitarianism."[41]

Early in May an embossed invitation was delivered to his hotel: "Their Excellencies, the Viceroy and Vicereine, request the pleasure of your company at Viceregal Lodge. . . ." Their Excellencies did not request in vain. In starched shirt and tails, he showed up at the appointed hour and entered a receiving line down which their Excellencies slowly processed. When Lord Willingdon arrived at Muggeridge, he extended his hand and said, somewhat grimly: "I have heard of you." Muggeridge was uncertain whether to be flattered or alarmed. After dinner, Lord Willingdon called him over and said: "You know people say this country is difficult to govern. Actually, it's not so. I've found it the easiest country in the world to govern—just be nice to these fellers and they respond."[42]

Walking back afterwards, and for years to come, Muggeridge kept turning over the Viceroy's words in his mind: ". . . the last Viceroy but three, up there in the Raj's mountain retreat, his guests around him, his A.D.C.'s at his elbow, his rumbustious lady within hailing distance, the band playing Elgar . . . and this grey, fragile-looking old gentleman telling me how easy he had found governing India and managing these fellers within so short a time of the Raj's total collapse."[43]

In Simla he managed to finish off (in every sense) Samuel Butler, and he dispatched the manuscript to Cape. Cape was appalled. What had been planned as a tribute to Butler on the centenary of his birth was instead a hatchet job, exposing the hypocrite who exposed the hypocrisy of Victorianism, pushing him off his pedestal and gleefully kicking at the pieces. The Victorians had sought to escape reality in emotions; Butler, Muggeridge contended, sought to escape reality in ideas. "He was a pioneer ideologue. His mind was his refuge; and he lived secure among its shadows and fantasies." When the book finally appeared, in August 1936, it was published not by Cape but by Eyre and Spottiswoode.

Muggeridge sent advance copies to his friends Hesketh Pearson and Hugh Kingsmill and received cautionary replies. Pearson wrote: "The book is splendid, but my God! You'll be excommunicated, blackballed by the Athenaeum, assassinated by Erewhonians. To debunk a debunker is, I should say, a capital offence. Anyhow, congratulations. You've done it unanswerably."[44] Kingsmill warned that he would be "flayed alive by every single critic"[45] and recommended extensive revisions and deletions.

Muggeridge made no changes, and Kingsmill's prediction was vindicated. Critics were outraged. The Butler tide was at its crest (how little one hears of him today!), and here was this brash young author portraying Butler as an even greater humbug than the Victorians whose balloon Butler had pricked. Desmond McCarthy, who was rumored to have been so disgusted that he flung the book into the Adriatic, devoted two full pages in *The Sunday Times* to a defense of Butler. Rather petulantly, Muggeridge replied, and this set off an acrimonious joust in the correspondence columns. E. M. Forster said the book constituted "an attack so disgruntled and so persistent that it may well be the result of a guilt complex"; while *The Daily Herald* called it "an extravagance of peevishness and spitefulness." But it was Stephen Spender in *The Listener* who raised the most intriguing question: "By the time the reader is half way through it, instead of mentally inveighing with the writer against Butler, he is asking himself why Mr. Muggeridge detests Butler so much?"[46]

Why indeed? No doubt the circumstances in which the book was written were partly responsible. In a nearly unrelieved state of torpor and melancholy, it is difficult to write appreciatively or even objectively; like expecting a condemned felon to appreciate the merits of capital punishment while waiting at the gallows. Even more important, Muggeridge saw Butler as the progenitor of nonconformity in all matters, casting off the shackles of tradition, but putting what in their place? In political terms, substituting state tyranny for aristocratic authority, as in Russia; in personal terms, substituting egotism for patriarchy, and carnality for morality. He saw himself and his generation as sprung from Butler's loins and, in hating himself and them, hated Butler. This is particularly evident in those passages where he heaps blame on Butler for developments for which it would be absurd to hold that ridiculous old boy responsible. In this passage, for example, there is clearly more autobiography than biography.

> *The Way of All Flesh* has born a rare progeny of young men and young women living their own lives in their own way in their own rooms and in front of their own gas fires, of earnest promiscuity—he matters to her, she matters to him, may matter, once mattered, matters no longer, mattering and not mattering and perhaps mattering: of poets in coloured shirts who love one another, and are Communists, and sing of the worker in his factory, the miner in his mine; of quiet, kindly, solitary persons who take each other's arms, and smile weakly as the kettle boils for tea, and go for country walks discussing the League of Nations on their way; of other novels—how many other novels! which empty out the insides of their authors as Butler in *The Way of All Flesh* emptied out his inside, dissecting relationships, streaming consciousness.[47]

Years later, after Muggeridge became friendly with George Orwell, Orwell wrote to him saying that he "enjoyed" but "did not approve" of *The Earnest Atheist.* "I know that you feel that people like Butler, who are disintegrators, prepare the way for dictatorships, etc., and I can see the connection between Butler's revolt against his parents and your experiences in Moscow. But I do earnestly think you are wrong. The real division is not between conservatives and revolutionaries but between authoritarians and libertarians. However, it's too complicated an issue to be argued in a letter."[48]

Muggeridge's attack on Butler is too unrelenting and unbalanced to be good biography. Nevertheless, *The Earnest Atheist* is a remarkable book in its way, full of insights rather than pedantry, genius not scholarship. Despite its critical reception, it helped to alter the prevailing view of Butler. Muggeridge's heresies have become so widely shared that in the unlikely event such a book were published today, it would either be ignored or its author condemned for putting out stale, conventional stuff about a man who was, at most, a minor thinker and a period piece.

One person the book pleased, and whose praise mattered most, was his father to whom the book was dedicated "With gratitude and affection." In his parents' own copy, he inscribed: "To Dad and Mother, who gave so much and got so little." H. T. had said little about his other books; *Three Flats* had too much sex; *Autumnal Face* was, on any showing, a cruel caricature of his parents; and *Winter in Moscow* had exploded myths that H. T. continued to hold dear. But he had only praise for *The Earnest Atheist*; "I can scarcely express my joy over your new book,—somehow it seems my triumph because in spite of (not because of) your other books I always believed in you and your calling someday to do something great that will help our bewildered and lost world. This is it."[49]

Shortly before he left Simla, Muggeridge met Amrita Sher-Gil, now generally considered to have been one of India's foremost painters. He was introduced to her at a club and asked her to dance. The first thing he noticed about her was "a kind of black down on her chin and eyes that were very bright."[50] A few days later he went to her house, which was also her studio, to see some paintings. Thus began ". . . one of those obsessive relationships which for a while occupy one's whole being; then come to an end as suddenly as they began." Under Amrita's spell he so neglected his reporting duties that he failed even to answer telegrams inquiring as to his whereabouts, or if he were alive or dead. Needless to say this occasioned consternation at the *Statesman*, but he was past caring. Later he embodied the bizarre situation of a newspaper that cannot locate its own correspondent in a short story, *Summer in Simla*, which was read on the BBC. Nearly every day he spent at Amrita's studio, where she painted his portrait, which now hangs in the National Gallery in Delhi.

Amrita's parents were a curious pair. Her mother was a red-haired, earthy Hungarian woman, who eventually committed suicide. Her father was a Sikh nobleman; a bearded, gnome-like, Tolstoyan man, who lived ascetically and spent each evening on the roof studying the movements of the stars through a telescope. Amrita was their eldest child, born in Budapest in 1913. She had studied at the Ecole des Beaux Arts in Paris and painted in a postimpressionist manner at times reminiscent of Gaugin. Their affair was as passionate and as intense as it was brief: "Why I love Amrita is that she, like myself, is a bare soul, without any allegiances or beliefs or hopes, just a sense of animality, so strong that she can paint as I write, reproducing the bare form of life without idealizing upwards or downwards. By the time she's my age, she'll be as ready to die as I am."[51]

Amrita Sher-Gil died at Lahore on December 5, 1941, at the age of twenty-seven, so this prophecy too came to pass. The exact circumstances of her death were never clear. She was cremated on the banks of the river Ravi, her father having abandoned his telescope to light the funeral pyre on which her body was cremated.

In August 1935, Muggeridge out of the blue received a telegram from Percy Cudlipp, editor of *The Evening Standard*, offering him a job on the Londoner's Diary at twenty pounds a week. He wired off his acceptance and notified Kitty that he was at last coming home. Amrita saw him off at Simla station and, when the little mountain train whistled for passengers to board, she embraced him and said: "I want you to be happy" and then, switching to French, *"J' ai en des beaux moments avec lui."* He waved out the window as long as she remained in sight.

Another platform, another parting, another person he would never see again. In his diary he wrote this sentence of James Boswell's: "When I survey my past life I discover nothing but a barren waste of time, with some disorders of body and disturbances of the mind, very near to madness, which I hope that He who made me will suffer to extenuate many faults and excuse many deficiencies."

·7·

The DARKNESS and The LIGHT

Tumult and peace, the darkness and the light
Were all like workings of one mind, the features
Of the same face . . .

William Wordsworth, *Authentic Tidings*

* * *

As far back as 1926 Muggeridge had written: "One early knows what to say; the difficulty is how to say it."[1] In the four years remaining before the war, he was to try essay, parody, drama, fiction, and social history to say what he had to say. It was a time of his most original, perhaps also his best, writing. But it was not to appear in *The Evening Standard*, a Beaverbrook paper, where work involved dressing immaculately ("or at least as immaculately as I can") in a black suit with pinstripes, wearing gloves and a black felt hat, and walking up Fleet Street carrying a furled silk umbrella, to Shoe Lane, usually arriving there about ten. Then tapping out a paragraph or two: It might be a bit of society gossip, a death, an honor or appointment conferred, or a breath of scandal. With no less than six full-time contributors, the Diary was overstaffed, and a paragraph or two from each was considered full measure. If he was absolutely stuck for a subject, he consulted the Diary's editor, Leslie Marsh, but usually elicited no more from him than the laconic query: "Have you checked the stiffs?" Since the Diary went to press at noon and was seldom altered for the later editions, Muggeridge was away by midafternoon. Unedifying, yes, but it bought bread. "Inside there is the same old loathing and disgust. I hurry along Fleet Street and hurry to and from the office library with papers in my hand, yet there is no reason why I should hurry . . . ."[2]

Lord Beaverbrook seldom appeared at the office, preferring to run the paper by telephone and leaving its day-to-day administration to his minion, Captain Michael Wardell, a man whose black eye patch suggested an early prototype of the Hathaway shirt man. Wardell eventually became publisher of the Fredericton *Daily Gleaner* and a sometime wheeler-dealer in Canadian politics. Muggeridge's only contact with Wardell was the occasional order to produce a "must" paragraph for the Diary; such instructions originated, of course, with the Beaver himself but were reverently communicated, like a sacrament, to the chosen hack by Wardell. One such "must" paragraph with which Muggeridge was entrusted was to point out that the bronchial ailment from which Sir James Barrie was reputedly dying was so painless that it was known as "the old man's friend."

"The reason was clear: Beaverbrook, an asthmatic, expected to die of a similar complaint, and wanted to be assured that it made for an easy death by reading it in the Diary. Harley Street was unresponsive when asked to provide confirmation, but the Diary nevertheless made the point . . . ."[3]

The Evening Standard was produced in one large room with tables everywhere and the usual newspaper hubbub comprised of disorder and noise. Street sounds occasionally drifted in above the din; on one occasion Muggeridge heard the strains of revivalist singing and reflected: "The singing was rather attractive. Anything to do with religion attracts me in a sort of way, but not as much as I think it does. The things that I really love in life are worship, sincerity, love, and great literature. The things that really touch me are innocence, weakness, poverty, and child-bearing."[4]

By January 1936, he was fed up with the *Standard*, with Lord Beaverbrook and Captain Wardell, and with the Londoner's Diary: ". . . grim work, revolting, futile and yet exhausting."[5] To ponder the future, he and Kitty went for a brief holiday at the Albany Hotel on the seafront at Hastings. This worthy establishment had belonged to Sir Henry Lunn and was a favorite haunt of his son, Hugh Kingsmill, who felicitously described its rich, retired clientele as "excrement living on increment." The Muggeridges arrived at the hotel to discover that a guest named Potter, whom they vaguely knew, had just fallen down the stairs and died. "All the other residents referred to him, not as having died, but as having fallen downstairs, as though, apart from such accidents, there was no such thing as death."[6]

From neither a vocational nor matrimonial point of view could the expedition be said to have been a success. His diary relates:

The sitting room is draughtless and warm and inmates move to and from it and the dining room like a herd of cows to and from pasture. Between meals they rest and ruminate. It's strange to see marriage in such circumstances, withered old men resentfully following withered old women. Like children, they make a lot of going to the lavatory, or going to lie down, since, as with children, these are important events.

On Sunday morning Kit and I walked to Bexhill. It was a dreary road amongst a litter of already broken down post-war houses. Kit had lived in Bexhill with her father and mother, and described how they used to go along this road quarrelling with one another. In the afternoon Hugh came round, and I talked to him while Kit rested. We laughed as we always do. After Hugh had gone Kit looked angry. We walked along the front arguing about living in the country, and about whether we should live together at all. The waves pounded in, and I thought how, if I'd been a Victorian novelist, I should have seen my own mood in their angry movement. I thought it might be better for me to leave Kit then and there, or to kill myself. Melancholy possessed me; I felt bewildered and tired . . . .[7]

His melancholy only disappeared in the company of Hugh Kingsmill, with whom he now spent many hours, in Hastings, or in London at the Author's Club or their favorite pub—the Horseshoe on Tottenham Court Road. It was here that another friend, Arthur Dawe, a civil servant in the Colonial office, once came upon Muggeridge and Kingsmill deep in conversation and described Muggeridge as "mobile, arrowy and missing nothing." Hesketh Pearson, another friend, frequently joined them there. The story of their friendship has been told with great sensitivity and affection by Richard Ingrams in God's Apology (Deutsch, 1977). Muggeridge was devoted to Kingsmill as this diary entry, typical of this period, reveals: "I love Hugh more and more. His company delights me, so that however depressed or ill I'm feeling, I never notice this with him."

By 1936, Kingsmill had written several biographies (of Matthew Arnold, Shakespeare, Samuel Johnson, and Frank Harris—the latter Muggeridge considered "a comic masterpiece") all of which were too unpretentious and perceptive for reviewers, whom Kingsmill described as "poor, soured devils who once thought they had some talent and are now a mass of nerves and without any convictions at all, except the very strong conviction that anyone more alive than themselves ought to be sandbagged"; at the same time, his biographies were insufficiently lurid or dramatic to appeal to that tiny, shrinking fragment of literate humanity who actually buy books. From a financial point of view, it was a ruinous combination, and Kingsmill's efforts to remain solvent resembled, as he put it, "a man leaping from ice floe to ice floe across a wide and rapid river. A strenuous, not a dignified, spectacle."

Kingsmill's genius found its natural outlet in conversation, a vivacious if slapdash mixture of ebullience, mirth, and understanding—much like that of his mentor Dr. Johnson. It was Kingsmill, incidentally, who brought Muggeridge to a full appreciation of the great Dr. Johnson—the man and the writer he admires above all others. On May 20, 1936, Kingsmill and Muggeridge visited Johnson's house just off Fleet Street, and Muggeridge wept when the curator related several instances of Johnson's benevolence and selflessness.

Like Johnson's conversation, Kingsmill's talk made a lasting impression on those who heard it. Alec Waugh (Evelyn's brother) wrote: "He is like the sun shining on you. You become happy. The present is rich. The future radiant. You talk well—he envelops you with warmth and friendliness."[8] This was so, Muggeridge decided, ". . . because his interest in people and things is, as far as it is possible for a human being's to be, detached from his own personal interests."[9]

Muggeridge said then and maintains now: "He was the only human being I have ever known in whose company I never suffered one moment of boredom, whose solid figure I never once saw looming up and whose voice I never once heard, except with unalloyed happiness."[10]

Together they conceived a project for starting a weekly humorous magazine, to be called *Porcupine*, and in January 1936, Muggeridge inserted this advertisement in *The Times*: "A group of writers who believe that there is room for a weekly which would deal wittily and honestly with the modern world would be glad to hear from anyone interested in financing such a venture."

"We were very excited about it," he wrote, "and felt quite confident that there would be a rush of rich men to finance so sensible and timely an adventure." They immediately set to work, drawing up a prospectus that promised "commentary on the passing scene, written intelligently and wittily," an editorial policy "individual and independent," above all "resistant to any of the herd emotions of today, Fascism, Communism, Douglas Credit, or any other nostrum." In the first blush of enthusiasm they were well pleased with the result; however, on rereading it, Muggeridge ruefully concluded that the generalities and empty phrases of the prospectus were "just the sort of thing that *Porcupine* was against."[11]

The response to their advertisement, when it came, was not encouraging. The first letter was from a home for indigents, ". . . a kindly, but not particularly helpful communication which expressed the hope that we would 'get the money (I having none by the way)' but 'still more, that you will put honesty before wit.' "

This was followed by two letters from promoters offering to demonstrate, for a nominal fee of £25, how a company could be formed

". . . the way the people do who make potato chips, or soap, or substitute butter, and then ask the public to subscribe." These possibilities were not pursued.

The only other communication received was from the publisher of a magazine for badminton players. "With some difficulty, on a grey, January day, we found the office of this publication and had a brief conversation with its editor and publisher. In selling a magazine dealing with badminton, he said, the first step was to locate circles interested in the game. If, by the same token, we could indicate to him where circles interested in humour were to be found, he felt sure that he would be able to meet with a corresponding success with a humorous publication. We agreed that this was the nub of the matter, and said that if we could think of a formula for tracking down the humorous with the same certainty that he had been able to track down badminton enthusiasts we would communicate further with him."[12]

Thus ended *Porcupine*.

At Kingsmill's urging, Muggeridge quit his job at *The Evening Standard* and, in May 1936, moved to the Mill House at Whatlington in Sussex. It was (and is) a large, charming eighteenth-century house, formerly an inn, which would have made a suitable headquarters for a temperance hall, being situated halfway down an incline running from the pub to the cemetery. The previous occupant had recently slit her throat, and this grisly occurrence had depressed the asking price to £800. Even so, it was beyond their resources and was bought only through the magic of mortgages. "It was," Muggeridge recalled in his memoirs, "a fairly austere existence; water came from a well which had to be pumped by hand, and drinking water from a spring some little distance away. Each day I fetched two bucketsful. Bathing was done in a small metal bath in front of a kitchen stove; there was no heating apart from fires and, of course, we had no car. The nearest shopping centre was Battle, some two miles away; and we would usually walk or cycle in and out."[13] Its chief attraction, as far as he was concerned, was its proximity to Hastings where Kingsmill lived.

For the next three years Muggeridge's only regular income was five pounds a week for reviewing new fiction in *The Daily Telegraph*. It meant reading novels, or trying to, which ". . . gave me a distaste for new novels in dustjackets which I feel to this day." Women novelists were particularly trying: "Very few women should be allowed to write novels; their vanity is too voracious."[14] Otherwise the family of six (a son, Charles, being the latest addition) survived on whatever odd writing jobs turned up—and some were odd indeed. For example, Muggeridge contributed two chapters to a book called *The Fifty Most Amazing Crimes of the Last 100 Years*; his contributions were *The Terrible*

Fate of Mrs. Staunton and, perhaps in the interest of sexual equality, *The Case of J. B. Trappman: Fatal Obsession of a One-Track Mind:* "He might have been a famous scientist—he possessed the perseverance, single-ness of purpose Instead . . . ." He also translated Caulaincourt's memoirs at thirty shillings a thousand words. And he wrote free-lance articles, particularly in *Time and Tide,* a vaguely feminist paper owned by Lady Rhondda, of whom Kingsmill once said that although not quite a *grand prix* bore, she was nevertheless a perfectly respectable yeoman bore. Some of Muggeridge's most trenchant journalism, such as "Why I am not a Pacifist," "The Materialist Conception of Culture," and "Dictatorships from Below," appeared in *Time and Tide.* [15] The paper also had a regular feature called "Notes on the Way" to which various people contributed somewhat eclectic jottings on the human condition, and this column provided an outlet for some of his earliest religious writing. In fact, many of his contributions to "Notes on the Way" read like an early draft of *Jesus Rediscovered.* He seldom passed up an opportunity to demolish phony or sentimental illusions about prog-ress, democracy, or his special *bête noire,* the League of Nations. He wrote: "To me, the League seems just idealism, rootless belief, pretence that things are so and so because it would be nice if they were so and so, a manifestation of an attitude of mind that has haunted the postwar epoch as morality haunted the Victorians, and with the same disastrous results." [16] Such sentiments did not sit well with some *Time and Tide* readers, nor with the owners and editorial staff. Miss Ellen Wilkinson, M.P., replied to his comments about the League of Nations by suggest-ing that a new verb be coined: "To Muggeridge: to deny the value of anyone's efforts to improve the evils that one sees, and at the same time to do nothing in particular about it oneself." [17] For its part, the paper printed this "Statement of Editorial Policy": "We disagree with quite nine-tenths of what Mr. Muggeridge has to say. His views on the League of Nations seem to us not merely nonsense but, if they were to be held by many, dangerous nonsense. Nevertheless, he seems to us the kind of person who should—occasionally—be heard. He is thinking hard. If his horror of smugness in every form leads him to empty out every baby with every bath—if his blind and feverish search for spiritual values has as yet led him no further than a violent rejection of what is after all a quite commonsensical and useful material basis . . . that is not to say that he is not both a brilliant writer and one symptomatic of a number of his own generation. So, strongly as we disagree with him, we gladly give him space to pick the world to pieces to his heart's content." [18] After such patronizing nonsense, the wonder is that he ever wrote a word for them again.

Financially, he was in no position to be choosy. No doubt

Muggeridge's continuing inability to say no to any project that is put to him derives from these financially lean years. Until he was forty, his only bank entries were overdrafts. Even so, when Kingsmill was most hard-up, Muggeridge offered to get a second mortgage on his house and give him the proceeds.

Away from Kingsmill, he was gloomy and introspective although never quite as melancholic as he had been in India. He still found himself torn between society and solitude. He remained prisoner not master of his emotions. The stench of flesh was always in his nostrils, yet still his appetites tormented him. In *Comrade Caliban*, an unpublished play from this period, he wrote: "I feel as though my will is being corroded from within; there's a kind of moral lassitude which has got into my very being."

His diary for 1936 is replete with scriptural admonitions about the transitory nature of life, about living in the spirit rather than the flesh, and about men loving darkness rather than light because their deeds are evil. This entry is typical of his blacker moods.

> No way lies there to ease my saddened heart—
> Not in the ecstasy of sense, nor in domestic peace,
> Not in success, the taste of power and wealth.
> The way that I must take lies clear before,
> And yet I falter, stop irresolute,
> Prefer the petulance of discontent.
> How shall I purify the soul within?
> How be a mirror to the truth without?
> Through mists of envy and of appetite,
> I see Eternity, and turn away,
> And groan, and contemplate interior darkness.[19]

All his lighter moments were spent in Kingsmill's company. Together they wrote a series of joint "Literary Pilgrimages" for a short-lived humor magazine called *Night and Day*, begun by their friend Graham Greene. These took the form of dialogues, loosely held together by some literary association, in which each man's contribution reflected his own personality; Muggeridge, impulsive and dogmatic; Kingsmill, temperate and reflective. One which gave particular satisfaction was a visit to the Wimpole Street house where Tennyson's friend Arthur Hallam had lived. Muggeridge and Kingsmill prepared themselves for a dawn visit by spending the night in a Turkish bath being ". . . kneaded, thumped, soaped and sluiced under the masseur's hands."

It was dark in the streets at six-thirty, but the clouds were turning a dull grey. We passed the British Museum, where a yellow light shone through tall windows, as though some secret trial were in progress. The darkness thinned away in Oxford Street, and in Wimpole Street it was already day.

After the carefree variety of architecture in Wigmore Street, Wimpole Street was narrow and monotonous and hardly changed at all in the hundred years since Tennyson stood there at the same hour. Already, milk bottles had been left at doors. There were the doctors' nameplates. Up above, a light here and there in a servant's bedroom, but no one stirring in Number 67.

Muggeridge: What a place to see as a deserted shrine! What desolation!

Kingsmill: *Dark house by which once more I stand*
Here in the long, unlovely street
Doors, where my heart was used to beat
So quickly, waiting for a hand . . .

Muggeridge: How he must have loved him to face the dawn in Wimpole Street! These rich houses, this ghastly mausoleum of affluence!

Kingsmill: *And like a guilty thing I creep*
At earliest morning to the door . . .

We pictured him striding in from Wigmore Street, tall, sallow and unshaven, not a man, we thought, that anyone would ask the way of, his eye fixed on Number 67.

Kingsmill: I wonder whether it would have made any difference if Hallam had lived?

Muggeridge: I can't see why. If instead of dying in Vienna, he had survived in Downing Street, Tennyson would still have watched by that dark door, and groaned as the blank day broke on bald Wimpole Street.

Kingsmill: I suppose so.

Muggeridge: A doubly barren love.[20]

Another of their joint ventures, only slightly more successful than the stillborn *Porcupine*, were two books, *Brave Old World* (1936) and *Next Year's News* (1937), both parodies of the popular press. Their aim, to adapt Robert Burns's words, was to send up ourselves as others see us, the others being the press. Both books fell victim to the satirist's nemesis; namely, the reader's inability to distinguish between reality and parody. Douglas Jerrold, their editor at Eyre and Spottiswoode, a tall, balding, severe-looking man whom Kingsmill once described as looking like an inflated hors d'oeuvre, had predicted that ". . . people simply won't understand it as satire," and he was proved right. Their mimicry was too subtle and too exact; for example, *The Church Times* informing its readers: "The Church of England is getting down to its autumn work, and persons of imagination are asking themselves the searching question: 'What exactly are we trying to do, and how are we

117

to set about it?' " Or this burlesque of a *Times'* report of the Archbishop's New Year's message (and who would be surprised if it somehow came to light that a Lambeth Palace drudge had actually cribbed a line or two from it?): "The world was becoming a wiser world. It was becoming a happier world. Above all, it was becoming a more honest world. The keynote of the age was a mistrust of phrases, an almost alarming sincerity in word and deed. Speedier communications, improved housing conditions, facilities for education and travel brought within the reach of the humblest, the miracle of wireless which carried culture to the fireside—all were uniting to knit men together and make of them one family. 'In a long lifetime' the Dean said in conclusion 'which has seen many changes, and most of them emphatically for the better, I have never looked forward to a New Year with such a sense of opportunities for service opening out on every side, and hands and hearts eager, under Providence, to grasp them.' "

Even their political parodies, no matter how they let their imagination soar, whatever flights of fancy they indulged, fell flat because reality kept overtaking them. By the time the books appeared, their efforts seemed tepid compared with the day's papers, more like yesterday's than tomorrow's news. The most dramatic example of this occurred in *Next Year's News* where they envisaged a secret meeting between Hitler and Stalin: "The dictators were together for three hours and twenty minutes. On parting they shook hands warmly." On August 24, 1939, what they fantasized came to pass with such exactitude that one might be forgiven for suspecting that the idea of a Nazi-Soviet pact first originated with them. Muggeridge had long said that communism and national socialism were the same thing except that one was a Slav version and the other a Teutonic version. Now it was clear for all to see.

Given their straitened financial circumstances, both men nursed what turned out to be extravagant hopes for these books. Kingsmill, in particular, envisaged piles of copies being sold in railway stations to the vast amusement of countless commuters; at one point he suggested that they might insert this advertisement in the trade press: "According to the authors, who appear to have private sources of information, *Brave Old World* is in wild demand." Actually, neither sold well, although Muggeridge continued to remember both books with particular affection because of the circumstances in which they were written: "Kingsmill would usually lie down on the sofa, and I would make notes, and then we would begin our labours, often interrupted by irrelevancies, and sometimes by a pleasant walk. At a certain point Kitty would bring in the tea, a meal to which Hughie was deeply devoted; and as we sat in my old study at Whatlington we would watch the evening come down, never failing to find the spectacle delightful, and reluctant to turn on the light and disturb the exquisite dusk which we both loved."[21]

Through the prewar years, the two met most days. Either Muggeridge cycled down to Hastings, where they used to walk along the cliffs to a little cemetery that overlooked the old town and gave an unobstructed view over the downs; or Kingsmill took the bus as far as Battle, and Muggeridge would set out walking along the road to meet him, ". . . delighted when his solid figure loomed up and he began to wave and shout his cheerful greeting—'hullo, old man, hullo . . . .' Never have I seen him without a warm rush of happiness. He created this feeling—a delight in the prospect of his physical presence, more strongly than anyone I have ever known."[22] These words, as it happens, convey exactly what several of his closest friends say about Muggeridge.

Muggeridge has always formed deep and possessive friendships, and this was especially true with Kingsmill; to the point that Kingsmill said he "felt uneasy" about it. Muggeridge resented any intrusion, even from men like Hesketh Pearson and William Gerhardi, who had known Kingsmill longer than he had. In fact, his possessiveness touched off the only acrimonious exchange to mar their friendship. Kingsmill wrote, chiding him for ". . . the amount of will you put into your friendships. There is bound to be will in every relationship, but their oughtn't to be much in friendship . . . Realizing that you feel possessive about your friends, and noticing some examples of it, I have become uncomfortable, being certain that when the occasion occurred you would attribute the same feeling to me."[23] It was a minor ruck and soon smoothed over.

The corollary to Muggeridge's possessiveness is his loyalty. To close friends, he turns a blind eye to faults, defends them against adverse (even if deserved) criticism, and is exceedingly generous. He brooked no criticism of Kingsmill; if any was proffered, he would simply say that the balance of obligation was so much on his side that, whatever Kingsmill's faults, he had already excused them.

What bound the two men together, apart from their love of literature, was a highly-developed sense of humor. Their laughter had a curious way of getting on other people's nerves. On buses or in pubs they would get disapproving looks, and patrons would shift their seats further away. Once, strolling together down Portman Place, Muggeridge remarked that it was a fine street, among the most beautiful in London, marred only by the statue of Quintin Hogg that cast a gloom over it. Kingsmill agreed and said that the Langham also made him sad because it was here that Oscar Wilde got into trouble with

Alfred Douglas. "At this we laughed uproariously and various passers-by stopped, wondering what was the matter with us."[24]

To the solemn and portentous, their laughter was an affront, grit in the eye. The literary agent, David Higham, remembered Hugh Kingsmill as ". . . a large, rollicking man—always laughing loudly. *He annoyed people.*" (Kingsmill, incidentally, nursed the hope that after Higham's death, his head might be mounted and put on display at the Author's Club.) Laughter belongs to the individual, not to the herd, and is therefore repugnant to the herd and to those whose concern is the welfare of the herd. Since laughter emanates from the imagination, it is resented by those who are dominated by the will. King John speaks for all such when he expresses abhorrence of ". . . that idiot laughter/ A passion hateful to my purpose."

If they could not meet in Hastings nor in Whatlington, Muggeridge and Kingsmill spent hours talking on the telephone, which became something of an ordeal for their wives. Kitty put an end to one marathon telephone conversation by hurling a book at her husband with sufficient velocity to break its spine; "Unfortunately," she was heard to remark, "not his."

Marriage continued to have its trials, and whatever ascetic aspirations he had, his personal conduct could hardly be described as monkish. He was often in a state of "frenzied indecision" about love, marriage, and how he should live. Two diary entries, in August 1936, illustrate this. On August 19, he wrote: "I'm still not smoking and am determined never to again." Carnality, he wrote, presented greater problems: ". . . I have not made up my mind whether to forego fornication, because I love it so, and because I still cherish the illusion that it's possible to have it occasionally without hurting anyone." Then, four days later, after reading a study of mysticism, he resolved to live according to the following precepts: "(1) subjection of the self; (2) mastery of the flesh; both of its ills and its raptures; (3) absorption of the principle of love which governs the universe." The thought of starting forth on this narrow path filled him with delight; then he thought of the many "weary, fearful hours" of stumbling and turning aside and was full of foreboding. Ruefully, he noted: "I have already wrestled long enough with myself to know that the will cannot be willed away."

His religious convictions were no less changeable. One day he resolved to subordinate his ego and his appetites, and to seek submission only to the will of God. "If I fail to find it my life will have been a failure, if I find it, my life will satisfy."[25] Then, the next week, he wrote: "It is inconceivable to me now that I should ever believe either in a personal God, or that Christ's claims to be God's son in a special sense were, insofar as he made them, anything but bogus."[26]

He had frequent bouts of depression. In September 1936, he wrote: "I'm having one of my blackest of black patches, with the queer pain at the back of my head I always have with them, and uncontrollable longings to die. Kitty is like an angel. I can't work. Everything worries me. I'm indecisive, sitting down, getting up again, starting for a walk. It's a wonderful, bright, clear autumn day, with the leaves just beginning to turn. As I walked along this morning I wrestled with myself, but all my efforts were drowned in a conviction that as I am now so I shall remain, that is I'll always be the same. The world is lovely and life is lovely, but I seem to have no part in their loveliness, except for occasional fleeting moments. Perhaps I'm diseased. Whom the Lord loveth, He chasteneth. He chasteneth me."[27]

They were now living on the dwindling remains of a £300 advance from Jonathan Cape for a book tentatively entitled *The Bewildered Soul.* The details had been worked out through Rupert Hart-Davis, then on Cape's staff. What Cape expected was a systematic study of contemporary religious attitudes and practices, rather in the vein of William James's *Varieties of Religious Experience.* The manuscript had been promised by the end of the year but, typically, Muggeridge allowed himself to be easily distracted from it. In the summer months he neglected it entirely while completing another novel, *The Steps of the Sun,* which was never published.

Another temporary distraction was his latent political ambition. Not surprisingly, his writing had made him an outcast in the Labour party, and he now turned wistful eyes on the Conservatives, even to the point of inquiring about constituencies where a nomination might be available. Like a suitor trying to impress prospective in-laws, he agreed to speak at a Conservative rally at Chester in November 1936. "I spent time I could ill afford preparing an elaborate address which, when I delivered it, was a complete failure . . . . The audience did not understand what I was getting at, which is not surprising, because neither did I."[28]

At Crew railway station on the way home, he saw Winston Churchill ". . . looking pale, I thought, and unsure of himself"; they had a brief, inconsequential chat. Thus ended his last political foray.

Incidentally, it must be counted a blessing for all concerned, not least himself, that his political ambitions, such as they were, foundered. It is difficult to imagine anyone less suited to political life. Prophets seldom make effective politicians. Political bargains are based on give and take, and Muggeridge is too much an absolutist to be any good at compromise. In the unlikely event that he had been successful, his demagogic skills and volatile moods would have made him dangerous. In the course of a review of Ignazio Silone's *The School for Dictators,*

Muggeridge gave his own prescription for the successful dictator's temperament: "He must not be happy because happiness makes him serene, rather a sufferer from insomnia, headaches, nervous disorders, solitary, melancholic, given to fits of hysterical rage and suicidal despair."[29] He can hardly have failed to realize how aptly he was describing himself. Anyway, so dreary and portentous a pursuit as politics would undoubtedly have drained him of the wonderful zest and humor that make his company so particularly delightful. Fortunately, he henceforth took to heart Dr. Johnson's admonition that while the lust for power is "strongly entwisted" in human nature, it is to be "pitied in others and despised in ourselves."

On December 16, he and Kingsmill accompanied Leonard Dobbs, Kitty's brother, to Lewes for Leonard's divorce hearing. It was Muggeridge's first contact with divorce courts, and he was fascinated and repelled by the tawdry spectacle.

> Outside the court, barristers in wigs and gowns were whispering and their clients, apprehensive, were wearing their best clothes. A policeman walked up and down shouting "Silence!" The court was small and we went up into the gallery. The Judge had a lean, ruddy face, kindly and tired. He lolled indolently in his seat. As case after case came before him, each the same squalid tale—first the oath administered by a dark-suited man with immense gusto; then the barrister asking his questions, photographs passed up to be identified, then the Judge's "Well, well," and the name of the next petitioner called out. It was dreary beyond words, Brighton boarding-house keepers testifying that such a couple had taken a double room on such a night; vacant men and faded women asking for the dissolution of long ago dissolved marriages; hard-boiled private detectives describing how they had broken in upon adultery . . . .
>
> Four minutes settled each case. To such a small compass had passion been reduced. What a concentration of scenes, guilty assignations, indecision, corroding suspicion and shrieking hate! Perhaps at Judgment Day whole lives may make as poor a showing, sifted of irrelevance, their shifting emotions and appetites compressed to a few bare questions. Life is full of strange consequences, as Lambeth Palace being a consequence of Calvary, or striptease of the Pilgrim Fathers; one of the strangest is that the play of the same impulse which brings young lambs in spring should lead to the enactment of this curious scene in a little County court—the aged Judge in red, the respectable clerk in black, the lawyers in their wigs and gowns measuring out adultery with practised hands, like a draper measuring out cloth.[30]

Early in the new year Kitty went to Switzerland for a two-week vacation with her parents. Malcolm stayed behind to look after the children. It was then that the Webbs paid an unannounced visit to

Whatlington. Since his return from Russia, and particularly after the publication of *Winter in Moscow*, relations with Aunt Bo and Uncle Sidney had been strained. No doubt this unexpected visit was intended to smooth things over. Unfortunately, this was not the result. "They were just the same, rather self-consciously affable, as though insisting: 'Of course, we know you'll attack us and the Soviet régime, but we're people who don't mind in the least being disagreed with. That's your point of view; this is ours.' I felt flat and unhappy and we showed our anger once or twice, as when she said if Russia and Germany went to war, Germany would be 'soundly whipped'—and I said, à-propos of her having got a certain novel because she'd read that it had sold a million copies 'That's a good example of how bestsellers come to pass.' The children came to see them off, and shook hands with them as though they were strange sea monsters."[31]

Looking after the children helped overcome his melancholy. Their innocence contrasted vividly with the sophisticated corruption of life going on around him—the abdication crisis, the inevitable buffooneries of politics, and the ominous, gathering clouds of war. The notion that one must become as a little child to enter, or even see, the kingdom of heaven, began to make sense to him. Life increasingly seemed a remorseless struggle for dominance between the will and the imagination. This was the fundamental dichotomy on which Hugh Kingsmill based his creative writing and, more particularly, his literary criticism. Muggeridge was strongly influenced by Kingsmill to adopt this view. Out of the imagination came love, understanding, goodness, and self-abnegation—every true synthesis capable of being understood, every true way of living worth striving for; from the will came lust, envy, vanity, and hatred— every false antithesis ever propounded, every collective Utopian formula ever attempted. The family seemed to be a manifestation of the imagination, just as the pursuit of power was a manifestation of the will. In his diary he wrote one evening: "After I had bathed the children and put them to bed, I thought how deep in human nature was the idea of a family, of a man and a woman and their children forming a unit; and how false the denial of that idea, as in Plato and in all collective systems, and especially in the present tendency to separate out sensuality and value it apart from procreation . . . . Children are the everlasting new start, life springing up again, joyous and undefiled. I know that my children must make every mistake that I have made, commit the same sins, be tormented by the same passions, as I know that a green shoot pushing up from the earth must ripen and fall back, dead, on to the same earth; yet this does not take away from the wonder and beauty of either children or the spring."[32]

Shortly after she returned from her vacation, Kitty became ill and was rushed to Hastings hospital where she was put on the danger list. She desperately needed a blood transfusion. Malcolm's blood type was checked and found suitable. A physician linked them up by a glass tube with a primitive bicycle style pump in between, and Malcolm could actually watch the life-giving blood being pumped from his veins to hers. Later, he wrote that as he saw Kitty's pale cheeks begin to flush and quicken "I understood how Christ gave his blood that men might live because he loved men. He washed away their sins, that is death, with his blood. His blood flowing into ashen souls quickened them."[33]

Kitty was in the hospital for several weeks. After one visit to see her, he and her brother Leonard went for a walk past Hastings pier and, on impulse, went in to a fortune-teller. "Her finger nails were long but not coloured. She had a queer sort of sincerity about her which disinclined us to facetiousness." After reading cards and looking at his palm, she told him some vague claptrap about money and happiness and so on. When she perceived that he was beginning to mock her, she dropped the generalities and told him: "Someone very near to you is sick . . . a priest is your friend . . . you've been in Egypt and you will be going to Africa . . . I can't see what you do but you are always scribbling . . . ." Somewhat subdued by this news (more accurate than he then knew as he was to spend much of the war in Africa), he and Leonard left and strolled up and down the pier while Muggeridge marveled at "what a queer process life is," and both men speculated on how such a creature ended up telling fortunes on Hastings pier and "how she'd grown up and what mother had borne her." When he got home, he wrote in his diary:

> "Men and women strolling by the sea,
> What are you hoping?
> Men and women strolling by the sea,
> What are you leaving?
> That makes your eyes so wilful, sad?
> Men and women
> I watch you passing to and fro,
> Shadows, oh shadows."[34]

In September 1937, he told Douglas Jerrold that he wanted to write a book on Germany, examining Hitler's rise to power, the realities of Nazi practices, and the prospects of war. Jerrold knew that his religious book for Cape was by now nearly a year overdue and replied that it should be completed first. In any case, Jerrold was not encouraging: "I very much doubt whether it is possible to write a brilliant book on Germany today. You're under constant supervision the whole time you are there, your telephone is tapped . . . and you have little chance of finding out what is going on under the surface."[35] Given Muggeridge's prophetic instincts, in retrospect it is a pity that this book was never attempted.

Still restless, he next considered going to South Africa, either as a correspondent for any newspaper that would have him or to free lance. He actually discussed this with several Fleet Street acquaintances, but this plan too came to nothing. Late in 1937, he completed *The Bewildered Soul* and dispatched it to Cape. Rupert Hart-Davis, who was the first one to read the manuscript, enthused about it: "I think it is damned good, Malcolm, and there is some grand writing in it. It is a bit fierce in places, of course . . . ."[36] The manuscript next went, anonymously, to William Plomer who reported that it was ". . . too long, too incoherent and inconsequent . . . ."[37] Jonathan Cape then read it and concluded that, whatever its merits or lack, it bore no resemblance to what they had contracted for, namely an objective study of contemporary religious beliefs. Instead it was a brooding, sensual, contemporary *Pilgrim's Progress* or, as one reviewer suggested, *Pilgrim's Regress*. Despite Rupert Hart-Davis's insistence that they were letting "a masterpiece" go, Cape decided not to publish. The manuscript went the rounds until May 1938, when it appeared as *In a Valley Of This Restless Mind*, published by Routledge's. Muggeridge's original intention had been to use a pseudonym, T. Wildish, and the original manuscript included a long introductory memoir of Wildish (who is supposed to have died just before publication) written by his closest friend, an Anglo-Catholic priest who had known Wildish since their Cambridge undergraduate days. The author chose anonymity, the memoir explained, in the hope that the book, "a kind of spiritual autobiography," might be judged on its own merits and not by association with the author's earlier books—which reviewers had sometimes condemned for "fantastic and often tedious obsessions."

In addition to being the earliest fragment of autobiography, this fifty-page introductory memoir is fascinating for the glimpse it provides of how Muggeridge (who, of course, wrote it) believed that Alec Vidler (its ostensible author) perceived him. It is not a particularly flattering picture: "What was there in his personality, I ask myself now, that made it somehow vivid and striking, if often disappointing? His intellectual gifts were not great; his conversation was sometimes lively, but often tediously earnest as well as irritating. The sincerity on which he prided himself, however real it might be at a particular moment, was subject to bewildering fluctuations. How often with him have I found today's enthusiasms become tomorrow's abominations."

The memoir gave an exact summary of Muggeridge's career to date;

socialist childhood; Cambridge; India and Egypt; leader writing; Moscow; Geneva; the I.L.O.; and free-lancing. In fact, the chronicle of events is so precise, and the portrait of Wildish so unmistakably Muggeridge that, had it been included, the author would have failed to remain anonymous. So, too, Routledge's concluded, and the memoir was dropped from the published version that appeared under his own name.

In the memoir Wildish dies at the age of thirty-seven from undisclosed causes; this accords with Muggeridge's own premonitions frequently recorded in his diary. The memoir finishes up this way:

Gertrude [Wildish's wife] told me that his last words were [after old Pointifex in *The Way of All Flesh*]: "Goodbye sun, goodbye sun!" . . . it was rather absurd, Gertrude said, since the sun had long since set, and yet somehow more moving than if the sun had been just sinking below the horizon, because so like him. The last thing he cared about when he felt an occasion had arisen for saying goodbye to the sun was whether it was in the sky to say goodbye to. Another characteristic thing, she said, was his asking to be buried in the village churchyard near their house with an inscription to the effect that he was sleeping out Eternity in the place where he belonged. "After all," Gertrude said, "We've only been here just over a year, and he had already begun to talk about going to South Africa."

She and I spent the evening before the funeral together in Wildish's room. His books lined the wall, and his papers were scattered over a long table by the window, just as he had left them. We sat there while the room slowly darkened. The children had been sent away, and everything was quiet.

"He had a bit of genius," Gertrude said.

I wondered if this were so.

Aware of my doubts, she went on: "Oh yes, he had a bit of genius. What is genius?—it's exuberance mitigated by disinterestedness, or disinterestedness enlivened by exuberance. A woman tenderly looking after an idiot child is genius. He had that sort of quality, along with much that was showy and cheap and greedy."

In the now quite dark room we both cried, not so much because we should never see Wildish again or hear his voice, as for the strangeness of human life; love lavished on an idiot child, its sublimity and its horror, its incomprehensibility.

Wildish was buried in the village graveyard, more because it was convenient than because he had expressed a wish to be buried there. Even in the disposal of his bones he showed his knack for making an aspiration of convenience. The local clergyman conducted the service, and the mourners numbered about a dozen, mostly local people. Gertrude sensibly altered the inscription he had suggested to: "Who is sleeping out Eternity where he last saw the sun"; and I persuaded her to add two lines from a passage in *King Lear* which Wildish had often misquoted to me:

The Darkness and the Light

"And take upon's the mystery of things,
As if we were God's spies . . ."

With or without the introductory memoir, *In A Valley of This Restless Mind* is Muggeridge's most original and unforgettable book. It is full of ecstasy and despair, interspersed with satire, parody, and malicious caricatures of recognizable people. If he will forgive so trendy a comparison, it is like a discotheque where strobe lights play over random figures, garishly illuminating first this one—then that one—as they throb and twitch for a moment's scrutiny before subsiding into oblivion. It is both fact and fiction, yet it has no plot. There is little action and no clear resolution. At times there is no narrator; at other times there are three narrators—Wraithby, Motley, and Flammonde—each an embodiment of a different facet of Muggeridge's complex and divided personality.

It is virtually impossible to say what the book is about although, in 1938 and since, several doughty reviewers have tried. At the time, Evelyn Waugh wrote: "It is not an easy book to describe. It has affinities, in form, with *Candide* and, in temper, with *Voyage au Bout de la Nuit*. It is a highly symbolized and stylized autobiography . . . lust and money and God are the topics of Mr. Muggeridge's enquiry . . . His attitude to lust is that of the surfeited and rather scared Calvinist . . . His conclusions about money are that it has become the symbol in terms of which the greater part of mankind measure happiness and well being; that it is in fact trash . . . His quest for God, for 'Purity of Heart' does not take him very far . . . His is that particularly English loneliness of a religiously-minded man suddenly made alive to the fact that he is outside Christendom."[38] Forty years later Waugh's son, Auberon, called it a ". . . monument to a doubting, troubled mind."[39] A few reviewers recognized its unique genius; one called it ". . . piercing, brilliant and profoundly disturbing,"[40] another ". . . a title deed to immortality,"[41] but most held their nose and turned away from the savage lyricism of Muggeridge's prose. Since this haunting masterpiece is again in print (Collins, 1978), each reader may judge for himself.

Among the most telling caricatures in the book is that of the Webbs who, as Mr. and Mrs. Daniel Brett, pass their lives drafting blueprints for new civilizations and useful lives in a booklined study with twin desks and a cleared space for walking up and down between them. Beatrice Webb purported to be undismayed and wrote to her sister, Kitty's mother, that she considered "The caricature of us was by far the sanest and most pleasant part of the book . . . . Some of it is brilliant, but really I think he overdoes his obsession about lust and dirt and cruelty. The human race is not quite so bad as that."[42]

127

One hilarious chapter records an actual visit Muggeridge paid to an archdeacon, badgering him incessantly with the question: "Is there a God?" Since no archdeacon attains eminence without mastering elementary diversionary skills, Muggeridge was invited back to breakfast. After eggs and toast and bacon, the archdeacon knelt behind his chair and prayed that his guest's darkness might be lightened. Leaving the archdeacon's house, nourished but no closer to an answer, the narrator ponders the incredible sequence of events from Christ's lone agony on the cross to the archdeacon breakfasting. "I marvelled at the strange sequence of events—a crucifixion worked on, digested, for two thousand years, and lo! the Archdeacon in velvety black with a silver cross hung on a chain around his neck."

Hesketh Pearson wrote to say that, while he ". . . roared with laughter" at the scene, Muggeridge should have realized that archdeacon's gaitors were specifically constructed so as to prevent them kneeling down to help anyone. "No Archdeacon that I have ever met or heard of would sink to his knees for anything except a preferment, and wouldn't do so at the breakfast table even for that. Now that the facts are laid before you, I feel sure that you will wish to undo the harm you have unwittingly done to a very fine body of men."[43]

Pearson also sent along some unsolicited advice in connection with an extended verbal battle Muggeridge was then fighting with the playwright Sean O'Casey. "Crucify him with kindness," Pearson suggested. "Offer him champagne instead of vinegar, taking the precaution to tell him that you've pissed in it first."

What happened was this. On March 9, 1938, Muggeridge wrote an article in *The Daily Telegraph* critical of the Moscow trials of Bukharov, Zinoviev, Radek, and others, which had ended in all the accused being convicted of treason and sentenced to death. Sean O'Casey responded with a long, maundering letter that *The Daily Telegraph* did not print. O'Casey then expanded, without clarifying, his letter and published it as an article "The Sword of the Soviet" in what was the only paper likely to print it, the Communist *Daily Worker*. Muggeridge saw this article but considered it ". . . so confused and incoherent" as not to warrant any reply. O'Casey responded to his silence by calling Muggeridge, in print, "a cock that won't fight," whereupon Muggeridge immediately challenged O'Casey to debate ". . . at any time and in any place . . . his and my attitude to the Soviet regime" —an invitation O'Casey scrupulously ignored throughout all the subsequent sound and fury. Muggeridge went on to say: "Mr. O'Casey is so fine a dramatist that I cannot help being surprised at such folly in him. He, an Irishman, with a vigorous independent mind, not to be brow-beaten by authority in any guise—he, of all people, comes forward and insists on the validity

Manchester Guardian, 1932,
shortly before leaving for Moscow

Kitty Dobbs, shortly before
marriage to Malcolm in 1927

With Amrita Sher-Gil and
her parents in Simla, 1935

Amrita Sher-Gil's portrait
of Muggeridge, 1935

of a series of charges, so fantastic that if they were made in a British or a German, still more an Irish court, he would be the first to laugh them to scorn; insists that confessions often containing obvious absurdities (as at the Ramzin trial, when interviews were confessed to with men dead at the time the interviews were supposed to have taken place), unsupported by documentary or other evidence, are to be implicitly believed; that Yagoda in his capacity as head of the G.P.U., was discovering traitors at the same time as, in his capacity as a German-Japanese spy, he was being one; that . . . But why go on?

The Dean of Canterbury, Professor Laski, the Duchess of Atholl, Sir Bernard Pares, the Webbs—these I can understand; but the author of *Juno and the Paycock*—I admit I was surprised."[44]

When *The Daily Worker* refused to print this letter, Muggeridge sent it to *Forward*, where it appeared on April 30, 1938. O'Casey replied, in a rather whimpering tone, promising ". . . to be chary about talking of cocks again when replying to Mr. Muggeridge" and trying to blame his predicament on *The Daily Telegraph* for not printing his first letter.

Muggeridge then shifted the forum to *Time and Tide* where, after outlining the sequence of events, he urged adoption of the French system of a right of reply to anyone attacked in the press: "Especially is such a provision necessary when, as in the case of Mr. O'Casey, the attacker, not content with his immunity from a counterattack, actually indulges in public boasts that the absence of one proclaims the invincibility of his arguments and the cowardice of his victim."[45] Two weeks later, *Time and Tide* ran two responses, one from O'Casey, whose bravado was now reduced to a barely audible hiss, the other from Idris Cox of *The Daily Worker*. Muggeridge finished them both off in his final reply: "If you [O'Casey] have decided to plump for Stalin and throw in your lot with his comintern sycophants inside and outside the U.S.S.R., then cut out talk about fair play and freedom. That kind of cant I expect from Idris Cox, but not from you, who must know that if you went through a *Daily Worker* file, and through a file of every Soviet newspaper ever published, you would not find one single word criticizing the Soviet government, its acts or policies or extant personnel."[46]

Thus ended the verbal war; tomorrow the real war was to begin. Its coming was no surprise. Muggeridge had foreseen it and written of its inevitability, in astonishingly accurate detail, as early as 1934. While not wholly immune to the enthusiasms of the period, he took a decidedly somber view. Expecting little of human nature in peace, he feared little from it in war. Hitler's and Mussolini's aggression, and Britain's and France's resistance to it was, he believed, but another act in the cheap melodrama called history. As an Englishman his sympathies were with England, but he never deluded himself into believing that thereby he was championing God and opposing Evil. With all restraints on the exercise of power gone, there must, he knew, be calamities and suffering. But what was life, for most people most of the time, but a series of more or less random calamities? He once wrote to Kitty: "Life is mostly suffering, or at any rate enduring, but the same for all."[47] Now the calamities might be more planned and coordinated (although at the beginning of the war even that modest expectation seemed highly doubtful), but the fundamental question of human existence was not Lenin's Who, whom? which was the only question that war might answer, but Why? and, to that question, war provided no answers.

He and Hesketh Pearson put this point of view in a play on which they collaborated at this time, *Harvest Thanksgiving*. Here the coming of war is treated as farce rather than tragedy. Given the jingoistic spirit of the day, it is not surprising that the play was never performed.

One year before the war, he had written again of its inevitability and this time added: "The whole distinction between peace and war is as arbitrary and illusory as the distinction between health and sickness. When has there been peace on earth except in this heart or that suddenly confident that (as the first epistle of John so sublimely puts it) 'All that is in the world, the lust of the flesh, and the lust of the eyes, and the pride of life, is not of the Father, but is of the world; and the world passeth away, and the lust thereof, but he that doeth the will of God abideth forever'?"[48]

·8·
WAR

Religious canons, civil laws are cruel
Then what should war be?

Timon of Athens, Act IV, Scene III

* * *

After Neville Chamberlain's three obsequious trips to Germany in a vain attempt to placate Hitler, Muggeridge wrote that ". . . England has surrendered to coercion . . . because of cowardice and unenlightened self-interest." War, he declared, would come sooner because of appeasement: "I have seen as in a nightmare broken-down politicians disporting themselves, aged clowns put on to hold the audience while the real play prepares. Yet a little while and it will be ready, the curtain raised and these aged clowns bundled off the stage, away, anywhere."[1] Privately he remarked that if Hitler had treated dogs as he had the Jews, the British people would have clamored for war two years earlier.

His own participation was never in doubt. Having missed the first war, he was not about to be left out again. In fact, he longed for war, less from patriotism than sheer excitement. "War, like lust, is exciting but not interesting," he often said. It would provide a blameless opportunity to desert domestic and financial obligations with a clear conscience. Pacifism held no attraction. Although he had several Quaker friends and retained a tarnished but nevertheless real admiration for Mahatma Gandhi, neutrality was not part of his combative makeup. One who enjoys the relative security of England, he wrote, must not disdain the means by which that security is maintained, and that is force of arms. Such freedom as mattered to him, to live where he wanted to live and to write what he wanted to write, existed only because men were willing to risk being killed to keep it so.

131

If I believed that the soldier who killed in defence of his and my country, or the sailor patrolling the coasts within which I live, was performing a shameful act, I should first dispense with their protection—that is renounce my nationality; then renounce the possessions they enable me to keep. Only then, naked on the naked earth, should I be in a position to preach the abomination of all warfare, and to pledge myself never to take up arms. Perhaps I ought to be naked on the naked earth. Until I am, however, it is hypocrisy for me to dissociate myself from armaments which enforce domestic order and prevent invasion, and so enable me, within limits, to live my life in my own way. . . .

In peace my English citizenship brings me benefits, in war responsibilities. I cannot have one without the other.[2]

After Munich, he wrote an open letter to the cabinet in which he claimed that "no words exist to express my scorn" and then, typically, went on to find appropriately scathing words: "I ask myself whether if you had been asked to kneel down together, the four of you, and with your faces in the dust sing the Horst Wessel song, you would have raised any objection? I do not think you would have . . . although, of course, you would have preferred someone else to act as your proxy."[3]

Sunday morning, September 3, 1939, was sunny and cool, and the Muggeridges walked over to a neighbor's cottage to hear the wireless, a luxury beyond their means. On the way they passed the vicar, looking solemn, and making for Whatlington church at a quickened pace; before they had a chance to say "Good morning," he blurted out: "We're all in God's hands now," repeated this twice more, and strode off. When they heard Chamberlain's pathetic voice (Muggeridge was uncertain whether it quavered through anger, fear, or just senility), they all rushed outside and stood gazing up into the clear sky expecting to see it fill with bombers—and barrage balloons rising to meet them. He wrote in his diary: "For long I had foreseen it, and now, I thought, it has come. Catastrophe often envisaged, and now to be gratefully endured. Lord, now lettest thou thy servant depart in strife."[4]

First thing Monday morning he caught the bus for Hastings to join up. The recruiting office, it seemed, was in Brighton. To save bus fare, he walked the seven miles home. On Tuesday morning, he packed a suitcase as a precaution against being sent straight off to camp, bade a solemn farewell to his family, and left for Brighton. At the Oddfellow's Hall a long queue had already formed; ". . . it might have been a queue of unemployed outside a labour exchange; indeed probably for the most part *was* a queue of unemployed."[5] Most of the men, he noticed, were as old as he was, men who had narrowly missed the first war and were determined to get into this one. When his turn came, he was taken into a room festooned with recruiting posters: "Join the army and see the world"; another showed a soldier cheerfully jerking his thumb in the direction of a tank and saying, "We're mechanized, mate." Muggeridge was asked perfunctory questions about age, medical history, and previous military training. When asked his occupation, he replied "Journalist." The recruiting officer scowled and muttered that this was a reserved occupation. Malcolm went to another table and this time answered "Author," then, in succession, "Book reviewer," "Clerk," "Schoolmaster," even "unemployed." All, it seemed, including the unemployed, were reserved occupations. Finally, the officer in charge—a large and genial Irishman—took him aside and confided that middle-aged, inexperienced scribblers were not high-priority recruits, and added: "I think you should go home and look after your family." It was as though an eager flyer had pushed his way through to join the few during the Battle of Britain only to be told that there were already too many. There was nothing to be done except to go back home ". . . feeling somewhat foolish," back to domestic cares, back to five novels a week in dustjackets, back to his study where he was walled in by moldering piles of *The Times* going back for the last ten years, the raw material for a social history of the thirties he was working on.

In that first week of the war, he tried recruiting offices in Tonbridge and Maidstone with similar results. He was obsessed with joining up. Several attempts to use highly placed contacts in the R.A.F. to pull strings on his behalf proved fruitless. He became desperate. "War" all had said, some with terror, some with rage, he with exultation—and lo! there was no war. He was a man looking for a war.

After several frustrating weeks, he was finally offered a position in the Ministry of Information, which had recently taken up quarters in Bloomsbury. It was scarcely hand-to-hand combat, but it seemed better than nothing. His job, so far as one can be said to have existed, was to write morale-boosting articles for foreign consumption. No matter where he found himself, however acute the external crises or peril might be, his fate seemed always to be plunked down before a typewriter and told to pontificate. Given his somber expectations about the war, it would be interesting to cast an eye over these cheerful efforts but, unfortunately, they have long since turned to dust. In any event, he did not write many. He spent most of his time drinking tea, which was in plentiful supply, with a man named Palmer with whom he shared an office. Palmer was one half of a mystery-writing team, and Muggeridge grew so fascinated by the idea of an uneasy literary collaboration that he later wrote a novel, *Affairs of the Heart*, based on the idea of two thriller writers who have a falling out and plot each other's death. Some days he simply talked with two colleagues, Graham Greene and R.H.S. Crossman, both of whom had washed up on the same strand. For them it was phony war, fought with words; an exercise in fantasy, enemies unattacked, victory without bloodshed.

He was staying at a house in Chelsea. The blackout was in effect, and he would stumble back after work, often losing his way or missing a turn in the aphotic night. "Thus groping my way about blacked-out London, a phrase took shape in my mind: Lost in the darkness of change. I said it over and over to myself, like some incantation momentarily crystallizing our human condition."[6]

The circumstances by which he finally got into active service had a characteristic element of farce. *The Daily Telegraph* published a satirical piece of his saying how, unlike the last war, real combat positions in this one were as difficult to come by as tickets for the Royal Enclosure at Ascot or invitations to the Lord Mayor's Banquet. This drew an unexpected response from a Major Davies, in charge of Field Security Police, saying that if Muggeridge was serious about joining up he should present himself at Mytchett Hutments, Ash Vale, without delay. The day before he received the major's letter, Muggeridge had been offered a Ministry promotion that would have involved a substantial raise in salary and allowances. As always, the lure of making off proved too great, and he presented himself at Ash Vale where he was outfitted in riding breeches, puttees, a high-necked tunic, and a peaked hat, sworn to allegiance to king and country, and discovered that he was now an unpaid lance-corporal in the just-forming Intelligence Corps. Meanwhile, Sir Edward Grigg, parliamentary secretary to the Minister of Information, rose in the House of Commons to forcefully deny rumors that Muggeridge and Crossman had resigned from the Ministry ". . . because there was no work for them to justify them receiving their salaries."[7]

It was at Ash Vale, on one of fifteen bunks in a long, narrow barracks, that he finished *The Thirties*. Its theme was not new, in a sense it was the theme of all his writings and could be summed up in the sentence: "Blessed are the pure in heart for they shall see God; cursed are the impure of heart for they shall see men." It was his first and, as it turned out, last attempt at social history; a companion study of the forties was never completed. The thirties was a perfect decade for his talents; its humbug, ribaldry, and bombast exactly suited his witty misanthropy. The decade began, Muggeridge wrote, in the illusion of progress without tears and ended in the reality of tears without progress.

The exquisite prose one expects of Muggeridge is here buttressed by clever insights and a clear perception of the drift of future events. Also present, of course, is his unfailing humor. If the book has a fault it is only that he packs his wit and perception so densely into its pages that the reader must occasionally break off and cry, "Enough." In one reviewer's opinion, it was like an egg boiled so hard that the reader cracked his teeth on its diamond-like shell.

Commercially, it was his most successful book to date. It drew enthusiastic reviews from Graham Greene (". . . breathlessly horrifying . . . the unity and mood of a poem . . ."), Sir Hugh Walpole (". . . amusing, witty, most readable and astonishingly comprehensive"), and George Orwell (". . . the Book of Ecclesiastes with all the pious interpolations left out"), among others. It was a Book Club choice (although the Book Club insisted that an unflattering reference to their operations be deleted) and brought in some needed income. And it has been more or less continuously in print since 1940.

As an exercise in prophecy, the book is fascinating to reread. Muggeridge seldom bothers about detail, is contemptuous of what are called "facts," and yet somehow he foresaw, with great acumen, the future consequences of the tumultuous events happening all around him. In 1967, when *The Thirties* was reissued, several reviewers noted this, most perceptively Philip Toynbee who called the book ". . . a strange visionary portrait . . . the deep, penetrating boom of a prophet in full flight."[8]

Prophet he might be, combatant he was not. On May 22, 1940, he got a commission, becoming Lieutenant Muggeridge. Immediately he asked to be sent off to France or Norway or the Middle East, as some of his fellow officers were. No luck. Despondent, he shambled into the officer's mess and was there greeted by a guard's sergeant major: "Well, Muggeridge, and what were you when you first came here? Nothing but a weedy-looking writer. And now you have the makings of quite a promising N.C.O."[9]

His job at Mychett Depot was to give lectures on security. All he knew about the subject came from the Encyclopedia Britannica and a few anecdotes passed on, like family heirlooms, from the time of the First World War. These he supplemented by a little play about a secret agent who is detected because he forgets to conceal a ballpoint pen for writing in invisible ink. For his special lectures on propaganda he discovered that the experience of writing "must" paragraphs for Lord Beaverbrook stood him in good stead.

To Hugh Kingsmill, now a substitute schoolmaster at Marlborough, he wrote on November 20, 1940:

My Dear Hughie:
Please forgive me for having been so long in answering your letters. There's no excuse except inertia. I've had heaps of time, and not a hair of my head has been endangered. The forces are the sheltered life in this war; women and children last its slogan. I've just been going on from day to day

waiting for the sirens, as residents in the Albany Hotel used to wait for the post; not expecting a letter, yet anxiously awaiting the postman's appearance because it was something to wait for.

London is very strange now; Barcelona in England's green and pleasant land. It conforms to what I've always felt it should have been. Who could have cared for Carlton House terrace when Curzon lived there; even less when the Savage Club and Herr von Ribbentrop succeeded him? But now, a ruin, with gaping, glassless windows and shattered walls, it's rather lovable.

. . . From this you will gather that I'm not what Churchill always says the army is, "in good heart". At the same time, I shouldn't say I was unhappy. I've known unhappier times. This war has, in comparison with previous ones, many advantages. Since the attack has been directed exclusively at the civilian population we are spared Sassoonery. No one can say "What you need is a bit of France", when all, or almost all, have had a bit of London. The non-combatant is as foolish as the combatant; and in the underground are many mansions of darkness and hate. Nor do I anticipate much post-war romanticism. . . . There are two states after drunkenness—the carry-over and the hangover; similarly after fornication, war or any other indulgence of the will. In the present case, I gratefully expect hangover, rather than, as after the last war, carry-over— hand, somewhat shaky, reaching for aspirin; step, somewhat uncertain, homewards turning; gaze, somewhat confused, resting uneasily on an abhorrent but inevitable scene.

I've just spent a week's leave in Whatlington. There, too, they have their crater, a proud possession. Any faint expectation I had that coming from the metropolis, I might be received as a tired warrior needing rest was soon disappointed. As there are now no schools in the vicinity, Pan and John go each morning to the Battle curate. John told me proudly that he was learning divinity. I asked what divinity was, and he said: "Well, I drew a sloping line and underneath I writ: 'The Upward Struggle.' " For such an answer he deserves to be made a Bishop in the Anglican church at once.[10]

Muggeridge's closest brush with action came on a temporary assignment on the Isle of Sheppey where, it was feared, a German invasion might be attempted. Each man was equipped with a rifle and twelve rounds of ammunition, all that could be spared for the purpose. All night they prowled up and down the coastline, listening for the sound of enemy aircraft and peering into the darkness for the outlines of a convoy. "Once we thought we heard aircraft overhead, and Captain Partridge told us to throw ourselves on the ground, which we did with alacrity, my rifle, to my great shame, going off in the process. This caused near panic; everyone thought the invasion had begun. One lance-corporal insisted that he heard church bells ringing—another that he clearly saw the outline of a boat approaching the shore. It was a case,

Captain Partridge explained, of fighting to the last man and the last round of ammunition; which in my case would now be the eleventh round instead of the twelfth."[11] In the result, his accidental shot was to be the only one he fired through the whole war.

A transfer to headquarters, located at the time in Kneller Hall, came as a relief. The war had now been on over a year, and still he was no closer to combat. Perhaps now he would taste fear, make heroic sacrifices, see the whole of his life pass before his eyes in a fleeting moment of death.

It was not to be. Life here all too soon developed a stale routine. Tea was brought at six-thirty by his "batman," a quick glance out the window at the streaky morning sky, ". . . the momentary illusion that a day of some significance was beginning," a hot bath, shave, dress and uniform, breakfast and newspaper devoured in the same voracious yet unsatisfying way. Then what? Like a boat without a sea or a tiger without prey, he was a soldier without a war.

"After breakfast I report to the Colonel, though with nothing to report. I say my nothing and he listens to my nothing. Thus exchanging nothings we pass some twenty minutes."[12]

Morning report having been concluded, he usually proceeded to an office in the front room of a suburban house. "Perhaps I go out here and there, driving along or motorcycling; perhaps tormented with indecision—debate whether to move or stay stationary." Then lunch, meals providing the only fixed points on the day's compass. Afternoons were spent laboriously shifting paper; it might be an application from a cottager in a military zone seeking to extend his garden patch, or an irate father upset because some officer billetted in his home had made a pass at his nubile daughter. Documents to be initialed then recirculated, coming and going, saluting, briefings, driving about consuming petrol in his camouflage-painted Austin Minor, his only wartime casualty—victim of an unyielding lamp post at a traffic island on Blackfriar's bridge that somehow obtruded itself in his path after a night of carousing.

Initially there was a shortage of accommodation at Kneller Hall, and he had to pitch a tent on the grounds. Then, when headquarters was transferred to Hammersmith, he found rooms. On weekends he was issued with a travel pass to go home, made out: "For the purpose of proceeding to Battle"—about the only soldier in the British army, he reflected, then so bent. During the week he often visited Hesketh Pearson, then living in Hampstead. On one occasion they went together to the House of Commons: " 'Malcolm wanted to see the revolting swine in session for the last time,' Pearson told Kingsmill. They sat in the Distinguished Stranger's Gallery trying hard to pick out a face 'that hadn't crook or fool written all over it.' 'Their time is nearly up,' Muggeridge trilled: 'We shall not see them again.' "[13] In this prediction, he was wrong; although when the House of Commons was bombed in May 1941, it did not seem far wide of the mark.

Throughout the blitz he spent his nights wandering aimlessly about the vacant, blacked-out London streets, sometimes with Graham Greene, usually heading in the approximate direction of the loudest explosions. One particularly fierce night he stood on the roof of St. Paul's school, beside an "aged crotchety Colonel," watching the shells burst in the night sky like shooting stars. "We're all mad," the aged colonel muttered, "people less mad than we are have spent their lives in lunatic asylums."[14]

On such nights Muggeridge experienced a kind of exultation in the blitz: "The empty, dark city, torn with great explosions, racked with ack ack fire, lit with lurid flames, acrid smoke, its air full of the dust of fallen buildings." This was no death wish or suicidal impulse; there are, after all, plenty of quicker and surer ways to kill one's self. Instead, he was fascinated by the spectacle of destruction for its own sake; history toppled, monuments reduced to rubble, the struts and props of a materialist society heaving and groaning and collapsing. The blitz was impulsive, wanton, random, and ruthless. He was impulsive, wanton, random, and ruthless, and he reveled in it. "I long for the siren to sound because in my heart I want the destruction, the violence. As a hart panteth for the water-brook so panteth my heart for thee—oh, destruction!"[15]

But what had been an exciting spectacle in darkness became flat and depressing in daylight when he made his morning inspections. "Like newspapers, wreckage must be new to be interesting. A two-day-old crater or heap of debris once a house is scarcely worth a glance."[16] Oddly enough, the human tragedy of the blitz did not become real to him until the bombardment left his own parents homeless.

In April 1941, he was transferred to Longford Castle near Salisbury as Security Intelligence Officer with V Corps. Montgomery was in command, and a kind of wary esteem, occasionally lapping the bounds of friendship, grew up between them. They corresponded after the war and, when Muggeridge was Deputy Editor of *The Daily Telegraph*, Montgomery occasionally passed on confidential information to which he had access by virtue of his position as Deputy Supreme Commander of the Allied forces. One such scoop was Eisenhower's impending resignation as Supreme Commander. Once when Muggeridge visited Montgomery at Bentley, Monty pressed on him two sheets of paper on which he had distilled, in his own schoolboyish handwriting, the four cardinal principles of good generalship. These were:

(1) Pre-determined framework:

Therefore, firm grip on battle: not only to keep developments within a pre-determined pattern of action, but also so as to get quick reaction to operational situations, both favourable and unfavourable.

(2) Clear-cut long-term relationship established between operational intentions and administrative resources; from the inception of a campaign or operation.

Operational and administrative planning will then proceed concurrently throughout the execution of the task.

(3) In the end, war becomes a matter of movement and supply: given, of course, capable commanders, a sufficiency of good manpower with high morale, a national will to fight, and a "desire" to get things done.

(4) A C.-in-C. must strive to read the mind of his opponent, to anticipate enemy reactions to his own moves, and to take quick steps to prevent enemy interference with his own plans.[17]

But in 1941, even Monty could not get him what he most wanted—an active posting. Even a personal letter, pleading that he had joined up ". . . in the hope of exchanging torpor for activity" and adding ruefully: "This hope has so far been disappointed"[18] brought no results. Do they also serve, Muggeridge wondered, who only sit and think?

One task that fell to the Intelligence Branch was to construct a dummy German soldier so that the men coming to and from the mess might familiarize themselves with what to expect. Having rigged up an approximately accurate replica, Muggeridge was seized by ". . . an irresistible impulse to make him wounded and bloody; with his arm in a homemade sling, and a bloodstained bandage round his neck. Then, warming to the work, I put him on a crutch, and finally amputated one of his legs. It was another of the occasions when I did something which caused almost universal offence, without any deliberate intention, or even awareness, of so doing."[19] He was let off with a reprimand, and the maimed dummy was hurriedly removed.

Christmas 1941 was a gloomy time. By the luck of the draw he failed to get home leave. On Christmas morning he attended Salisbury Cathedral but found the music "thin and far away" and the sermon "empty." A few days later there was a special officer's mess during which, he told Kitty, ". . . the men got very noisy and (would you believe it?) pulled off each other's trousers and pulled each other around by their ties. Most of the men were around forty. I went up to bed and lay there thinking somewhat sombre thoughts."[20] Somber thoughts, added to his generally pessimistic attitude about the outcome of the war—no matter which side ostensibly won—did not go down well in the mess. In September he was expelled, and even threatened with arrest, for insubordination. When he asked his accuser, an Irish major who was mess president, to give particulars, he refused to be drawn. It was nothing specific, the major said, just his talk, the whole tenor and tone of it, everything.

His work involved liaison with neighboring military bases, zooming about the countryside on his motorcycle with documents to be initialed and packets to be delivered. It provided an opportunity to visit his parents, then living close by in Christchurch. His father was observably failing. After one visit he wrote to Kitty: "He is almost blind and his heart is very weak indeed. He has become very childlike, worries about getting his tea and how his flowers are arranged. Milder weather may revive him a little but I doubt if he has very long to live."[21] Nor did he. Within a year (on March 25, 1942) H. T. Muggeridge was dead. Malcolm was then enroute to Africa and unable to attend the funeral. H. T. was buried in a shady corner of Whatlington cemetery underneath a stone with his name engraved on it. Years later his sons added the inscription (from the Old Testament prophet Amos): "He was a good man and a just."

Muggeridge continued to chafe under the lack of action. Across the channel men were dying while he marked time, full of "vile inertia." One day all the officers were trooped into a cinema in Salisbury to view a German propaganda film about the conquest of Poland. "There we sat, row on row of staff officers, and watched the Germans conquer Poland; spared none of the horrors, able to take it all in there in plush seats in a quiet, preposterous cathedral town."[22] Though he had time on his hands, he found he could not write. The less he did, the more time dragged. "It's all so dreamlike and unreal. No one will ever believe it afterwards. I doubt if I shall myself—the strangeness of carrying on pretence activities when such real dangers threaten; like hanging on to a cliff with one hand and giving a BBC talk on the pleasures of mountaineering in the Dolomites at the same time. I just drift along like everyone else, and I shall deserve like everyone else the retribution when it comes, as it must."[23]

Deliverance from such monotony came in the form of a telegram instructing him to appear, for an undisclosed purpose, at a given address in London. The purpose, when it was disclosed, was M.I. 6.

After perfunctory training in the bizarre customs of espionage—like how to make invisible ink from bird droppings; how to cipher and, what was infinitely worse, decipher; how to plant deceptive materials; and so on—it was revealed that he would go to Lourenço Marques in Mozambique. His assignment was to gather intelligence on German disruption of Allied shipping around the South African coast. "I said that nothing could suit me better, implying that Lourenço Marques was a place I had always been interested in and wanted to visit, though in point of fact I had never before heard of it, and had no idea where it was."[24]

Ironically, after all his strenuous and unavailing efforts to become a combat soldier, he now became a civilian again, issued with an identity card and passport, once more making off, this time for a mythical position on the staff of the British Consulate-General in Lourenço Marques.

His first stop was Lisbon where there was little to do except hang about the street cafes, read newspapers, pace up and down the streets, and make a minimal effort to learn Portuguese. He was, in intelligence parlance, establishing a cover. It was in Lisbon that he heard from Kitty of his father's death. "Death seems to release the memory, and now a hundred memories of Dad, of long ago when I was a little boy, come pouring in on me,"[25] he wrote back.

To Hugh Kingsmill he wrote on May 6, 1942:

> Some days ago I climbed up a hill near Cintra (you will remember Wordsworth on the Convention of; Byron, also, dealt with the same subject but, I understand, characteristically described the wrong building as the scene of it being signed, and probably the wrong Convention) to a little deserted hermitage where five monks lived for several centuries. There were their little cells and a stone slab they used for a table, and a chapel, and one of the most wonderful views I have ever seen; all so quiet, so remote. At first I thought: How fortunate they were! Then it occurred to me that probably one of the cells was rather less draughty than the others, one place at the stone slab to be preferred to another, and that as much passion would have been expended on those conquests as by, say, Hitler on his.[26]

At the end of May he left Lisbon by ship for Lobito. For security reasons, he was not permitted to disclose even to Kitty his final destination. "The scene when the boat left Lisbon was very touching, hundreds of people waving handkerchiefs at each other and finally breaking down and sobbing. I had no one to wave to, but participated in the emotion of the others. . . ."[27] On board ship were a loquacious French naval attaché and an equally loquacious Japanese businessman, both bound for Tokyo; the three of them talked much on the voyage. The Japanese businessman's command of English was somewhat shaky and once, when Muggeridge tried to buy him a drink, he replied: "No, thank you, I'm on the water closet."

To Kitty he wrote that his thoughts were in the past. The present seemed aimless, the future full of foreboding. "I suppose in such a mood one might write one's memoirs, but so far I've resisted this dangerous temptation. Like Hazlitt, I've had a happy life. Every life is happy which brings illumination; the only unhappy lives are those which remain imprisoned in their own limitations."[28]

From Lobito he went by train to Elizabethville in the Congo, then to Nairobi and, finally, by flying boat down the coast to Lourenço Marques. He put up at the Polona Hotel where his opposite numbers, the Italian Consul-General, Senor Campini, and the Abwehr agent, Dr. Wertz, also resided. It was inevitable that they would meet occasionally, if only in corridors, public rooms, or the lavatory; when this happened ". . . we pass by with a haughty stare. Very silly, but then war is silly and so is peace."[29] Muggeridge feared his room might be bugged, and so early on he made a thorough reconnaissance of the hotel in the course of which he discovered a way of peering unobserved into Wertz's room. This seemed to open up limitless prospects but, in fact, ". . . the only discovery I made was that Dr. Wertz wore a hair net—an interesting, but scarcely significant, item of intelligence."

By the end of the summer he had evolved a routine—enciphering messages to London and deciphering the responses, watching the comings and goings of foreign ships and personnel, and recruiting a network of informants—bizarre, improbable activity that seemed infinitely remote from the war. Still, it kept him occupied and helped stave off his recurrent bouts of melancholy. "I just go on from day to day," he wrote home, "reading newspapers, discussing the war, working, taking a turn in the sea, and then suddenly, as ever, in the middle of the night or the early morning, or just inconsequentially anytime during the day, wondering: Why?"[30]

The most perplexing problem he encountered was recruiting reliable informants. The reliable were seldom informers, and informers were notoriously unreliable. When the two contradictory attributes were conjoined in one person, that rare specimen was usually already in the pay of *Senor* Campini or Dr. Wertz, sometimes in the pay of both. Gradually, though, he established "contacts"; a policeman here, a prostitute there, a shipping agent, and a taxi driver. Inevitably the question of money arose: "I found that bribing . . . had as many subtleties and diversities as seduction. Thus, in certain circumstances the passing of money had to be engineered in such a way that it seemed to happen of itself, which, in seduction terms, was the equivalent of lolling or reaching out an arm as though by accident. Alternatively, there were occasions in which one yelled or banged the desk, insisting that not a cent more would be forthcoming. This might be compared with violent assault . . . incidentally, the same word is used for both— to pass money or to make a pass. I became quite adept as time went on, knowing just when to show the colour of my (or rather H.M.G.'s) money, and how much was needed to provide the necessary incentive in this or that case."[31]

His operations met with considerable success—more than the self-depreciating account in his autobiography suggests. He engineered the escape of a group of South African sailors. He arranged the kidnapping of a German undercover agent and subsequently had him returned to England for interrogation. But Muggeridge's most spectacular success was to contrive the sinking of a German submarine that had been harassing Allied shipping. Despite the Inspector Clouseau tone of his memoirs, he was an intrepid player of the "game of the foxes," as befits a cunning chess strategist. No doubt he also enjoyed the whole business more than he is now prepared to admit. After the war, his achievements were honored by several decorations, among them the *Légion d'Honneur* and the *Croix de Guerre* with palm.

He wrote weekly letters home (which took up to two months to arrive) but little else. Occasionally, he started on something, completed a few pages, and then it would trail off—sometimes literally in mid-sentence. Among these incomplete efforts that have survived are a series of *Letters to an Enemy*, a sort of dialogue with Baron Werner von Alvensleben, a German escapee from Rhodesia, who, oddly in light of Muggeridge's position, became one of his closest friends in Lourenço Marques. Even his diary, *The Diary of a Sad Man* he called it, received only sporadic attention.

The heat, the war, most of all the necessity of engaging in the preposterous fantasies of intelligence work, all combined to drain his imagination and energy. He was listless and lonely. He doubted that he would ever write again. Occasionally something would happen to lift his spirits momentarily, but he soon slid back into the slough of despond. In November 1942, he wrote to Kitty. "I've just read *Anna Karenina* again, and it was like a wonderful draught of fresh water when one is parched. Far and away the best novel ever written, a true image of life, like life just as boring and with its moments of ecstasy. No one has ever described happiness as well as Tolstoy. . . . Like all great books it gave me a passionate longing to write again. I bought a notebook, got as far as that." He got no further. "I sometimes try but it always ends in nothing."

He took to the bottle and to Hélène, a nightclub dancer at the Café Penguin. Once when they were driving together his car careened out of control and narrowly missed a row of trees. Closer inspection revealed that the steering column had been tampered with, most likely the work of Campini's *apparat*. Life was pointless and degrading. He plumbed the lowest abyss of his forty years. "Much of the time I spend wishing I was dead," he wrote Kitty, "wondering why I am doing what I have to do, putting up my own faint struggle with the tedium of time."[32]

The second volume of Muggeridge's autobiography describes, in quite considerable detail, his suicide attempt by drowning at this time. Driving out along the deserted coastline, undressing in the darkness, wading out until the cold, inky water rose around him, swimming out further and further until the glimmer of light from a coastal nightclub was just barely visible. Then, suddenly, overcome by a longing to live, by a mysterious certainty that all life is good and that all the strands—the suffering, self-betrayal, loneliness, and degradation no less than the ecstasy, creativity, and peace—all come together to form a unity, and behind and within that unity, animating and giving it meaning and purpose, a spirit not of malignity or indifference but of love. A spirit so ineffable that men were reduced to the monosyllable—God. Then, floundering and stumbling his way back to shore and to life.

He says this experience left an indelible impression on him. Yet there are several curious aspects to it. Muggeridge's writing is not prone to understatement, hesitance, or qualification, but his account of this episode is: "Even this dying seemed false. Was it me, wading on to the open sea? Was it really happening? . . . The next day I took the precaution of reporting to London, giving the impression that I had gone through the motions of trying to drown myself as a deliberate ruse to delude Wertz into thinking I had completely lost heart. In the end, I began to wonder whether after all, it *had* been a ruse. In all deception . . . the ultimate danger is that the deceiver comes to believe in his own deceits."[33] Curious, too, that such a spiritually formative incident was never subsequently communicated, even to someone as close to him as Alec Vidler, who first heard of it when he read Muggeridge's memoirs. Nor is the incident related, or ever once referred to, at the time or since in his generally frank diaries.

Strangest of all, though, is the fact that Muggeridge had written a fictional account of just such a suicide attempt ten years before in his unpublished novel *Picture Palace*. If the alleged incident at Lourenço Marques was a case of life imitating art, it did so with remarkable exactitude. In *Picture Palace* he wrote:

[Mrs. Boswell] rushed from the room, and down to the beach, now deserted, a stretch of quiet sand gently washed by the sea. I'll drown myself, she thought. Drowning was said to be an easy and perfect death . . . She took off her clothes and swam out about a quarter of a mile.

The water was tepid and full of moonlight. Her arms, making strokes underneath the water, were like flashes of light. She looked up at the stars, thickly in the sky; and, treading water, watched the lights along the shore, and heard music coming from a dance band. It sounded clear over the sea.

Not death that I'm seeking, she thought, but life. A great longing came to her for happiness, nestling against the sea, enclosing moonlight and stars and the silky darkness in her arms. Her troubled spirit dissolved in the wash of the sea, and found peace for a little while; her restlessness dissipated itself in the twinkle of lights on a distant shore. She swam back.[34]

At many times in his life, including this period in Lourenço Marques, Muggeridge has been depressed enough to consider suicide, perhaps even to attempt it. But he was then so enmeshed in a world of fantasy that it is impossible for anyone, even him—perhaps, especially him—to say whether or not this incident ever occurred, and, if it did, whether it was seriously intended or simulated. After the war the historian David Irving unearthed a reference in some German Foreign Office papers to a telegram sent by Dr. Wertz to his *Abwehr* bosses "re Muggeridge's attempted suicide." When the story hit the papers, Muggeridge denied it: "It was purely a matter of deception. I never tried to commit suicide. It was staged as a plot to fool the Germans."[35]

He left Lourenço Marques in July 1943. His last weeks were particularly uncomfortable because of stomach pains that became acute when he landed at Kampala airport in Uganda. After being rushed to a hospital, an emergency appendectomy was performed. When he had recuperated, he was flown on a Belgian plane to Lagos to await a flight back to England. To his annoyance, a one-legged colonel pulled rank and bumped him off the first available flight. This flight crashed near Shannon airport with no survivors. Kitty had been alerted that he was on this plane, so his eventual appearance at Whatlington was greeted rather in the manner of Lazarus's emergence from the tomb. "It was tempting to regard my ejection from the crashed plane as a kind of miracle . . . but, on reflection, such a view seemed disrespectful to the memory of the one-legged Colonel, who would certainly see the incident in a different light."[36]

On the first day of October 1943, he reported back to Section V, now installed in premises on Ryder Street. As there was no point to be served in maintaining the pretense of his consular position, he was inducted back into the army, now a major. Subsequently, he was sent to North Africa with instructions to report to *Sécurité Militaire* as liaison officer. On his second day in Algiers, the car in which he was being driven was involved in a crack-up, and he was rushed to the hospital with a concussion. He came to, he told Kitty, with a feeling of complete weightlessness, floating free, unconnected to anything, and suspended "between time and eternity belonging to neither. In a way I understood and felt quite reconciled. But of course the next morning the noise of life began again—and I began to plot to get out of the hospital and about again."[37] Although he was under doctor's orders to rest, he conspired with a visitor to get some civilian clothes and slipped unobserved out of the hospital.

Liaison with the *Sécurité Militaire* meant familiarizing himself with the Free French forces and their leaders, particularly Jacques Soustelle, de Gaulle's chief of intelligence. The two got on well and remained in touch after the war when Soustelle became a member of the *Assemblée Nationale* and a Gaullist minister. Later Soustelle arranged for Muggeridge to interview de Gaulle when the General was at the nadir of his political life. For now, Muggeridge only glimpsed him from afar, but even then was struck by de Gaulle's bearing: "The face of a man born to lead a lost cause with the additional sorrow that it would ostensibly triumph."

He found Algiers "horribly crowded," particularly with Americans whose noisy, gaudy ways and humorlessness made ". . . all the others, even the Arabs, seem agreeable." As an Englishman, he told Kitty, one became popular simply by proceeding ". . . side by side next to an American," thus becoming accepted ". . . as a sort of idiot version of Thomas Cook."[38]

His duties were ill-defined but included briefing senior British and American military officials on decoded intelligence coming through the Enigma system from Bletchley, arranging for local police to take care of informers, and planting misleading information on German agents. Plunged back into the fantasy world of espionage, he quickly became dispirited. On Christmas Day 1943, he lay sleepless on his bed ". . . full of hateful thoughts and images; a sense of being imprisoned, of being diseased and distorted, of corruption."[39]

Insomnia, a recurrent torment, became acute. At the best of times, Muggeridge is a light, restless sleeper and an early riser. When depressed, he is unlikely to sleep at all. In one of his bedside anthologies, these lines of Robert Herrick's are scrawled across the title page:

> "When the house doth sigh and weep,
> And the world is drowned in sleep,
> Yet mine eyes the watch do keep,
> Sweet spirit comfort me!"

His main consolation in Algiers was literature and this, too, affected his moods. Carlyle's essays he admired but found "physically tiring." He turned to that favorite of melancholics, Johnson's *Life of Savage*, and found it immensely comforting. "The contrast was quite extraordinary—mental refreshment, serenity, etc. I thought a lot about the contrast between C. and J., and came to the conclusion that it was due to the fact that J. was an integrated man, C. not; J. a product of an integrated civilization, C. of an already disintegrated one."[40] Reading revived his fear that he would not be able to write again, that five years of the monstrous buffooneries of war had drained his imagination and creativity. "My nightmares of never being able to write again continually haunt me," he lamented to Kitty. More than concern for his own safety or the outcome of the war (which seldom gets a mention), this fear of being unable to write predominates throughout his wartime correspondence.

On August 12, 1944, Muggeridge went to Paris to continue intelligence liaison work with the French *Sécurité Militaire*. As Orly and Le Bourget airports were out of action, his little plane landed at an airstrip about sixty miles from Paris from where he hitched a ride with some American officers in a staff car in the vanguard of the liberation. Along the road were clusters of people waving and cheering and pressing brandy on the liberators. "As the brandy with which amiable patriots plied us took effect, we responded to the public's warmth with mounting enthusiasm. Paris, when we arrived there, was, not surprisingly, in a state of great confusion and a certain amount of street-fighting was still going on. In the circumstances there seemed little liaising to be done and I abandoned myself to the prevailing celebrations."[41] He finished up in a nightclub where his euphoria dissipated when a shabby entertainer ". . . completely bald, with a large, sad clown's face, was intoning a soliloquy, in which he recalled all the terrible things that had happened to him since the Germans came to Paris. *Et maintenant*, he concluded, with an expression of infinite woe, through which he struggled to break into a wry smile—*Et maintenant, nous sommes libérés* . . . Somehow it seemed the most perfect comment on the situation, and ever after, when I have thought of the liberation, I have seen again the solemnity of his vast expanse of face, and heard his woeful declaration. Only clowns and mystics ever speak the truth."[42]

His new assignment was to secure the release of British agents who had been arrested and wrongly accused of collaborating with the German occupiers, ". . . the only worthwhile thing I did in the whole war." One of his charges was P.G. Wodehouse who, early in the war, had made what were thought to be seditious broadcasts from Berlin. Muggeridge found Wodehouse at the Bristol Hotel ". . . standing by the window; a large, bald, amiable looking man, wearing grey flannel trousers, a loose sports jacket and what I imagine were golfing shoes, and smoking a pipe." Wodehouse seemed as little perturbed by the accusations now being flung at him by the Allied side as he had been when the Germans had arrested and interned him in a prison camp at

Tost. He simply went on writing his stint each morning and spent his afternoons reading, looking out the window, and smoking his pipe. By war's end he had completed five novels. Muggeridge was immediately drawn to this kindred spirit: ". . . a man singularly ill-fitted to live in a time of ideological conflict, having no feelings of hatred about anyone." Wodehouse's political views, Muggeridge wrote, were limited to ". . . expressing the hope that this or that august personage might be induced to return to his padded cell." Wodehouse and his wife, Ethel, were actually arrested and put in jail at one point, but Muggeridge obtained their release after much bureaucratic wrangling and form filling.

A less celebrated but poignant case involved an attractive French girl who had fallen in love with a German soldier billeted in her parents' home. After all, she told Muggeridge, despite the war the German soldier remained a man and she a woman. Since the liberation, she lived in fear that she would be seized as a collaborator and have her head shaved or worse. Fortunately, Muggeridge was able to prevent this from happening, but her plight so interested him that he wrote a play, *Liberation*, based on it.

In the play Françoise's German lover, Karl, stays behind and is hunted down and executed by Free French insurgents. Françoise is betrayed as a collaborator by her fanatical brother, Gerard, who defends his action to her grandfather by saying that Karl was a fascist and a German first, and only secondarily the man whom his sister loved. The grandfather, an old man, replies: "I wonder. It seems to me that the real difference was that she loved him and you hated him. Love, like light, discloses the individual, and hate, like darkness, effaces him leaving only that terrible abstraction, the herd, the mob, the collectivity. The individual climbed out of the herd to become a man capable of loving, but he can always sink back into it again, reverting to the herd and capable only of hating."

Although her lover is dead, Françoise finishes up as the only person in the play who has been truly liberated. The other characters remain in thrall to the will and the will's empty slogans. For her alone, love has elevated her vision beyond passion and power; she has escaped from the will to the imagination.

As with his prewar play, *Harvest Thanksgiving*, the theme and tone of *Liberation* ran directly opposite to the spirit of the time and, despite its dramatic power, it was never professionally staged.

In November 1944, Churchill came to Paris, and Muggeridge described the scene in a letter to Kitty: "I saw him walking down the Champs Elysée with de Gaulle and I must say felt most moved. He looked so pink and happy as the crowd cheered him; even de G. melted somewhat and waved his arms in the air in his ungainly way."[43] After the war, Muggeridge's friend, P. J. Grigg, who was then on Clement Attlee's staff, described arriving at Number 10 Downing Street with Churchill. It was very late at night and ". . . they decided to relieve themselves in the Garden. In the course of this operation, W. remarked 'I wonder if Gladstone ever did this?' "[44]

When Muggeridge was editor of *Punch* he was pilloried for running a cartoon that urged retirement on a puffy, maundering old Churchill, declining into senility, thereby giving Muggeridge an undeserved reputation for hostility to Churchill. In fact, he had publicly referred to Churchill's wartime record as that of ". . . a giant among pygmies," and he believed that precisely those qualities that made Churchill so extraordinary a leader in the extraordinary circumstances of war, particularly his extravagant and bombastic oratory, unsuited him to the more restrained exigencies of peacetime politics. Remove the threat to the nation's survival, and Churchill's rhetoric became hollow and portentous. Whether one accepts Muggeridge's assessment or not, it was never based on dislike or belittling of Churchill; yet such was Churchill's symbolic status that any comment short of sycophancy was enough to provoke righteous indignation. Much the same thing happened, as will appear later, in the row over the monarchy.

With normality more or less restored in Paris, it remained only to have a look at blitzed Berlin, by now a slagheap of rubble, albeit one from which a gleaming new city of chromium and glass would soon push upwards. Then the war, whose coming he had so clearly envisaged and whose combat he had so eagerly sought, was over. For him it ended, as it began, in farce. In April 1945, he simply took off his uniform and went home, effectively demobilizing himself. "I just wound up my military service myself, becoming, I suppose, technically a deserter, until some months later I received my demobilization papers, went along to Chelsea barracks and collected my discharge and civilian suit and message of appreciation from the King. . . ."[45] Fantasy to fantasy—oh war, where was thy sting?

What had the war accomplished? What had it all signified? Was it a struggle between good and evil, light and darkness? Was it a parable about the fall of man, played out on a global stage? Had there been a victor and a vanquished, or was victory, like liberation, one more fantasy? The Axis was defeated, but in Eastern and Central Europe police states under Russian tutelage emerged that produced, sometimes in even more exaggerated form, all the most hateful features of Nazi rule. His friend A. T. Cholerton said that Hitler had won the war in the guise of Stalin. Who, then, had lost it? At the time, Muggeridge would have agreed with Arthur Koestler that the outcome was ". . . the victory of a half truth over an absolute lie." Now he would be less sure.

Shortly after he got back to London he bought tickets for his children to see a performance of *As You Like It* at the Old Vic.

I was only able to get to the theatre myself after the performance had begun. Not wanting to create a disturbance by making my way to my seat, I stood at the back waiting for the end of the first act. I could see Kitty and the children quite clearly. In that perspective, the four of them seemed to be grouped round her rather than seated side by side in a row; their faces riveted by what was happening on the stage, not just attentive, but utterly absorbed. There they were, caught up, compacted, by the enchantment of Shakespeare's comedy; and there was I, looking at them, and recalling that it was thirty years since I had likewise sat in that auditorium as a child, and been enthralled by *As You Like It*. On this occasion, the theatre was still very battered from the blitz; part of the auditorium roped off as dangerous, and the stage similarly restricted, the roofing reinforced by a tarpaulin, but in places the sky and the stars nonetheless clearly visible. A very gallant and splendid effort, I thought, to have a performance at all; like a ship limping into port after battling its way through a terrific storm. The actors were very young—they might even have been RADA students—but they spoke the lines charmingly, bringing the Forest of Arden to pass in Waterloo Road, and Rosalind to life amidst the debris of a war fought and a victory celebrated. After all, then, something *had* been salvaged from the world's wreck, as there might still be something to salvage from my life's wreck. At the back of the Old Vic auditorium, I had my own private V.E. Day and then, when the lights went up, joined the others.[46]

·9·

OUR OWN CORRESPONDENT

The only fun of journalism is that it puts you in contact with the eminent without being under the necessity to admire them or take them seriously. It is the ideal profession for those who find power fascinating and its exercise abhorrent.

Malcolm Muggeridge, 1964

* * *

The war is over and I find myself sitting in my old room at Whatlington exactly as it was when it began. There is a fire burning, Kitty is downstairs in the kitchen, everything is as it was, except that five and a half years have passed, and my hair is grey, and I am tireder than I was. During these five years I have been here and there, and I suppose that sometime I shall write about it all. For the moment I have little desire to write about those years, or indeed anything; all I really want to do is sit and look out the window . . . . Even now the war seems like a dream and might never have happened. I might have been sitting here in this room all the time instead of going here and there. Looked back on, the war had no substance. I can recall different incidents, different places where I went, but only as one recalls a dream. Action, a product of the will, leaves no trace behind; only the imagination is permanent.[1]

His first requirement was a job. A press attaché opening in Brussels looked promising at first but failed to materialize, as did a Colonial Office posting to Nairobi. What he really wanted was to get back into journalism, and to this end he sounded out acquaintances like T. S. Eliot, Anthony Powell, George Orwell, and Hugh Trevor-Roper.

Trevor-Roper came to stay at Whatlington in early May 1945, and once, apropos of nothing, remarked how Malcolm looked like he imagined the devil to look like, ". . . sometimes truly evil, sometimes with goodness uppermost." This observation must have struck home, for Muggeridge recorded it in his diary, and added: "Dr. Jekyll and Mr. Hyde—true of all existences, collective and individual; take, for instance, monstrous lust on the one hand, on the other ecstasy and the ego's momentary disappearance, in its being swallowed up in everlastingness, as a little ship on the horizon is swallowed up in the sea's immensity."[2]

As usual, idleness made him morose and ill. He had severe chest pains that were diagnosed as lung trouble. Heavy smoking did not help. Were his ailments physical or psychological? "I am supposed to be ill with something wrong with my right lung," he wrote. "Sometimes I think it is really bad and will be the end of me, and sometimes I think it is nothing at all, just an outward and visible manifestation of an inward and invisible desire to escape from the bondage of human life. All my desire is to turn my eyes away from time and towards eternity."[3]

He marked the official end of the war by attending a local service of celebration during which the vicar prayed that a new and better world might come to pass. "What a foolish prayer!" Muggeridge jotted in his diary. "Better the old prayer for that peace which the world cannot give, and for the granting of desires and petitions as may be most expedient." Then he and Hesketh Pearson, who had moved to Whatlington in 1941 to escape the Blitz—to the occasional discomfiture of local residents as, for instance, when Pearson took to denouncing the Archbishop of Canterbury as "Public Enemy Number One"—repaired to the nearby Red Oak pub for a celebration of their own. The deeper in their cups they got, the more misanthropic the conversation became; they finished up agreeing that Shakespeare had taken much too charitable a view of the human species when, in *Measure for Measure*, he referred to men as "angry apes."

On May 18, 1945, Muggeridge was interviewed by Arthur Watson, the editor of *The Daily Telegraph*. Watson first asked about his politics; Muggeridge replied that he had been brought up a socialist but now considered himself free of all political allegiances. Watson then asked if he could write leaders? "I said that I could (could I still?)." Then Watson put the critical question: Did he believe in private enterprise? "I hedged, genuinely unable to say whether I believed in it or not, it seeming to me not a matter susceptible of belief. He set his little grey mouth and said that he believed in private enterprise. It seemed to me that he clung to this belief savagely, it being the only belief he had; if so, a foolish one, I thought. We parted amicably."[4]

A week later Watson wrote offering him a job—leader writing at £1400 a year. He started on June 1, attended the morning editorial conference, and was assigned a leader on the situation in Burma; "on

Burma I duly typed, writing almost automatically after so many years, easy-coming, complete rot."[5]

With a pang the Mill House was sold, and the family moved from the tranquility of Whatlington to a London flat on Buckingham Street that overlooked the Thames and the Embankment Gardens where, on warm summer evenings, bands played. He and Kingsmill (now at *Punch*) liked to stand looking out the window and listening to the music, feeling part of the scene yet agreeably detached. On the South Bank, they could see the Festival of Britain taking shape, ". . . one of those macabre enterprises to which declining regimes are addicted." With Kitty and the children in tow, he wandered around the Festival's dimly lit streets (lighting was then still economized): "My mind went back to my perambulations through the streets of Moscow, and the conviction I had so very poignantly then that this was to be the future—an unending procession of anonymous people padding noiselessly through darkened streets. Certainly there was little evidence of festivity . . . ."[6]

The Daily Telegraph, of course, came out strongly for the Conservatives in the July 1945 election. Muggeridge took little notice and felt neither elation nor dismay when Labour won decisively. "I cannot recall a single election in which I have not hoped for the defeat of the incumbent side. This might seem a very negative and irresponsible attitude, and the only justification I can offer for it is that, since being able to turn a government out is almost the only advantage parliamentary democracy offers, one might as well enjoy it as often as possible. As far as the sense of being in the enemy camp—it didn't weigh much with me, since I had no expectation that Attlee and his colleagues would be able, or even seriously try, to achieve the things that had seemed so wonderful a prospect when I was lurking in the red cosy-corner in our Croydon sitting room to avoid being sent to bed, and listening enthralled to the Saturday evening talk of my father and his friends."[7] In any case, he had come to realize that the equalitarian ideas which the Labour party espoused in practice meant little more than stifling individual initiative and achievement.

From Heinemann's, Muggeridge obtained a commission to edit an English version of the secret diaries of Count Galeazzo Ciano, which had been smuggled out of death cell 27 in Verona jail where Ciano had spent his last days before being executed in 1944. As well as being Italy's foreign minister from 1936 to 1943, Ciano was Mussolini's son-in-law, and his diary thus provided a unique glimpse of both the politics and the personalities of the climactic period of Italian fascism. Apart from its obvious historical importance, the diary was also a fascinating human document since, despite his inordinate pomposity,

Ciano was a lucid, observant writer. Day by day he recorded his thoughts, hopes, conversations, all that happened to him, expecting to have completed, if the Nazis triumphed, a meticulous exposition of his own brilliant part in their victory, and if they were defeated, an *apologia* that would no less brilliantly excuse himself and lay the blame where it belonged, at the feet of his father-in-law and former patron Mussolini. "What he achieved actually," Muggeridge wrote in his introduction, "was to provide the world with one more record, incomparable in its naivety, of how futile a pursuit is power, and how certainly those who pursue it become enmeshed in their own deceits and stratagems."[8] Later, Muggeridge edited a companion volume of Ciano's diplomatic papers, a more formal record of the years covered in the diary. When, in 1952, an earlier fragment of the diary came to light, he again wrote an incisive introduction to the English translation.[9]

Muggeridge has always been fascinated and repelled by the spectacle of power and those who wield it, although few cut as bizarre a figure as Ciano. Power is to the collectivity, he believes, what lust is to the individual—"an expense of spirit in a waste of shame" in Shakespeare's elegant phrase. Through the practice of half a century of journalism, and particularly since the advent of television, he has been brought in contact with prime ministers, potentates, and despots, people who have achieved power over their fellowmen by acclamation, birth, persuasion, the ballot box, or the barrel of a gun. Its effect on almost all of them, he has observed, is to corrupt—not in the more obvious sense in which Lord Acton spoke of power corrupting, but in subtler, more insidious ways; principally, by diverting their attention from what is enduring, true, and worthwhile to what is evanescent, circumstantial, and tawdry. "Here am I, Captain of a Legion of Rome," runs an inscription Muggeridge is fond of quoting, "who served in the Libyan desert and learns and ponders this truth—there are in life but two things, love and power, and no man can have both."

His view has partly been shaped by his own experiences; of the New Civilization proclaimed in the Soviet Union, which finished up in the far-flung camps of the Gulag Archipelago; of the man of destiny seizing power in Munich, which finished up in the mass, anonymous graves of Auschwitz; of *Il Duce* who made the trains run on time and finished strung up by his heels in the marketplace at Milan; of ballot boxes and interminable parliamentary debates in Paris and London and Washington, which finish up in societies so aimless and enfeebled that they are unable to resist either external aggressors or internal terrorists, yielding simultaneously to barbarians from without and within, and in their last legislative gasp striving to extinguish individual freedom through the closed shop and individual life through legalized abortion.

Why? Why did the exercise of power, even by democratic means and in pursuit of seemingly humanitarian ends, invariably lead to destruction? The reason, Muggeridge concluded, is that a civilization, like a dwelling, must have a stable foundation or it collapses. Christianity was the foundation on which laws, customs, and regulations—a whole civil order, as well as our art, music, and literature, rested. In other words, it provided the moral imperatives from which civil authority derived; destroy that foundation and the whole edifice topples. "Where there are neither religious values nor an accepted manner of behaviour to impose a moral pattern on life, all that is left is the pursuit of power as such."[10]

Yet it is truth, not power, which endures and which provides individuals with whatever security is ultimately attainable. For western Europeans, Christianity expressed that truth. Undermine Christianity, venerate humanism in its place, and a true, immutable foundation, capable of withstanding the buffeting tides of history, has been replaced by a false, shifting one. Instead of life being understood as a pilgrimage and man as a wayfarer, seeing at best through a glass darkly and fitfully, yet with a sure guide and a certain hope—a sojourner in time whose true home is eternity, humanism proclaims that life is a contest for survival in which man, having proved the fittest, has come of age and is capable of charting his own course, master of his own destiny. On such a foundation, Muggeridge contends, nothing can be constructed except fantasy; and there is no power, whether derived from wealth or arms, which can for long sustain fantasy.

Still, power fascinated him, and he did not hesitate, when the opportunity came up in April 1946, to go to Washington to observe how the world's other great superpower, the leader of what was then unashamedly still called "the free world," actually operated.

The plan was for Kitty to join him during the summer school vacation when he had located a suitable house, preferably in the country but within easy range of Washington. For the moment the boys, Leonard, John, and Charles, would remain at school in England, while daughter Val would come to America with Kitty as soon as he was settled. Both Malcolm and Kitty entertained the thought that the family would eventually emigrate and settle permanently in America. He soon changed his mind. A foretaste of what lay ahead came at Liverpool where he embarked; a brusque American immigration officer, "a gaunt hag-like female," demanded: "Now what *exactly* do you expect to get out of going to America, Mr. Muggeridge?" He replied wearily: "A living."[11]

He passed the transatlantic voyage playing chess with a Czechoslovakian Jewish émigré or just pacing up and down the deck, thinking of ". . . you [Kitty] and Hughie and Tony [Powell], the three persons whose company I love most . . . There's no delight in life now other than in talking about it." Even before the ship reached America, he wrote to Kitty: "I never approached a new country with less desire to see it."[12]

He docked at New York and spent some time there covering the Security Council debates of the fledgling United Nations, a spectacle ". . . full of quiet entertainment for one who, like myself, likes to keep watch o'er man's insanity."[13]

First impressions of a country are usually lasting, and his were unfavorable. Things in the United States seemed "in as great a muddle as in England" and, worse, the hotels seemed incapable of providing tea in the morning. In contrast to England, where shortages were common, the shops were bursting with food and merchandise. "When it comes to the point, however, I find I don't want to buy anything."[14]

No sooner had he arrived in New York than he heard from Kitty that their landlord had unaccountably locked the family out; he fretted about this, regretted ever having come, and fell into one of his black moods of "frenzied inertia." Already he was "inconceivably depressed" about America, and the thought of settling there "fills me with horror."[15] To Kitty he wrote: "It's difficult to convey the curious mixture of utter melancholy and excitement which this country generates. There's a kind of infinite futility about it, a kind of senseless energy rather like your mother's which makes one want to shout aloud."[16]

On Easter Sunday he watched the traditional fashion parade down Fifth Avenue: ". . . masses of well-dressed and well-fed people aimlessly drifting to and fro in bright sunshine. After all the desolation of Europe, it was in a way impressive, and yet I don't know. I didn't envy them particularly, or feel any greater confidence in their future than in that of their shabby, hungry equivalents in Paris or London. The skull beneath the flesh I always seem to see, perhaps morbidly, and I have too keen a nose for mortality."[17] Beneath the glittering surface of America, he sensed doom: "This country is in the process of going up in smoke or I'm much mistaken. I felt it in my prophetic soul from the moment I landed here. In the end I think the mess here will be even worse than the mess in Europe." Muggeridge wrote those words on May 12, 1946, when the greatest economic boom in American history was just about to begin. So, in this prophecy, Muggeridge may be said to have been wildly wrong. Or was he? Might he not say, with Kipling: "I saw the sunset ere men saw the day"?

To Kingsmill he wrote:

There is something very wonderful about this country, but not for me. In no country that I've been in have I felt so completely an outsider as here. It makes me very lonely even when you see a lot of people. Though they speak English, and go to church, and wear pyjamas, they make me feel much more alien than even the Russians did. I'm hopeful that being here will, for some reason I can't explain, cure me of my Russian obsession. Already I find myself less heated in my denunciation of Russia, and though I won't say that it would not give me the most exquisite pleasure to hear that Molotov was dying by slow torture, a very delicate instrument would I fancy detect an appreciable modification of my attitude towards him after one of Truman's press conferences.[18]

In Washington he settled in a small apartment in a house owned by an aged French lady who, despite forty years in America, spoke practically no English—"for me, *toujours les frogs.*" Americans, he told Kitty, ". . . are the most terrible bores the world holds; they only really want to talk about themselves and that's a soon exhausted subject."[19] Fortunately, he ran across a friend from Moscow days, William Henry Chamberlin, whose garbled, yet perceptive conversation and "real oddity" cheered him up; ". . . No doubt my pleasure in his company is increased by virtue of the fact that he has learnt pages of my works and recites them often."[20] Also, Huntington Harris who had been a friend in Lourenço Marques turned up.

News gathering developed its own ritual. He had breakfast seated on a stool at a drugstore lunch counter and then set off for the *Telegraph* office in the National Press building from where, within a mile or so, was the greatest concentration of wealth and power ever to exist on earth. In military terms, the Pentagon; in executive terms, the White House; in financial terms, the Treasury; in diplomatic terms, the State Department; in legislative terms, Capitol Hill. He first picked up copies of *The Washington Post* and *The New York Times* ". . . through whose stagnant columns I swim lazily for an hour or so." Then there might be a congressional committee or a senate debate: ". . . shabby, noisy, vulgar, egotistic men, bellowing and waving their hands about, power at its dregs."[21] Failing that, he would trudge along Massachusetts Avenue to the British Embassy, then presided over by the odd figure of Lord Inverchapel; that source, however, dried up when Muggeridge was barred for what was termed "unhelpful" reporting—". . . a term which, in the trade, signified letting your own cat out of someone else's bag."[22] A presidential press conference, rarer then than now, was a highlight. Muggeridge was intrigued to learn that the "S." in President Harry S. Truman stood for nothing at all and thenceforth took to calling him "Harry S. (for nothing) Truman." His parents must have exhausted

157

their imaginative powers when they thought of Harry, he decided, and just threw in the "S." in case he or anyone else might be able in the future to put a name to it. To Kitty, he wrote: "When you consider that this little fish has to look after the atomic bomb and a country in dissolution, it's pretty amazing. I think of him every time I go past the White House, sitting there, S. (for nothing)."[23]

The whole production seemed unreal. Pentagon generals and admirals waiting for orders that never came; up in the White House a forlorn little man without a middle name; Treasury full of depreciating paper; a State Department made of cardboard; legislators on Capitol Hill always just about to be, or just having been, elected.

Afternoons he usually spent in his cramped office, barely room for a desk and two ticker tape machines that spewed out copy so relentlessly that if he left the room, even just to go to the lavatory, he had to fight his way back in through mounds of accumulated paper. On Sundays, when all the political mills closed down, he dredged the Sunday papers for whatever snippets might catch the fancy of *Telegraph* readers back home. "I worked out once that it took something like 420 acres of forest land to provide the newsprint for a bumper Sunday issue; staggering under the weight of several of them on my way to my office on a Sunday morning, I used to see in my mind's eye the wide expanse of trees against a grim Norwegian or Finnish sky which had been hewn down to provide my load."[24]

When the U.S. Air Force carried out its atomic bomb tests at Bikini, he described the operation to Kitty as "inimitable": "The airplane that carried it was called Dave's Dream and a pin-up girl was painted on the bomb before it was dropped. Apparently scarcely any damage was done at all. A flock of goats left on the island appeared unperturbed afterwards." Later he learned that the pin-up girl on the atom bomb was actually Rita Hayworth and that she had wept at learning of this signal honor. When the Bikini goats, along with some radioactivated pigs and rats, were brought back to the U.S. for observation, he went along to see them and concluded his account for Kitty's delectation: "They were all receiving blood transfusions and vitamins in air-conditioned pens. A press handout answering criticism of humane societies that it was cruel to submit animals to atomic explosions contained the delightful phrase: 'They have not died in vain.' I suggested there should be a tomb to the unknown pig on which visiting statesmen might lay a handful of acorns."[25]

If each trade has its own fatuity, journalism's is a fetish for the reaction of a ubiquitous, rather odious creature called "the man in the street." From time to time, Muggeridge would get a cable demanding "urgentest, quickest, fastest, immediate reaction man in street stop appointment X firstlord admiralty," or some other such momentous event, the assumption being that in the slums of Detroit as across the wide plains of Montana and in the cotton fields of Alabama, brave men went pale and women clutched babies to their breasts every time another game of musical chairs was played at Whitehall. He eventually developed an effective *modus operandi* for dealing with such requests: "The editor of *The Washington Post*, at that time a delightful Yorkshire-man, once in a while permitted me to contribute a small editorial piece of my own to his columns, preferring that it be on some topic considered to be important in England but for one reason or another overlooked by the American press. So I would tap out a little item on the recent appointment, press a sentence or two of it on Reuters, and lo! I could give the *Telegraph's* English readers the *Washington Post's* reaction to this world-shattering appointment— sometimes in the manner of an exclusive scoop even before it appeared in the *Post*. Thus were the preoccupations of the Old World duly taken account of in the New."[26]

He also discovered Scotty Reston and used him as an unfailing source, like a serviceable clotheshorse on which any odd article of clothing may be hung. "I've used him as 'a source close to the White House', as a 'high State Department official', or just as 'usually well informed.' Thus attributed, one could whisk off some of his more sagacious and prescient sentences to London, where, with a bit of luck, particularly in the somnolence of a summer evening, someone would whisk them back to Washington. It was a kind of trans-Atlantic tennis which hurt no one, and greatly enriched Western Union and Marconi."[27]

Despite such shortcuts, the job of singlehandedly covering Washington, and frequently New York too, was extremely demanding. He complained to Kitty that he was "dog tired" with no chance to read anything except newspapers, or think of anything except news. "I work more or less all the time and really have no leisure anymore . . . Something's always happening, suddenly and unexpectedly, and I quite often don't find out until too late and then I get a telegram complaining. The sight of a telegram now makes me shudder—horrid, little yellow envelopes."[28] He threatened to resign unless the *Telegraph* provided additional help, and went so far as to write to Heinemann's inquiring about the possibility of work in publishing. He was wasting his time, he told Kitty, but then added: "The idea of wasting one's time is, after all, pretentious, based on the assumption that how one might otherwise have employed it would have been of great importance, which obviously it wouldn't."[29] When Kitty and daughter, Val, finally arrived in October 1946, he became more content and put aside thoughts of resigning.

Most of the news stories he covered in his eighteen months in America have long since been forgotten, although tattered cuttings survive; loans to England, the Marshall Plan, extension of price controls, and the mine workers' strike in which union boss John L. Lewis forced President Truman to take over the mines. Then, as now, trade union politics brought bully boys to positions of authority, and Muggeridge minced no words in describing John L. Lewis: "Ruthless and at the same time astute, violent yet knows how to wait, greatly hated and at the same time respected, full of rancour over past failures and unforgetful of past quarrels, and determined to exploit to the limits his present advantageous position irrespective of the consequences to the nation. . . ."[30]

Amid the dross of this far-off daily journalism there are one or two nuggets, such as Muggeridge predicting that General Eisenhower, then just about to vacate his chief of staff position to take up the presidency of Columbia University, would be the successful Republican presidential nominee; and that the Democratic party must soon split, giving rise to a third party candidacy by Henry Wallace. Certainly his superiors at the *Telegraph* were well-pleased, and by the time he left America, his journalistic stock was high.

He finished his American stint by making a motor trip down to the South, across the Midwest, and out to California, listening by car radio as he went along to the bewildering variety of religious broadcasts that fill the American airwaves. A Christian Scientist who referred to Jesus as ". . . of humble station but nevertheless highly successful and influential"; Roman Catholics ". . . clever and pessimistic"; and Methodists ". . . making vehement pleas against licensing liquor shops," which led Muggeridge to conclude that in Tennessee ". . . the only permitted indulgences were eating and domestic fornication."[31] In Memphis he had dinner at a squalid, circular restaurant with a dance floor and a band blaring. Diners came equipped with their own bottles, and at the next table a man passed out and was sick on the floor. The women, he noticed, were as drunk, loud, and obnoxious as the men, as well as being "hideous." "Can these save Western civilization," he asked himself: "No, not even the Great Western Railway." Thinking it over, he decided that Americans were ". . . the only case of a people who'd become decadent without ever going through the stage of being civilized."[32]

In Little Rock, Arkansas, he listened to General Eisenhower address a group of war veterans and wondered if such a figure, ". . . made up and play acting," could possibly lead America and the free world? In Nevada he visited gambling casinos and divorce courts: "Thus the two great mysteries of American life—marriage and divorce—celebrated in

Liberator, Paris, 1944

Hugh Kingsmill, August 1939

Hesketh Pearson and Malcolm Muggeridge, 1950

this one State."[33] Then on to Los Angeles, California, movie town, wealth and beauty capital, ". . . where lovers are forever young and forever desirable, dates are endless and inexhaustible, appetites forever being satisfied and never sated—the American dream, in technicolour, here perpetually being fashioned."[34] He was grateful to spend his last night in North America, as the year 1947 came to an end, in the austere surroundings of Anchorage, Alaska, on ". . . a pale Arctic night with clear cold air and snow mountains all around."[35]

From Anchorage he flew to Tokyo to begin a *Telegraph* Far Eastern series, starting with the trial of General Tojo and the Japanese war criminals who, he reported, all sat listening impassively and without the slightest flicker of emotion to the full catalog of their crimes which the prosecution went into in shuddering detail: "They might themselves be judges instead of accused so imperturbable is their bearing. . . ."[36]

In something of a journalistic coup, he sought and obtained an exclusive interview with General Douglas MacArthur. He was received in MacArthur's office, the general seated with his back to the window and smoking an exceptionally large black pipe. His article described the general's conversation as "resonant and fervid," but his diary was more candid: "He talked at me for nearly an hour. His inconceivable theme was that the U.S. army brought democracy and Christianity to Japan, and had thereby wrought a revolution unique in history. He spoke of the Sermon on the Mount, producing an exceptionally large number of cliches ('Freedom is heady wine', etc.). I was bored and embarrassed. He seemed to me like a broken down actor of the type one meets in a railway train or boarding house in England who complains that his recent production of Hamlet at the Pontypool Repertory Theatre was badly attended whereas the circus was crowded. Occasionally I made feeble efforts to check the flow of words, but with no avail. It had to run irresistibly on . . . an inconceivable performance."[37] With relief he made his way back to his military billet, where trays of highballs were brought in from 4 p.m. onwards, and the only interruption was an occasional shriek as some Japanese girl resorted to Jujitsu in self-defense against the more intimate assaults of some American apostle of democracy and Christianity. "Heady wine indeed, I thought."

The next day Muggeridge indiscreetly recounted his "interview" with MacArthur to an American State Department official who was greatly amused. Their conversation happened to be overheard by one of MacArthur's officers who reported it to the general, thereby touching off ". . . a first class departmental row,"[38] which resulted in the State Department official being sent home.

By special train (on which the Emperor Hirohito and his entourage were traveling), Muggeridge went next to Hiroshima to assess the aftermath of the dropping of the first atomic bomb. He had never been among the doomsayers who prophesied apocalyptic ruination from the atomic bomb. In fact, he was closer to P. G. Wodehouse's attitude; when Muggeridge once referred to the possibility of the human race being made extinct by atomic warfare, Wodehouse's laconic response was, "I can hardly wait." Kitty's reaction to the dropping of the atomic bomb had been to wonder if the army recruiting posters would now be modified to read "We're atomized, mate." However destructive atomic weaponry might be, Muggeridge contended that the human condition was fundamentally unaltered. "It was the will to destroy rather than the means which mattered." The crossbow in its time, he recalled, had been condemned by the Vatican as a weapon of such diabolical destructiveness that Christians could be relied upon never to use it. Between the crossbow and the atomic bomb were differences of degree, not of kind.

Emperor Hirohito wore a trilby hat which, in public, he continuously raised and lowered; his retinue of court officials, all resplendent in identical black cutaway coats with a tiny crysanthemum, symbol of the royal house, in their lapel buttonhole, had presumably told him that as he was no longer a sun god he must behave like an ordinary democratic monarch. "They neglected to point out, at the same time, that hats should thus be raised only for a particular reason, as in response to cheers; and he just raised and lowered his all the time—like working a pump handle."[39]

At Hiroshima, Muggeridge was particularly anxious to see the strange phenomena that had been widely reported to have occurred at the moment the atomic blast went off; a hand instantaneously fossilized in a stone wall, or the outline of a bicycle melted into a bridge. His most persistent efforts proved to be unavailing; although such incidents seemed to be universally believed, indeed had passed into the city's folklore, and despite the fact that plenty of people he interviewed claimed to have seen them, he was unable to find a single person who could actually take him to see one for himself. Only an old priest, an actual survivor of the bombing raid, was likewise skeptical of such stigmata. It was not the first time, nor would it be the last, when Muggeridge discovered that the only truly skeptical attitude belonged to the religious mind. It is the secular mind that is credulous and naive because, as G. K. Chesterton observed, the alternative to belief in God is not belief in nothing but—what is far worse—belief in anything.

Mulling over his experience at Hiroshima, Muggeridge concluded that it was a laboratory example of mythology in the making. The *Zeitgeist*, or consensus, had decreed that there were such stigmata; they were tangible representations of the guilt that moralists and psychiatrists said that all must feel at this great human tragedy. So exist they must. Contemporary man can be persuaded to believe any proposition, however absurd, so long as it is dressed up in pseudo-scientific or psychological terms. Thus Christians who accept the virgin birth find themselves ridiculed by practitioners of astrology, those who aspire to a broken and contrite heart are suspected of mental imbalance, and heaven is dismissed as a pipe dream by people who arrange to have their bodies quick-frozen and placed in cold storage vaults in the hope that eventually technology will be able to thaw them out and start them up again. (Incidentally, one such frozen corpse awaiting not resurrection but revivification is Walt Disney, the premier fantasist of the twentieth century—a good example of what Muggeridge calls "fearful symmetry.") Contemporary credulity was a theme to which he would often return, particularly after he began to do a lot of work on television, a medium that inevitably takes first prize in the fantasy stakes.

From Japan he went to Hong Kong, Bangkok, Singapore, Rangoon, Calcutta (where he recalled his *Calcutta Statesman* days ". . . another aimless period in an aimless life"), then to Cairo and finally, early in 1948, back to London.

Kitty and the family were now settled at 5 Cambridge Gate, just next to Regent's Park where nearly every day Malcolm would stroll with Anthony Powell, talking mostly of Powell's *Dance to the Music of Time*, which was then just beginning and which Muggeridge "liked and admired greatly."[40] His own literary efforts were concentrated on a novel, at this stage called *In Collaboration*, which he had begun during his frenzied days in America. In 1949 it was published by Hamish Hamilton as *Affairs of the Heart*. It was his last attempt at fiction and is quite different from all his previous novels. Gone is the brooding introspection, the sensual gloom and moralizing; instead it is a detective story, long on characterization, short on plot, gracefully and mordantly written, but unmemorable. It opens promisingly: Ossian Routledge and Philip Ambrose write thrillers in an uneasy literary collaboration under the pen name Anthony Anstruther. But it is Routledge who is deferred to by waiters and doormen, who reaps public acclaim and the lion's share of the royalities; Ambrose toils on in obscurity, sustained by a bitter, growing hatred of his partner. From the moment Routledge keels over in the reading room of the British Museum, his killer and the motive are obvious to the reader; the only question is How? Ambrose's self-imposed challenge was to devise a murder so subtle that Routledge will unknowingly have been plotting his own death in the pages of their last unfinished Anstruther thriller, called *Death by Collaboration*. Routledge's widow hires a down-at-the-heels literary hack to find the answer, ". . . to approach the problem from a literary, rather than a criminal angle, if you see what I mean," she none-too-convincingly explains.

The trouble with the book is that the literary hack never does find out how Ambrose killed his partner, and neither does the reader. Instead the plot just peters out meaninglessly. One cannot lead the reader on for two hundred pages wondering how it was done and then just finish up: "This, as far as I was concerned, settled things. It is true that certain details remained obscure; but the essential fact that Ambrose sent Routledge to die in the British Museum Reading Room seemed to me to be now established. Whether Routledge was due to die of heart failure was really beside the point as I saw it."[41]

But it is not beside the point—it is the whole and only point of the book. Given the author's inability to work things out, it is surprising that the book was published. When it was completed, in fact, his diary records that he was ". . . far from satisfied" with it. Had it been a first novel instead of a fourth, or preceded rather than followed his highly acclaimed *The Thirties*, it probably would have been rejected. As it was, it was his most successful novel commercially and was published in the United States twelve years after its first appearance in England.

It did not enjoy the favorable, often ecstatic, notices that his earlier novels had drawn, proving once again that there is little connection between the tastes of reviewers and buyers. Evelyn Waugh, effusive in praise of *In a Valley of This Restless Mind*, was this time succinct: ". . . despite the high gifts of wit, humour and observation, he cannot tell a story. His plot is elaborate, unintelligible and quite superfluous."[42] C. P. Snow called the ending "somewhat mysterious,"[43] while Peter Quennell wrote that "the plot dissolves in a mist of uncertainty."[44]

The least autobiographical of all Muggeridge's novels, *Affairs of the Heart* does contain one delectable real life characterization, that of his long-time literary agent, David Higham, the egregious Mr. Elphinstone of the book, whose deference towards author-clients is finely calibrated to their incoming royalties. "In the practise of his profession of literary agent he had acquired an unerring and useful facility for adjusting his manner exactly to the circumstances of the individual with whom he was dealing. He was a human barometer. You tapped him on the chest and he at once registered your worldly prospects."[45] Such was Higham's vanity that he not only praised *Affairs of the Heart* as Muggeridge's finest work (a ludicrous judgment from one who must be presumed to have at least nodding acquaintance with his author's *oeuvre*) but he actually drew people's attention to the fact that he was the model for Elphinstone and went on doing so until his death in 1978.

Leader writing at the *Telegraph* occupied less and less serious attention. With little thought or effort Muggeridge pontificated on the subjects assigned to him, as ready to deal with Ceylon's gain of Dominion status as de Valera's loss of the Irish premiership, afterwards pasting up the cuttings in his diary and giving a frank assessment of his own efforts; "sheer blather" and "boring" in the two instances cited.[46] Scarcely three months back in England, he had written in his diary: "Already I find leader writing infinitely wearisome, but it is easy money, and the great thing to do is just not to worry about it."

Occasionally he was called on to declaim the need for European unity in the face of the Russian menace, one of the *Telegraph's* pet themes. This he did with a heavy heart, not because he doubted the reality of the menace, but because he thought the whole idea of European unity was an illusion, ". . . a shadowy project like attempts to revive the Holy Roman Empire. Theoretically admirable, actually inconceivable, I fear. The march of events has its own momentum, and is clearly now directed towards the final destruction of what remains of Western European civilization, to clear the way for some new essay in collective living. To recognize that this is so does not imply an acceptance of its desirability. One belongs to what is to be destroyed, and to pretend otherwise, to oneself or to others, is both foolish and contemptible."[47]

Of the inevitable internal politics of a newspaper office, he took little notice—still less of the affairs of the union to which he belonged, the N.U.J. Only when several avowed Communists were elected to the union executive board did he become alarmed and resolved "to attend all meetings and, if necessary, undertake duties."[48] Actually, he could not have carried through this resolve because his name had been struck from the union's membership roll when the recording secretary received a mysterious telephone call saying that Muggeridge was dead. The identity of the anonymous informant, and the purpose behind this call, never came to light and later, of course, his membership was restored. Muggeridge clearly foresaw the consequences of left-wing domination of the trade union movement; on February 11, 1948, he wrote that Communists and their sympathizers came to dominate trade union affairs because ". . . they are prepared to undertake duties which others shun and were diligent in turning up at meetings. I realized that this was going on all over the country in all Unions. Highly dangerous, since such positions in many ways are more powerful and important than, for instance, being in Parliament." Given the shambles to which Fleet Street, and indeed the whole British economy, has been reduced by trade union thuggery in all its manifestations, who would now argue the point?

His apprehensions were reinforced when he covered the twentieth Congress of the British Communist party and looked over the sallow faces arrayed on the platform and shuddered ". . . at the thought that in many parts of Europe such people were already in absolute control."[49] When their leader, Harry Pollitt, spoke, Muggeridge was intrigued that the only non-Communist publications he cited with approval were *The Times* and *The Times Literary Supplement*. His dispatch drew attention to this oddity, but the *Telegraph's* editor, Colin Coote, cut that part out.

He also did a short stint covering the House of Commons. This was sufficient to dispel any lingering illusions he may have had about the foresight, resolve, or will of such absurd, lilliputian figures to resist what he increasingly saw as a total disintegration of Western European civilization. Clement Attlee had ". . . a faculty for being banal which must exceed in achievement anything in that line in the history of the world,"[50] while Winston Churchill, "looking like a moth-eaten old lion," whom Muggeridge had last glimpsed marching triumphantly side by side with General de Gaulle along the Champs Elysées, seemed irresolute and disspirited. "I felt a great affection and veneration for him, but it seemed a pity that after his great performance in the war, he should have to, or choose to, demean himself by bickering with fifth rate people."[51]

Later when he became deputy editor of the *Telegraph*, Muggeridge was invited to Westerham to interview Churchill, and his diary gives a vivid account of their meeting.

> Churchill walked in suddenly, wearing his famous siren suit and smoking a huge cigar—a quite astonishing figure, very short-legged, baby faced, immensely thick neck, and oddly lovable. I was expecting tea, but a tray of whiskies and sodas was brought in, and continued to be brought in at intervals. . . .
>
> He then spoke about the Germans and said it was absolutely essential to re-arm them. He mentioned that he'd been invited to go to Cologne where he was to address a huge gathering, perhaps 30,000, and he believed he would receive a great ovation. He then began walking up and down the room and, in effect, giving the speech he was to give at Cologne—a bizarre spectacle, the great wartime Prime Minister, rather tight, walking up and down reciting his speech which he proposed to give to a German audience from whom he expected warm applause. He obviously still has a great affection for Stalin. "What a pity" he said "that he has turned out to be such a swine" and went on "Why, he and Truman and Attlee could have governed the world—What a triumvirate!"

Then Churchill took Muggeridge to the garden where he showed off his goldfish in a pool. Churchill claimed the goldfish would assemble at the sound of his voice, but they had other ideas and continued to swim aimlessly about until he got some maggots that he threw into the water

. . . whereupon the goldfish did come and started eating them. He said that his whole standing with the goldfish depended on their associating the sound of his voice with the provision of maggots, and he laughed heartily when I said that he was in very much the same situation vis-a-vis his constituents. . . .

When he came to see me off he shouted to some odd characters who were waiting there, "I'll be back soon" and suddenly I was reminded forcibly of King Lear and his conversation with Poor Tom—the conversation in which he calls poor Tom "my philosopher." This sudden identification of Churchill with Lear made me feel full of pity for him, imprisoned in the flesh, in old age, longing only for a renewal of the disease of life, all passions unspent. He waved goodbye very cheerfully, and I waved back, and drove thoughtfully back to the D.T.[52]

Muggeridge also stayed in close touch with Montgomery throughout this period and got several important scoops on military stories from him. In July 1950, for example, Monty showed him a document he had prepared for the Brussels Treaty powers on the defense of Western Europe against Soviet aggression. The document concluded: "The plain truth is that there is no reality whatsoever in the general defence structure of Western Europe. We've plans and committees and papers and talks, but nothing of any real value if a battle should develop in the West . . . We're not moving steadily towards the achievement of our aim, but going backwards."[53] Muggeridge echoed this line in a feature article, "Facts We Must Be Told," which created a stir. Monty also briefed him on the political and military situation in Indochina before Muggeridge went there to do an extensive *Telegraph* series.

Muggeridge's diary is full of acerbic descriptions of those with whom he came in contact at this time and, for the most part, his first impressions have borne up well. Enoch Powell (whom he had briefly met ten years before in an army intelligence course): ". . . Mongolian features, very bright eyes, receding forehead, rather ridiculous sprouting moustache, an obvious power maniac . . . but if things get really tough, quite likely we will hear of him";[54] Harold Macmillan: ". . . rather nice . . . distinctly above average in intelligence. We talked about politics, present difficulties, etc. He, on the whole, very gloomy";[55] Hugh Gaitskell: ". . . soft-looking character, large face which always looks slightly unshaven, amiable, and, in his way, intelligent, rather like a certain type of High Church clergyman with a slum parish";[56] Richard Crossman: ". . . He looks extremely like an Indian Brahmin, and the temper of his mind more and more resembles one—singular facility for demonstrating a proposition, but the propositions themselves unconnected to any point of view";[57] Evelyn Waugh: ". . . quite ludicrous figure in dinner jacket and silk shirt . . . extraordinarily like a loquacious woman, with dinner jacket cut like a maternity gown to hide his bulging stomach. He was very genial, probably pretty plastered, all the time playing this part of the crotchety old character, rather deaf, cupping his ear,—'feller's a bit of a Socialist, I suspect'. Amusing for about a quarter of an hour, then tedious."[58]

On April 13, 1950, Lord Camrose, the *Telegraph's* owner, announced Muggeridge's appointment as deputy editor. Just before this, Muggeridge had discussions about taking the chair at *The Spectator* or at *The Daily Mail*. The new responsibilities—administrative memoranda, letters, people coming and going, ". . . all the curious pushing, intriguing, obsequiousness, and envy which goes, and ever must go, with the exercise of authority"[59]—he accepted with mixed feelings; appreciative of the extra £500 in salary, but nostalgic ". . . for the days when I contributed my little piece of folly to the larger folly and then pushed off."[60]

·10·
FRIENDS

The last word in wisdom is not to make disciples but to keep friends.

Hugh Kingsmill

* * *

The Muggeridges' favorite holiday retreat was at Roquebrun-Cap-Martin where his friend from Moscow days, A. T. Cholerton, had a villa. These holidays Malcolm considered ". . . the perfect existence," and set out his daily routine as follows:

> Rise about 7, drink tea, bathe, walk by the sea; 9 breakfast (crusty bread, butter, fruit, coffee) and then sit at a little quiet shady table looking straight on to the Mediterranean, write a bit, read, think; at noon long swim and lie in the sun until 1:30; then lunch (cheese, salad, ham, red wine, fruit) and after lunch doze and read; at 4:30 bathe again and in the evening walk either to Monte Carlo or to Menton, buy newspapers and sit in a café reading them and watching people; return leisurely at about 8:30 and dine either at villa or Mme. Ambert's solidish meal (chicken or omelette *au jambon* or Mediterranean fish) and enough red wine or rosé to feel drowsy; game of gin rummy with K., brief read and early asleep. That—for anyone who cares to know— is how I like to live; but I daresay, as K. pointed out, it wouldn't answer permanently. As a break—wonderful. [1]

Cholerton's company never failed to delight him; particularly his pungent observations as, for example, that liberty, equality, and fraternity soon gave way to cavalry, infantry, and artillery, or apropos the ideological gymnastics of the fellow-travelers who followed each twist and turn in Soviet policy: "The vomit returns to the dog" or, what Muggeridge used to call Chollie's theme song: "The woman Thou gavest me, Lord, is ending." Cholerton—with his "queer wistfulness, even hopelessness" and total impracticality; with Charlotte, his wife,

169

small, neat, and methodical; together they were a strange, lovable pair. For two hours or so every morning, Chollie would pour water on his tiny garden patch distributing, he told Malcolm, some two tons daily. "He likes to do the watering practically naked, gets himself covered with mud, and then plunges into the sea to clean himself."[2] Once when they were all staying together, Chollie suggested that they watch an eclipse of the sun. Since it was dangerous to view this with the naked eye, he brought out some photographic negatives to look through. When held up to the light the negatives turned out to be a recent series of X rays of Cholerton's bollocks.

In addition to leader writing, Muggeridge's job involved doing a regular column "Books of the Day," where his outspoken reviews occasionally landed him in hot water. When he called John Middleton Murry, author of *The Free Society*, ". . . a moral striptease artist without compare, gracefully and decorously bearing his bosom only in order to beat it,"[3] both author and publisher wrote letters of complaint. Still, Muggeridge always liked reviewing, both for itself and for the review copies thus obtained, which, at that time, he usually transformed into instant cash through the alchemy of Robert Gaston, a secondhand bookseller in the Strand. He and Kingsmill regarded Gaston, not without justice, as one of humanity's singular benefactors. "Gaston's attitude to books is one of extreme distaste. He always refers to them as a rather disgusting commodity; for instance, of a certain publisher, 'They shift the stuff.' "[4] Although Muggeridge's bank balance was slowly beginning to creep from red to black, Kingsmill remained hopelessly enmired in debt, and he was often to be seen outside Gaston's shop, hatless, clutching a pile of review copies under one arm and hastily scribbling down a few notes before parting with the books. Gaston paid half price for nonfiction, a third for novels, and only once turned Muggeridge down, refusing to accept a book called *Co-operative Movements in the Punjab* written by a graduate of Benares University; looking around, Muggeridge noticed that half a dozen copies of this momentous work had already found their way to Gaston's shelves. He and Kingsmill regarded the proceeds of this transaction by which books became sterling as the children of Israel must have regarded manna from heaven.

Muggeridge's days were full. With a break to stroll in Regent's Park, he worked through the mornings on reviews or *The Forties*; usually he met Kingsmill for lunch at the Author's Club, where they quite often lingered on through the afternoon in the Silence Room, talking and laughing; dashed off a short leader at the *Telegraph* or, if possible, avoided one; poked his head in at Heinemann's where he was now literary advisor; afternoon tea; drinks with friends, and a walk back home along the Embankment in the fading light. Only the evenings, when too often there was a cocktail or dinner party to be attended, were sometimes trying. His diary contains this account of a party given by Robert Kee to launch a new publishing enterprise.

It was in the house of Cyril Connolly who was of course there but nowadays we're not on speaking terms. Party was pretty macabre—first person I saw being Pamela Hansford Johnson who looked at me with an expression of deep loathing; with her, grotesque character called Kay Dick who wears an eyeglass and with whom George Orwell once took me out to dinner, also not very friendly. I grasped their arms and hurried on, falling into the arms of Higham, whose moustache seemed bigger and face grosser than ever. We chatted a few moments. Then saw Stevie Smith who gave me a dirty look because she'd sent me a copy of her latest book and I hadn't acknowledged, or indeed read it. I laughed this off as best I might. Waved to the Baroness Budberg who was charging about like a huge dreadnought. Masses and masses of people, mostly very unedifying, glad to get away.[5]

His melancholy had pretty well dried up, his journalism was read widely and respected, and he and Kitty cut a wide swath in society. "No one has the moral right to be disappointed after the age of forty,"[6] he wrote. He was now middle-aged and, for the first time in his life, relatively free of disappointment and morbidity.

His most serious concern was Kingsmill's health. The first time he saw Kingsmill after returning from America he had noticed how ". . . old and tired" his friend looked. In fact, Kingsmill was suffering from a duodenal ulcer, and the continuing failure of the medical profession to make a proper diagnosis eventually cost him his life. On March 3, 1948, he had a severe hemorrhage and was admitted to Royal Sussex Hospital in Brighton. Exploratory surgery was performed but proved inconclusive. Muggeridge filled in for him at *The New English Review* and on April 17 went to Brighton to visit.

I went to see Hughie in hospital, and was relieved to find him in quite good shape, though of course somewhat haggard and old-looking. He was asleep when I got there, but when he woke up and saw me sitting by his bed such a smile of happiness came on his face that I was deeply moved. We talked for about two hours and he was quite up to his old form. He is in a public ward and is quite a centre of interest to the other patients. He said that, as always happens, as they came and went, all the standard human characters appeared—a Dickens, a Hitler, etc. He had been reading Sherlock Holmes's stories, and said that, with all their inherent absurdity, they never quite lost their charm, especially when one is ill or fatigued. He quoted a line from Browning's *Andrea del Sarto:* "I am often tireder than you think" and said it was one of those everlasting remarks which could be described as "husbandly."[7]

On May 4, Kingsmill was discharged and went to stay with the Muggeridges to begin his recuperation. A week later he left for Folkestone. His farewell line was Matthew Arnold's, "Calm's not life's crown, but calm is well," which both men agreed was ". . . very expressive of middle age."[8]

In the summer and autumn Kingsmill resumed work and seemed to have at least partly recovered his old ebullience. On January 20, 1949, Muggeridge's diary records: "Hughie came to lunch and we were much amused by an extract from Archbishop Lang's memoirs in *The Sunday Times*, particularly the statement that on a deer stalking expedition, in order to protect the King from a heavy shower, 'the Archbishop, claiming the privilege of a subject to cover the person of his Sovereign, lay down on top of him.' On this awesome picture Hughie dwelt at great length, imagining what would have been the reaction of some Highland gillie who had come upon the monarch and the Archbishop thus disposed under an overhanging rock."[9]

Kingsmill had just completed reviewing proofs of *The Progress of a Biographer*, a collection of his wonderfully shrewd literary criticism taken mostly from *The New English Review*, when on April 10, 1949, he was readmitted to the hospital in Brighton. Three days later Muggeridge and Hesketh Pearson had lunch at the Author's Club, and afterwards, as they walked in Regent's Park, Muggeridge remarked that if Kingsmill died, half the joy of living would be gone at a stroke. Pearson agreed.

On May 7, Muggeridge went to Brighton and there saw his friend for the last time: "Very shocked to find him so haggard and white. He was delighted to see me. I tried to talk all the time to prevent him talking, but, of course, although forbidden to do so, he did talk and laugh as we always do when we meet. All the time I was with him a blood transfusion was going on, blood dripping into him drop by drop under my sight. He said he'd had twenty pints and all his arms were punctured from fitting on the instrument through which it is injected.

"He said that he hadn't liked to think about Shakespeare much, but rather Johnson because J. was never angry. He quoted a wonderful remark of Johnson's when he was dying, and someone arranged his pillow and asked him if it would do. 'Yes' he said 'it would do—all that a pillow could do.' "[10]

The prospect of death did not trouble him. To Hesketh Pearson, Kingsmill wrote: "Balmy spring breezes blowing in from the sea outside, and all past springs revive, but I hope that this decaying old husk will release me at not too long a date to recover all the beauty of those old days in some other form."[11] To Muggeridge, he said that he felt like an evacuee, confident that suitable arrangements had been made for his reception elsewhere, but who, if given the chance, would nevertheless prefer to remain where he was. That morning Kingsmill was amused to overhear a nurse tell a doctor that he was holding on to life "like grim death." As Muggeridge made ready to go ". . . he held my hand—an unusual thing for him, who was, by temperament, undemonstrative. He had, he said, some good news to impart; something wonderful which had come to him about our human situation. He never did manage to get it out, but nonetheless, unspoken, it often has comforted me." Years later, in his sixties himself, Muggeridge added this comment: "As I get older, and approach my own end, it even seems that I know what he had to communicate with ever greater precision and certainty."[12]

Kingsmill fell into a coma about midday on May 15, 1949, and died that evening. Muggeridge was the first person to be told by Kingsmill's wife, Dorothy, and immediately set down his thoughts for an obituary, which appeared in *The New English Review*.

Kingsmill, he wrote, ". . . was a unique person whose greatness lay, as all true greatness must, in his faculty to see into the mystery of things. In the light of this, all considerations of success and failure, of recognition and neglect, become utterly irrelevant. They are shed along with what he described as his 'decaying old husk.' What remains is the only thing that ever does or can remain—his deep and undeviating purpose to seek out the significance of life, as distinct from its phenomena; his unsparing and inexhaustible interest in his fellows, with all the bright hours it brought to those privileged to be his friends; the memory of him which they will always cherish."[13]

A memorial service was held at St. Paul's, Covent Garden, on June 9, 1949. Muggeridge read the lessons. Soon after he and Pearson began exchanging reminiscences of Kingsmill, and their letters to one another were published by Methuen as *About Kingsmill* in 1951. A labor of love, this form of memoir particularly suited their subject, a man always ready to lay aside his pen in favor of a talk with friends. Also each letter, as it was received, reminded the other person of incidents and anecdotes that might otherwise have been forgotten. Like everything connected with Kingsmill, the book made no splash commercially, but the letters have an immediacy and verisimilitude that is quite unique so that they manage to breathe life into their subject. Even those who never knew Kingsmill in the flesh may meet him "feelingly" in these letters. Some critics, such as Richard Ingrams, have contended that Muggeridge's finest writing is in *About Kingsmill*.

Kingsmill's influence on Muggeridge was subtle and pervasive. In common they shared a religious temperament—that view of life which derives less from thought than from intuitive conviction—that life is more than its external phenomena, which Kingsmill contemptuously called "the empirical," that what one sees is but an image of a larger reality and earthly life only a preparation for another life in eternity. Muggeridge did not learn this attitude from Kingsmill; he had it from the beginning, as his earliest letters and writings show. But Kingsmill refined it, developed it, and, most importantly, related it to the realm of literature.

It was in regard to literature that Kingsmill's influence was greatest. Kingsmill had thought out his own criteria for assessing literature, for distinguishing between the enduring and the ephemeral, the true and the merely sensational, criteria he distilled in *The Progress of a Biographer*. In this respect, Muggeridge could be said to have been his pupil. In fact their critical judgments were so similar that when Kingsmill was ill, Muggeridge wrote articles and reviews under Kingsmill's name for various periodicals with neither editor nor reader detecting any difference. Their tastes in literature were virtually identical: Shakespeare, Dr. Johnson (to whom Kingsmill bore an affinity and of whom Muggeridge wrote: ". . . of all Englishmen, he appeals to me most—the best, the greatest, the dearest"),[14] Wordsworth, Bunyan, and Blake.

Both men were mystics—in both the dictionary sense of believing it possible to attain insights into the mysteries of human existence and in that both had occasional, unanticipated mystical experiences. Once, for example, on a walking tour in France, Muggeridge's diary records how suddenly ". . . the elements and ourselves, all life, became one, nothing separate from anything else, as will be seen at the last."[15]

Also, both men believed that the imagination and the will were locked in perpetual conflict and that only by subordinating the will, by living in the imagination, could one hope to realize King Lear's desire to take upon himself "the mystery of things," as if he were "God's spy." The pursuits of the imagination were love, truth, and understanding; the pursuits of the will were power, lust, and all panaceas for creating better human societies through collective action. Kingsmill particularly scorned Utopians, whom he called "dawnists"—those deluded souls (if anything, *more* common today) who see in each new political creed or slogan or piffling cause some new dawn for mankind. Muggeridge had been sufficiently disillusioned by Fabian socialism, Russian communism, and American materialism to share this attitude, although he preferred the term "green stickery," derived from Tolstoy's childhood belief that somewhere there was buried a green stick on which words were carved that would abolish all evil in men's hearts and bring them everything good. The first step of maturity, both men agreed, was to discard such beguiling nonsense, to accept that in this vale of tears there will and must be shortcomings and suffering and imperfection, that the kingdom of heaven cannot be created on earth, and that what man's ineradicable yearning for perfection truly signifies is the reality of another mode of existence beyond the dimensions of time and mortality. Kingsmill summed up their view in his book *The Poisoned Crown.*

> Many remedies for a shattered world are now being offered to mankind, but they are all collective remedies, and collective remedies do not heal the ills produced by collective action . . . what is divine in man is elusive and impalpable, and he is easily tempted to embody it in a concrete form—a church, a country, a social system, a leader—so that he may realize it with less effort and serve it with more profit. Yet, as even Lincoln proved, the attempt to externalize the Kingdom of Heaven in a temporal shape must end in disaster. It cannot be created by charters or constitutions nor established by arms. Those who set out for it alone will reach it together, and those who seek it in company will perish by themselves.[16]

To be an individual in a collectivist age, an uncommon man in the Century of the Common Man, a mystic in a materialist society meant, in Kingsmill's case, being an ignored writer but a rare friend. Muggeridge acknowledged that Kingsmill taught him that ". . . the pursuit of understanding is so enthralling that all others seem, by comparison, lustreless; that, as he so often quoted, all the world's in a grain of sand, and ecstasy lies in holding it up to catch the light."[17]

Kingsmill died at the age of fifty-nine; Muggeridge is now past seventy-five and more than a quarter of a century has gone by. Yet there is no human being, alive or dead, to whom in conversation Muggeridge refers more often or more affectionately than "Hughie." As a result, several of Muggeridge's friends have come to discover Kingsmill's insightful books, the charm of his conversation (recorded in greatest detail in *About Kingsmill*), and even to consciously adopt his unruffled, benign approach to living in a world gone mad, thereby (as Richard Ingrams has said) finding something of Kingsmill's humor and happiness. "It is not true," Muggeridge said not long ago, "that when friends die one is cut off from them. Relationships based on passion soon pale and are forgotten. In any case, passion is available elsewhere or comes to seem tiresome or foolish. But relations based on friendship may actually become closer after death, and one goes on communicating, not through mediums or spiritualism or any such rubbish, but through the imagination, by a communion of spirit which grows deeper and more expressive as one moves towards the close of one's own life."[18]

Within a year of Kingsmill's death, another friend, George Orwell, died.

Muggeridge and Orwell became friends in 1944 in Paris where Orwell had gone as *Observer* correspondent to report on the liberation. Naturally they talked of writing, and Muggeridge took an "inordinate interest" in *Animal Farm*, which Orwell was then just completing. Muggeridge even suggested to Orwell that at the end of the allegory, when the animals start going about on two legs, a drove of fellow-travelers, such as the Dean of Canterbury, assorted *New Statesman* writers, and others, might put in an appearance going about on all fours. Orwell was amused but considered the idea "too unkind."[19]

After the war they dined together regularly, usually at the Bourgogne on Gerrard Street, often with Anthony Powell and Julian Symons. Symons has recalled how on these occasions Muggeridge would play an "impish, mischievous role . . . luring Orwell away from his sensible empiricism to wild flights of political fantasy, such as his view that the Labour government might induce the British electorate to accept a lower standard of living in exchange for an end to colonialism. 'Freedom For the Colonies, and a Lower Standard Of Living For All', that would have been his election rallying cry."[20] Or, Muggeridge would provoke him into a defense of one of his absurd but tenaciously held prejudices: "All tobacconists are fascists" Orwell would declaim, as though this was something so obvious that no one could possibly question the statement; or, one which particularly amused Muggeridge, that circumcision was the mark of the upper class.

Once when Muggeridge arrived ahead of his friend, he noticed as Orwell came in how tall he appeared, his height exaggerated by a gaunt, cadaverous frame on which his clothes, a battered sports jacket and corduroy trousers, hung like a flag on a windless day. "He looked exactly like Don Quixote, very lean and egotistical and honest and foolish; a veritable Knight of the Woeful Countenance . . . Hughie and Hugh Trevor-Roper joined us afterwards, and H.T.R. said foolishly that Orwell wrote like Johnson. Hughie, of course, would not have this at all, and shouted out: 'Cobbett! Cobbett!'. We all agreed on Cobbett."[21]

Often the talk was of the East, Muggeridge having been in India at the same time Orwell was in Burma. In this connection, Muggeridge maintains that Orwell and Kipling had much in common; in their exaggerated admiration for doers as distinct from thinkers; in that each found it easier to portray animals than humans in a sympathetic context, as witness *Animal Farm* and the *Jungle Books*; that each, if given authority, would reorganize zoos so that humans were kept on exhibit in cages and animals allowed to roam free outside. Again like Kipling (and also Swift), Orwell was melancholic; Muggeridge described him as ". . . an idealist whose hopes and dreams were so bitterly mocked by the ways of men that he turned in despair to creatures who at least had the merit, being speechless, that they could not lie, and being incapable of love, that they could not betray and deceive."[22] But when Muggeridge suggested the Kipling comparison directly to Orwell (who, of course, purported to find Kipling's views abhorrent), ". . . he laughed that curious, rusty laugh of his and changed the subject."[23]

Before Muggeridge left for America, Orwell made him promise to find him some boots that would fit his outsize feet. Muggeridge either forgot or couldn't find any, and the continuing failure of boots to arrive in the post agitated Orwell who, months later, inquired anxiously of Julian Symons: "Have you heard anything from Malcolm? He hasn't sent me my boots."[24]

While Muggeridge was away in America, Orwell took up residence on the remote Isle of Jura. As a result, Muggeridge saw less of him when he first returned to London. But when *Affairs of the Heart* made its appearance on Hamish Hamilton's spring list, he received a congratulatory note from Orwell indicating that he, too, had completed a novel while Malcolm was away: "I am not pleased with it but I think it is a good idea. It is a fantasy, really, a story about the future (after the atomic wars) written in the form of a novel."[25] It was, of course, *1984*, which Muggeridge called Utopia in reverse.

In 1949 Orwell left the Isle of Jura to enter a convalescent home for tuberculars at Cranham in Gloucestershire. Muggeridge and Anthony Powell visited him there: "We found George in very good shape in the circumstances, and the same old rusty, lovable egotist. He looked very thin and said that he would probably have to spend every winter henceforth in a sanitorium. He hoped, he said, to live for another ten years because of various things he wanted to do, and because by that time his little adopted boy would be fifteen. I am not sure he will pull this off. Though he has T.B. he goes on smoking cigarettes, and was able to produce a bottle of rum from under his bed which we consumed . . . we all talked eagerly and the three hours we were with him passed very quickly."[26]

Later Orwell was transferred to University College Hospital in London where Muggeridge frequently saw him. After one visit Orwell wrote a touchingly bizarre letter complaining, not of his own deteriorating condition, but of a magazine advertisement for "Wolsey socks" that claimed they were "Fit for the Gods," a phrase Orwell considered "really blasphemous."[27]

When Muggeridge and Powell visited Orwell on Christmas Day 1949, they found him ". . . very deathly and wretched, alone, with Christmas decorations all around. His face looks almost dead, and reminded me, I said afterwards to Tony, of a picture I once saw of Nietzsche on his deathbed. There was a kind of rage in his expression, as though the approach of death made him furious . . . Poor George,—he went on about the Home Guard and the Spanish Civil War and how he would go to Switzerland soon, and all the while the stench of death was in the air, like autumn in a garden."[28]

The last time Muggeridge saw Orwell was on January 19, 1950; "I doubt I will ever see him again,"[29] he wrote in his diary after that visit. Nor did he. Orwell died two days later of a hemorrhage. Muggeridge's first impressions, as recorded in his diary, were these.

> In a way his death was sadder than Hughie's because he passionately wanted to go on living, and thus there was no sense of peace or relinquishment in him. I thought much about his curious character, the complete unreality of so much of his attitude, his combination of intense romanticism with a dry interest in some of the drearier aspects of life—e.g. Gissing. Remembered Hughie's phrase about him—that he was like a gate swinging on rusty hinges, and that he only wrote sympathetically about human beings when he regarded them as animals. All the same there was something very lovable and sweet about him, and, without any question, an element of authentic prophecy in his terrible vision of the future. His particular contribution to this sort of literature was his sense that a completely collectivized state would be produced not, as Wells had envisaged, in terms of scientific efficiency, nor as Aldous Huxley had envisaged, in terms of a heartless but vivid eroticism, but to the accompaniment of all the dreary debris and shabbiness of the past—mystique of materialist Puritanism, the dreariest and saddest of all human attitudes which have ever existed.[30]

The task of arranging a memorial service and burial fell to Muggeridge and Powell. It took place in an unheated church on a wet and chilly day, January 26, 1950. "The service went off without a hitch, though it was obvious that a good many of those present were unfamiliar with Anglican liturgy. The thing that held my attention all the time was the enormous length of the coffin. It seems they [the undertakers] had difficulty in procuring one long enough."[31] Afterwards, the mourners retired to Anthony Powell's house for sherry.

Later, Frederick Warburg, who had published *Animal Farm* after it had been turned down by a host of London publishers, showed Muggeridge some of Orwell's verse. In light of Orwell's divided personality—claiming generic membership to the Left while increasingly belaboring everything Leftist—Muggeridge thought one poem in particular might well have served as an appropriate inscription on Orwell's tombstone:

"I am the worm who never turned,
The eunuch without a harem;
Between the priest and the commissar
I walk like Eugene Aram."

Orwell had stipulated that no biographies of him should be written, and that everything one needed to know could be found in his work. Nevertheless, it soon became obvious that several would be written, and his wife, Sonia, asked Muggeridge to undertake the authorized biography. Without a great deal of enthusiasm, he set about collecting letters and documents, interviewing people who had been connected with Orwell, and so on. Indolence, plus a vague feeling of disloyalty to Orwell's ghost, led him to abandon the project uncompleted.

With Kingsmill and Orwell dead, the lunches at the Bourgogne and lazy afternoons at the Author's Club and the Horseshoe came to an end.

Muggeridge saw more of Hesketh Pearson now. Recalling their times together Pearson wrote of Muggeridge: "He was a stimulating talker, a robust walker, a hearty laugher and a good quaffer. Though his main interest was in politics, he could discuss life and literature with rare appreciation and witty depreciation, and when not in a mood of profound melancholy his company was always invigorating and entertaining."[32]

When Kingsmill was alive he had been the magnet that had drawn Muggeridge and Pearson, otherwise rather opposite types, together. Had it not been for Kingsmill, Muggeridge and Pearson would have been largely indifferent to one another. As it was there was an undercurrent of hostility between them that occasionally surfaced and which may have been exaggerated by mutual jealousy for Kingsmill's attention. In the thirties, Muggeridge's diary contains one or two unflattering references to Pearson, and Pearson used on occasion to refer to Muggeridge as "Stalin" or "Hitler" when corresponding with Kingsmill. Before the war Muggeridge and Pearson had exchanged heated words over a review Muggeridge wrote of Pearson's biography of *Tom Paine* (a book written, incidentally, at Muggeridge's instigation and dedicated to him). Pearson particularly objected to Muggeridge referring to ". . . poor, besotted Tom Paine." Tempers only cooled when Muggeridge wrote a conciliatory note to which Pearson, whose temper was as shortlived as it was violent, replied as follows:

Dear Malcolm,
I hasten to tell you that there is not a grain of grit in our friendship so far as I am concerned. I like you because I like you, not because I agree with your opinions. . . . Difference of opinion among friends merely results in

lessening of admiration, not of affection, and the two things are or should be entirely separate. All of us admire people we don't like and like people we don't admire. When I read your "poor, besotted Tom Paine" I realized at once that you and I admire quite different things but it did not alter my feelings of personal affection for you by a gram (whatever a gram may be). . . . You are one of my very few friends. Please remain so in spite of Tom Paine.[33]

Now, in their grief and shared loss at Kingsmill's death, they were drawn together. Malcolm and Kitty frequently dined with the Pearsons at 14 Priory Road. The two men went on daylong country walks and literary excursions together, once to see A. A. Milne in a Tunbridge Wells nursing home. They exchanged reminiscences about Kingsmill and generally took a keen interest in each other's writing. It was Muggeridge, in fact, who suggested to Pearson that he write a dual biography of Boswell and Johnson, which Pearson did with great acuity and affection.

At the time of Kingsmill's death, Pearson was working on his life of George Bernard Shaw, and he once wrote to Shaw suggesting that Muggeridge might accompany him on his next visit. Shaw replied on a postcard: "Not with Mugg." When Pearson told him, Muggeridge wrote in his diary: "I was rather flattered to think that various cracks I'd had at the old villain had gone home."[34]

Pearson and Muggeridge were cross-grained companions. Pearson was a hero worshiper, the one recurrent flaw in his biographies, a trait Muggeridge has always despised. Also Pearson was more class conscious, more inclined to snobbery and affectation than Muggeridge. But the main dissonance between them arose over religion. By temperament (if not always conviction or practice) Muggeridge has always been religious; it is clear that he never conceived of the meaning or significance of life in secular or materialist terms. He accepted as intuitively obvious that the reality of life is greater than its phenomena and that it can be best understood, or at least apprehended, only in religious or mystical terms. This was anathema to Pearson who claimed to find ". . . my spiritual life in Shakespeare, Beethoven, the scenery of England, and a limitless interest in the characters of remarkable men." What appealed to Pearson, in life and in letters, was good nature, good humor, good sense, and good nonsense. Pearson used often to chide Muggeridge and Kingsmill for their religiosity; concerning Kingsmill, he wrote: "We did not often discuss religion because it meant very little to me; and Hughie used to get quite peevish when I bracketed him with any religious bunch. 'I'm not religious!' he once burst out, adding with a laugh 'thank—shall we say God? or Falstaff?'—this, because Shakespeare's Henry IV was my bible, and Falstaff was worth more to me than all the saints, martyrs and teachers who have afflicted the universe."[35]

Paradoxically, Pearson was closer to the institutional church than Muggeridge who used to contend that deep within Pearson there lurked a parson. Pearson came from a long line of clerics. He had been brought up in the Church of England, whose doctrine and liturgy he continued to love however much he affected to disbelieve it. One of his most sympathetic biographies was of a cleric, Reverend Sidney Smith (*The Smith of Smiths*). Even his personal mannerisms were redolent of the cloth; Muggeridge recalled how "His voice had a decidedly clerical ring about it, and in repose he was liable to press his fingers together and wear an expression of studied amiability in true parsonical style."[36]

In March 1951, Pearson's wife Gladys died, having borne a long and crippling illness with great fortitude. Later Pearson married Joyce Ryder, and throughout the fifties and early sixties, he continued to turn out highly readable biographies of Whistler, Sir Walter Scott, Beerbohm Tree, and others.

In March 1964, Pearson entered the hospital where a diagnosis of terminal cancer was made. This was kept from him, although his wife was told. He returned home, weak and tired, but convinced that nothing more was wrong with him than a minor stomach ailment. He asked Muggeridge if, as a personal favor, he would address the annual meeting of the Sir Walter Scott Club, of which Pearson was chairman, on March 6 in Edinburgh. Muggeridge did, and four days later received a letter from Joyce Pearson.

> Hesketh wants me to thank you so much for sending him the script of your Scott speech. I read it to him and he pronounced it really excellent. He finds any physical effort (even reading) terribly tiring, but his mind is perfectly clear and receptive.
>
> I often ask him if he would like to see any of his old friends but he says he is too tired. He dozes and sleeps most of the time and mercifully so far does not seem to be in any pain. He is depressed by his weakness but still thinks it is the result of the operation. We all pray that he won't have time to realize that there is any other cause.[37]

Muggeridge visited him on April 8, 1964. Pearson was in bed with a record player next to the bed playing Beethoven records, so that if he died this should be the last earthly sound he would hear. They talked mostly of Shakespeare, Pearson's favorite subject, and he was serene and cheerful. He said he had no regrets about his life and would contentedly live it all over again.

Hesketh Pearson died the next day at the age of 77. A memorial service was held at St. Paul's, Covent Garden. Since ". . . nothing would have excited his derision more than a contrived eulogy," there was only a two-minute silence and then a short organ recital during which mourners were invited to remember ". . . that although it is a man's mortality that has brought you together it is also an expression of the love which alone gives to life its meaning."[38] On the memorial card were printed two stanzas from a poem, *Elegy For a Man*, which had always been among Pearson's favorites.

> Leave nothing to repent
> Richly did he live.
> Prodigal of life, he spent
> All that life could give.
>
> Sing no dirges, ring no knell;
> All his spirits spurned.
> He who loved this earth so well
> Is to earth returned.

Writing his friend's obituary in *The Times*, Muggeridge chose to remember him in these words.

> Pearson loved the English countryside, and English bells sounding across it; the English language, and all who tried in however humble a capacity to use it worthily . . . with him and the late Hugh Kingsmill I spent some of the happiest hours of my life. . . . He could never manage to finish reciting Wordsworth's verses upon the death of James Hogg. The closing lines—
>> "How fast has brother followed brother
>> From sunshine to the sunless land"
> were too much for him. I shall always think of him stumbling over the poignancy of those exquisite verses, and hope that the land will, after all, turn out not to be sunless.[39]

Of Muggeridge's closest friends, only "the Dr." Alec Vidler, remains alive, as serene and imperturbable as ever, always managing to leave behind him a little of his own serenity. He lives now in the house in which he was born, Friars of the Sack, the only surviving part of a thirteenth-century friary in the ancient town of Rye in Sussex. Muggeridge and Vidler spend many days together—walking, talking, and laughing. Thus another of Muggeridge's prophecies, this one made in a letter written when he was eighteen years old, has come to pass; that in age as in youth, he and Vidler would remain together, insepara-ble companions.

·11·
CELEBRITY

*Alas, 'tis true, I have gone here and there,
And made myself a motley to the view.*

William Shakespeare, Sonnet CX

* * *

The first issue of *Punch*, "the London charivari" as its masthead proclaimed, went on sale on July 17, 1841, the fourth year of Queen Victoria's reign. It quickly established a reputation for trenchant commentary by publishing, in 1843, Thomas Hood's attack on the sweatshops of the Industrial Revolution, "Song of the Shirt," which had previously been rejected as too controversial by several other periodicals. In the First World War the magazine so lampooned the Kaiser that he put a price on the editor's head. But, after the Second World War, *Punch* had grown tame and soft, the Establishment's court jester; woebegone, unchanged in appearance, with creaking joints and hardened arteries, it now pandered to what it presumed its diminishing clientele had come to expect. A decline in sales and advertising revenues and a precipitate drop in circulation (to 133,000 in December 1952, near the magazine's all-time low) made drastic action inevitable.

When Bradbury, Agnew and Company, the owners, announced on November 29, 1952, that Malcolm Muggeridge would be the next editor of *Punch*, they broke with a 112-year tradition of never having chosen an editor from outside the staff. Moreover, they selected a man who had never written in the magazine's pages nor even so much as turned them over, except in search of an occasional book review by Hugh Kingsmill. To the extent that he could be said to have had an opinion about it, he would have called *Punch* stodgy, tepid, unduly fearful of giving offense, in politics infected by the virus of liberalism, and almost totally unfunny. "Nothing in his career seems to have led up to his arrival at

183

the head of 'the table' at *Punch*" commented *Punch's* American counterpart, *The New Yorker*, "which is exactly why so many people feel that the appointment may be highly stimulating for all concerned."

For the most part, the magazine's staff were hidebound, sunk in a rut, and extremely wary of a new editor who was openly contemptuous of those traditions, like caution and breeding and decorum, which *Punch* held dear. At his first meeting with the staff Muggeridge detected an "unsympathetic attitude."[1] What he did not know was that a cabal of those opposed to his appointment, led by former editor Kenneth Bird, had already held conspiratorial meetings. Had he known, it is probable that he would not have been much concerned because he had obtained a commitment of a completely free hand from the owners. The chairman of the company, Alan Agnew, had made it clear that Muggeridge was ". . . the right man for the job. He stands head and shoulders above the others."[2] Privately, Muggeridge was apprehensive: "I feel very doubtful and unsure about it myself."[3] His doubts were not assuaged when Ian Fleming told him that, had he not gone to *Punch*, he was about to be offered the editor's chair at *The Sunday Times*—a position he would have much preferred.

However, having made a commitment, he threw himself into it with zest, resolving to change not only the magazine but the mausoleum-like atmosphere in which it was produced. After the clatter of a daily newspaper, he arrived at Number 10 Bouverie Street to find the stale, Edwardian offices of *Punch* "quiet and strange,"[4] the denizens padding about as if afraid to reveal their presence and speaking in hushed voices. A cloud of solemnity, like the ghost of old jokes and feeble laughter, seemed to hang over the place.

Muggeridge soon changed that. Formalities were dropped. Contributors were urged to laugh or shout or bellow in the office or in print. Once he had satisfied the ritual of carving his initials on the *Punch* table (actually he only began to carve, leaving the job to his son Charles who pressed so hard that the knife went right through and the table had to be sent away for repair), he quickly established his ascendancy. He invited new contributors with fresh ideas; some of them, like Anthony Powell, John Betjeman, and Christopher Hollis became regulars. Table discussions were transformed into convivial, occasionally boisterous, occasions at which one *Punch* hand recalled, "Muggeridge threw off ideas like a catherine wheel. Often he thought of a story title first and only afterwards the story."[5] *Punch's* celebrated cartoonist, Leslie Illingworth, described the atmosphere of those early days as "electrifying," and called Muggeridge ". . . the most brilliant man, with the quickest mind, I ever met on Fleet Street."[6]

Another new recruit, brought along by Anthony Powell, was Claud

Cockburn, a former Communist and *Daily Worker* writer with whom Muggeridge had exchanged angry words in the past. When Cockburn's work began appearing in *Punch*, Muggeridge received a confidential visit from a CIA man, who labored unsuccessfully to persuade him of the danger of publishing contributions from a man with such a background.

In his lively autobiography, *I, Claud* (Penguin), Cockburn has given a vivid account of his first meeting with Muggeridge at *Punch*.

[Powell] made the suggestion that we now take a walk down the corridor and visit Mr. Muggeridge in person. I positively babbled. I tried, in a few hurried words, to explain the real relationship existing between this Muggeridge and myself. I tried to make clear that while it was already incomprehensible to me that Muggeridge should be publishing articles from me —it seemed to me that he must be imagining that I was a different, perhaps an Irish, Cockburn—it was certain that a personal meeting should at all costs be avoided. "I have every reason to suppose" I said "that he detests me as deeply as I detest him. Let us keep this thing as far as possible in the old-boy net—let me deal exclusively with yourself. A meeting with Muggeridge can end only in bitterness and disaster."

Pooh-poohing and laughing—idiotically, I thought—Tony insisted; in fact he actually held me by the arm and steered me down the passage and into the bugbear's den. Of that first conversation I remember very little, except that it was from the start tumultuous and at the end—hours later—hilarious. . . .

Within an hour of meeting Malcolm Muggeridge I was aware that here was the sort of man who, if he caught himself feeling comfortably convinced of anything for a longish period of time, would start ringing alarm bells in his own head and heart; a man who felt immediate guilt on discovering that he was taking anything for granted; that in fact to take anything for granted—even the truth if it were the truth—was more heinous than to spring up with a restless effort and, quite possibly, bound straight into an abyss of error. He was, in fact, an enemy of mental and spiritual placidity, one compared to whom many who believe themselves to have alert, inquiring minds, appear on the contrary sunk into comfortable complacency. . . .

Despite my general nervousness . . . I began to have the feeling that with this fiercely gentle, chivalrously ungentlemanly man on the far side of the grandiose editorial desk, jerking and flashing his eyes and from time to time cackling out a cacophony of furiously raucous expressions like a sailor's parrot loose in Mission Hall, something new and special in the way of clowning and satire might yet be made of this ancient publication. . . .[7]

Muggeridge began with a clear idea of what he wanted *Punch* to become: "The business of a humorous or satirical magazine must be to ridicule the age in which we live, and particularly those set in authority over us."[8] After several issues on his own, he doubted his ability to bring it off. "I feel at the moment that the task is hopeless."[9]

His own previous experience had been as a reporter and feature writer. Apart from occasionally filling in for Coote at the *Telegraph*, he had little editorial background and none at all in administrative, financial, or personnel matters. Like any recent incumbent, he was inclined to stress what he knew best and that was news. He dropped the pastoral sketches, the illustrated poems, the quaint anecdotes about marriage and children; in their place, he put satire, invective, gossip, and occasionally straight news stories. *Punch* became topical and opinionated. Putting the magazine to press, once a quiet, timeless ritual, took on the excitement of a newsroom covering an ever-changing news story; articles were jammed in at press time so as not to be left behind. He showed the way in trenchant and cutting editorials, and the cartoonists followed suit, turning their attention away from bumbling gentlemen in country houses to people in the news—politicians, archbishops, press barons, lords, and ladies. Tradition was broken by experimenting with *Punch's* cover, hitherto unchanged for over a century. Typography was streamlined. Parodies of British institutions and the press became regular features. The BBC, in particular, Muggeridge proclaimed "a heaven sent target" because ". . . it takes itself seriously, believes it has a mission, and is pompous about it—all things *Punch* is interested in puncturing."[10] *Punch's* humor was now acerbic and pointed as well as funny, as in this guide on "How to be a Successful British Diplomat":

> (1) When an international agreement is unilaterally denounced, insure that any formal protests you are instructed to make are as hesitant and equivocal as possible . . . (2) Remember that nowadays the glittering prizes are given for feats of demolition, not of construction . . . Every diplomat carries a peerage in his knapsack, provided only that he keeps retreating . . . (3) Do not allow seeming setbacks to lower your spirit. Rather, they should be made the occasion for displaying even more complacency and self-satisfaction than before; (4) In politics you should incline to the left. If you can combine this with ample private means and socially distinguished connections, so much the better. (5) No opportunity should be missed of taking a sly dig at Americans and their policies. Indeed potential allies everywhere should be treated as somewhat ludicrous if not downright despicable.[11]

He also invited contributions from distinguished authors, and many, like Joyce Cary, J. B. Priestley, Noel Coward, and Dorothy L. Sayers, accepted. When he called in an old wartime debt, the name P. G. Wodehouse reappeared in *Punch* for the first time in years. R. G. G.

Price, the historian of *Punch*, wrote of Muggeridge's early days at 10 Bouverie Street: "He bounced in determined to make changes fast while the revolution was in progress and to change too much rather than not enough, arguing that this was the only way in which change could be made."[12]

Results were soon apparent. Within months the drop in circulation had been arrested; by the end of his first year in the chair, circulation was up over ten percent.

But not all readers were happy. The Churchill cartoon, mentioned previously, touched off a terrific row, including a letter to Muggeridge from Randolph Churchill, who had been a former colleague at *The Evening Standard*, canceling their friendship as well as his subscription. The cartoon itself, skilfully drawn by Leslie Illingworth, showed the former prime minister slumped at his desk, the effects of a paralytic stroke of the previous summer evident on his face, and underneath it was the caption: "Man goeth forth unto his work and to his labour until the evening." In an accompanying editorial, Muggeridge wrote, ostensibly of the decline of a Byzantine ruler, Bellarius:

> By this time he had reached an advanced age and might have been expected to settle down to an honourable retirement. . . . Instead he clung to power with tenacious intensity. His splendid faculties began to falter. The spectacle of him thus clutching wearily at all the appurtenances and responsibilities of an authority he could no longer fully exercise was to his admirers infinitely sorrowful, and to his enemies infinitely derisory.[13]

The resulting storm was not unforeseen. Claud Cockburn met Muggeridge at the rail station in Limerick just before the Churchill issue appeared: "As he sprang from the train [he] remarked with profound satisfaction that the issue of the magazine he had just sent to press was 'likely to get us all in a lot more hot water.' "[14]

Among those upset were Bradbury, Agnew and Company. Only their public pledge of a free hand and their contractual commitments spared Muggeridge from being sacked.

Before the Churchill row had died down, another one flared up, this time over another Illingworth cartoon depicting Anthony Eden returning from Geneva in the same way that Neville Chamberlain returned from Munich. Eden, incidentally, was among Muggeridge's favorite whipping boys; in an article in *The New Statesman* he had included the sentence: "Better a Churchill senile than an Eden in full possession of his faculties, such as they are,"[15] thereby managing to give fresh offense to both camps.

Abusive letters and canceled subscriptions poured in, from maiden ladies in Bognor Regis, retired generals and admirals in Tunbridge Wells, from clerics in vicarages around the country—all readers who regarded humor as a sedative rather than a stimulant. Muggeridge was called cruel, disrespectful, ungrateful, a guttersnipe of execrable taste, unworthy of the editorial traditions of a once great institution, etcetera, etcetera. Few, however, managed to puff up their indignation as pompously or at such length as Beverly Baxter, M.P., who belabored Muggeridge through twenty-five hundred words and finished up charging him with ". . . grave disservice to the British people."[16] No less a personage than the Archbishop of Canterbury momentarily turned his attention from his dwindling flock to reprove *Punch* and its wayward editor. To His Grace's letter, Muggeridge replied:

> My Dear Archbishop:
> It was very kind and considerate of you to write to me yourself about the question of bad taste in *Punch*. I've thought and thought about this question ever since I became editor.
> My own conclusion is (and you probably won't agree with it) that humour itself is in bad taste, as also, incidentally, is truth. I'm sure that the Pharisees (men of taste) rightly felt Our Lord was often guilty of bad taste—for instance, when He said that the Sabbath was made for man and not man for the Sabbath. Equally, the gargoyles that adorn our cathedrals are in bad taste, though I personally love them, and always think of them when I am trying to convince myself that editing *Punch* is a worthwhile job.

Muggeridge's letter went on to define humor as the disparity between that perfection to which man aspires (the kingdom of heaven) and what he actually achieves (the kingdoms of the earth), and then concluded with this concise statement of his own religious position.

> I am, alas, not myself a believing Christian. I wish I were. But one thing I can say with the utmost sincerity, and that is that I grow evermore convinced that the Christian gospel was the most wonderful thing that ever happened to the world; that it represents the nearest to ultimate truth that has yet been revealed to mankind; that our civilization was born of it, is irretrievably bound up with it, and would most certainly perish without it; that the basic trouble with the world today is that false prophets (some of them professing Christians) preach that man can live by bread alone which is truly blasphemous. If anything ever appeared in *Punch* which contradicted these convictions I should be ashamed indeed. I don't believe it has.[17]

In print Muggeridge proclaimed himself "impenitently a champion of bad taste," and pointed out that it was a sign of decrepitude, not of strength, that brought forth charges of bad taste. Only when institutions and values have come to seem dubious are they so vociferously championed. Strength needs no such defenders. The row over the cartoons, he declared, was ". . . no more than a means of evading disagreeable truths, a smoke screen to protect a tottering citadel from assaults which it has little hope of being able to withstand." In any case, what good was a satirical magazine if not ". . . to provide a minefield over which politicians and administrators must proceed warily and at their own risk. They are repositories of bad taste or they are nothing."[18]

Another project Muggeridge conceived was to marshal the talents of *Punch* on stage. The result was a much heralded but little patronized production, *The Punch Revue*, at the Duke of York Theatre. On opening night, one voice could clearly be heard above the babble during the first intermission loudly proclaiming: "This is a flop d'estime." Probably Muggeridge derived as much satisfaction from that remark as he would have from a stage hit.

As editor, he was as generous with *Punch*'s money as he has always been with his own. As soon as he took the chair, he doubled the commission paid to writers and artists. Once, a writer acquaintance down on his luck rang up to ask for an urgent loan of twenty pounds. When he showed up at *Punch*, Muggeridge handed him a sealed envelope and they talked of this and that. When the writer left, he opened the envelope and found five twenty pound notes. Efforts to repay the loan later were spurned.

Never had the magazine had so controversial an editor, nor one so often in the public eye. Muggeridge was at the center of the row over commercial television, which he supported, and the BBC and many of the Establishment opposed. In the space of a month he debated the issue with Lord Radcliffe, Christopher Mayhew, Lady Violet Bonham-Carter, and Lord Hailsham. His advocacy of commercial television was based, not on any affection for the medium, still less on any sanguine expectation about program content (most of which he publicly dismissed as "nonsensical and bestial") but on the threat to free thought and the stultifying conformity of a government broadcasting monopoly. His favorite debating trick was to remind audiences that Churchill had been denied an opportunity to broadcast in the thirties because of his opposition to the policy of appeasement. "My purpose," Muggeridge declared, "is to break the monopoly of the BBC. . ." which without competition, he called ". . . a dangerous step in the direction of collective servility."[19] To the Overseas Press Club in New York he said: "Monopoly whether in terms of the monolithic totalitarian state, or of a national institution, like the BBC, is the enemy of freedom and produces at last, a hard, turgid monotony of thought and practise."[20] The campaign for independent television was ultimately successful, although the end result disappointed him. "Any hope that the BBC, confronted with competition, would lose some of its pomposity and unction has been disappointed, as has any hope that the commercial network would prove less essentially conformist in temper."[21]

While the commercial television debate was going on, he crossed swords with Tom Driberg, the Labour M.P. for Barking, who, in extravagant terms, had attacked American foreign policy as aggressive and imperialist and advocated British disengagement from Western Europe and withdrawal from NATO. Muggeridge replied in a full page article called "Anatomy of Neutralism" in *Time* magazine, in which he argued that the primary flaw in American foreign policy was that it was not aggressive or imperialist enough but rather sentimental and imprecise, seeking to evade the realities of international power politics in the abstractions of democratic theory. Driberg's "neutralism" he compared to the fellow-travelers in the thirties who had praised the Nazi-Soviet nonaggression pact as a way for Britain to steer clear of entanglement in an imperialist war against Germany. His conclusion to this article succinctly stated his own position on the topic that dominated public discussion in the mid-fifties, the Cold War.

> If I accept, as millions of other Western Europeans do, that America is destined to be the mainstay of freedom in this mid-20th century world, it does not follow that American institutions are perfect, that Americans are invariably well-behaved, or that the American way of life is flawless. It only means that in one of the most terrible conflicts in human history, I have chosen my side, as all will have to choose sooner or later, and propose to stick by the side I have chosen through thick and thin, hoping to have sufficient courage not to lose heart, sufficient sense not to allow myself to be confused or deflected from this purpose, and sufficient faith in the civilization to which I belong, and in the religion on which that civilization is based, to follow Bunyan's advice and endure the hazards and humiliations of the way because of the worth of the destination.[22]

This is as close as Muggeridge has ever come to an explicit declaration of political allegiance and, perhaps for that reason, he does not particularly like to be reminded of it. When *Things Past*, an anthology of his writings, was being prepared, this was the only quotation he proposed deleting. However, it stayed in.

Early in 1956 it was announced that Nikita Khrushchev and Marshal Bulganin would make official state visits to England at the invitation of the government. Together with Auberon Herbert and the anti-Communist Congress for Cultural Freedom (a curious organization, originally composed of Polish expatriates and financed mainly and

190

clandestinely by CIA money, which later midwifed the birth of *Encounter* magazine), Muggeridge set about mounting a protest. Petitions were circulated, letters written, speeches made, and all the activity was planned to culminate in a giant rally at the Albert Hall on March 25. Ten days before, and despite a firm commitment, the management of the hall canceled the booking. Efforts to book other locations in London proved unavailing. Finally (and at his own expense) Muggeridge got the Free Trade Hall in Manchester where the meeting took place a day later, on March 26, 1956. Dozens of telegrams of support arrived, many of them sent at some personal risk from East European countries; some came addressed not to the Free Trade Hall but the Free Speech Hall. The audience, estimated at three thousand, filled all available seats, and many were turned away.

"It is possible to guess," Muggeridge began his address, "who was behind the Albert Hall cancellation—after all, guessing has not yet been nationalized." He expressed delight to be standing on the same platform with "humble exiles" and the platform party—"a singularly undistinguished lot"—rather than "to be in the position of Her Majesty's government and be compelled to be engaged in amiable social intercourse with Marshal Bulganin and Mr. Khrushchev. . . ." He paid special tribute to the support received from two distinct groups, East European exiles and Roman Catholics.

"What we are protesting against," he went on, "is not so much a visit, or an ill-conceived or fatuous diplomatic initiative—although expecting B. and K. to reform their ways as a result of seeing our free way of life is like asking two professional ladies from the Moulin Rouge to attend Roedean in the hope that they will marry Archdeacons and settle down to a life of quiet respectability; no, what we are protesting against is evil itself."[23]

By all accounts the meeting was exciting, dramatic, and utterly futile. It finished up by passing a resolution saying that "However much the people of Britain may long for friendship with the Russian people, there can be no mutual trust while the Soviet Union remains Communist, maintains slave labour camps, attacks religion and persecutes those who practise it, and continues to hold in thrall the nations of Eastern Europe."[24] This resolution was to be forwarded to the prime minister at whose invitation the two ". . . seasoned professional terrorists and their grisly entourage of sycophants and gunmen," as Muggeridge called them, came in the first place. Still, one columnist wrote that ". . . the spectacle at the end of the meeting of that leading loyalist, Mr. Malcolm Muggeridge, joining lustily in the national anthem made the journey to Manchester worthwhile."[25]

When the Russian leaders actually arrived (to a nineteen-gun salute, smiles, and handshakes all around), Muggeridge traveled the length and breadth of the country holding protest rallies. In Coventry he admitted to feeling ". . . a brief pang of pity" for them [the Russian visitors] on learning that they had spent twenty hours at Number 10 Downing Street ". . . talking to the greatest bore in Christendom."[26] In Glasgow, he said that a queen, whose titles include Defender of the Faith "ought not to. . . ." He got no further. James D. Millar, a magistrate, leaped to his feet and shouted from the second balcony that Muggeridge must "withdraw that remark." Muggeridge managed to finish his speech without further interruption and later laughed off the rather improbable suggestion, apparently originating with Mr. Millar, that his opposition to the Russian visit was undertaken under orders from the Pope.

While Bulganin and Khrushchev were in London, Muggeridge led a march of twenty thousand people, the largest postwar demonstration in Britain, to the Cenotaph in Whitehall where wreaths were laid in memory of Polish freedom. Afterwards he delivered a petition to the prime minister containing sixty thousand signatures protesting against the visit.

The day after the Manchester rally, Radio Moscow proclaimed that Bulganin and Khrushchev ". . . care nothing for the emotions of the editor of *Punch*,"[27] while *The Daily Worker* lamented the decline of "poor old *Punch*" to "the house organ of a political crank."[28] When challenged to debate his position by a left wing M.P., Muggeridge went to the Oxford Union and successfully carried the motion—"This House refuses to believe that there has been any change in the Russian policy of world domination"—by a vote of 237 to 173.

Apart from receiving hundreds of letters, including some extremely poignant ones from former victims of the Gulag Archipelago, the main effect of his campaign was to make Muggeridge and his implacably anti-Communist position better known. He has since been much in demand as a speaker by exile and dissident groups. Inevitably this has led to some misunderstanding, because, while sharing their abhorrence of the Soviet regime, he does not share their sanguine expectations of the West. He has never conceived of the worldwide power struggle between East and West as susceptible to moralistic analysis, or as involving a righteous conflict between universal suffrage democracy and totalitarianism. In fact, it is the similarity between the two systems, their mutual and undeviating dedication to materialism, rather than their differences, that most intrigues him. Both ideologies appear to be agreed on the end to be achieved, i.e., a constantly expanding gross national product to satisfy the appetites of their citizenry; they differ primarily on means. What the people of the Soviet

Editor of *Punch*, 1958

Savouring a point

As the Gryphon in Jonathan Miller's
'Alice in Wonderland' dancing the
Lobster Quadrille with Alice
(Anne-Marie Mallick) and the Mock
Turtle (Sir John Gielgud), 1966

With Lord Reith during filming of 'Lord Reith Looks Back', 1969

Union want is not the dictatorship of the proletariat and the withering away of the state, but cars, refrigerators, and color televisions; Marks and Spencer rather than Marx.

The same principle applies, in his view, to comparisons of the media in each country. In Communist countries, all communications media are subject to central control and put out one line on public affairs; hence their excruciating boredom. In the West, by contrast, there are a variety of communications media, yet all purvey the same essential message—that the point of life is to pursue happiness, to be beautiful, successful, and wealthy, prepared to rearrange the natural life processes—indeed humanity itself—if necessary to achieve happiness. Like two adjacent rifle ranges; in one all the shots hit the bull's-eye; in the other they cluster around the target; but in both the marksmen fire in the same direction. The effect of the mass media in both countries, Muggeridge contends, is to induce in those subjected to them a mood of acceptance, in the one case total and specific, in the other vague and generalized.

In fact, Muggeridge does not distinguish between just and unjust governments at all, but only between bearable and unbearable ones. Thus, for example, he would say that Franco's Spain was more bearable than Tito's Yugoslavia, yet both are unjust, inequal, and unrepresentative. Similarly he would rather live in Washington than Moscow, or Japan than Communist China, while recognizing that in both the exercise of power leads to abuses and misfortunes. In the Soviet Union the bookstalls do not stock Solzhenitsyn (whom Muggeridge has called "the most noble and important man of our time") but nor do they stock the pornography that overflows the shelves in Soho or Washington, D.C. One's freedom to walk about the streets of Moscow is limited; in Washington one is free to walk anywhere but risks one's life to do so. And so on. He would never contend that there is nothing to choose between the relative freedom of the West and the relative servitude of communism—that is a truly wicked argument. What he would say is that power inevitably means that some wield it over others and so abuses—differing only in type and extent—there must ever be, and that those who repose their hopes for justice and freedom and equality in one form of ideology or another must ever be disillusioned.

Punch's owners were becoming increasingly disconcerted at the public visibility of their editor and by the extent to which the magazine increasingly reflected his political philosophy. The "Russian" issue in the middle of a state visit, while praised for its topicality and professionalism (the cover showed the prime minister pulling a carriage with B. and K. lounging in it, and the lead cartoon had the Queen offering a bun to a simian-looking Czar Alexander II) once again ruffled important feathers. Too many subscriptions of long standing had been canceled and while, from a purely economic point of view they had been more than made up for by new readers, the magazine's clientele was less well-placed and influential than formerly. The owners increasingly resented their editor's cavalier ways, such as telling a *New York Times* reporter exactly how profitable *Punch* was. And he increasingly resented having to justify his actions. A parting of the ways was inevitable.

No single reason was responsible for Muggeridge's leaving although the breakdown of plans for a Canadian edition played a part in it, as did the owner's decision, without consulting him, to remove some satirical verses about the Prince of Wale's preparatory school. Most important, though, was boredom. Throughout his life, in all of his jobs he has demonstrated a low boredom threshold which, when crossed, means he packs it in, usually with a well-timed elbow to his boss's teeth on the way out. Claud Cockburn, who called each Monday morning to sort out a topic for his weekly article, noticed a gradual change in Muggeridge's attitude.

> For a long time, these conversations were, as they say, "constructive", in the sense that I could hear the whole thing coming to life as we talked. . . . Gradually, however, he showed less and less inclination to talk about material for *Punch*, entertaining me instead with scandalous gossip or Christianity or television. Often, particularly if the long distance line from Ireland was in poor shape as a result of tempest or other interruption, I would suggest that since we might get abruptly cut off at any minute, we ought perhaps to turn to practical discussion of my next article. "Hell, my dear boy, I leave all that to you. Write anything you like." . . . Later still he once confessed to me that he found it nearly impossible to start reading any of the articles in *Punch* until the paper was actually in page proof. He had to postpone until the last moment paying attention to a matter which had come to bore him so cruelly.[29]

On May 7, 1957, his diary reads: "Usual office day. Increasingly bored by *Punch* routine. Ought really to give the job up, sometimes think of doing so; then hesitate because it's easy money, and, by virtue of being editor things turn up." He had been editor for nearly five years, and they had been hectic, draining years. Transforming *Punch* had been difficult; his journalistic output remained high, in *Punch* and elsewhere; he had campaigned up and down the country in support of his causes; he had undertaken grueling lecture tours in Australia, Canada, South Africa, and the United States; and he had established himself as one of the country's best known broadcasters. He was worn out. He smoked and drank heavily and had a reputation for womanizing, although few of his Fleet Street colleagues were entitled to cast a stone on that account. He was tormented by insomnia and required stronger and stronger sedatives to sleep. In fact, had it not been for Kitty's devoted ministrations, he would have destroyed at least his health, and perhaps his life, during this period.

Also, he wanted to return to his own writing. In April 1957, he wrote in his diary that he probably had only twelve to fifteen years of writing left and much to accomplish: "(1) Play—'Life and the Legend'; (2) long short novel: 'Love in the Fifties'; (3) series of long reminiscent biographical essays on the Webbs, Orwell, my father, P. G. Wodehouse affair, etc.; (4) long novel 'Hero of Our Time' starting with observation in Café 'I sometimes wonder if I'm licking the right boots.' "[30] Of this list it is interesting that only a few short biographical articles were ever done (although Muggeridge still darkly threatens to emulate John Aubrey and produce "Muggeridge's Brief Lives"—"absolutely scabrous, dear boy, absolutely scabrous"), and that his plan for George Orwell had already been scaled down from a full-length biography to an essay.

On July 27, 1957, Bradbury, Agnew and Company announced that ". . . having completed the period for which he originally undertook the editorship, Malcolm Muggeridge is resigning effective October 1, 1957." Publicly he said that the job had been "tremendous fun" and that he was leaving to get on with his own writing. On the *Tonight* program he claimed his relations with his employers had been characterized by "total amity," and that his purpose, namely to make *Punch* ". . . as acerbic and offensive as possible,"[31] had now been achieved. Actually, though his departure was amiable enough, it was so only because of a £5,000 severance payment which meant, he reflected privately, that ". . . the only way to make any money in journalism is to be sacked or to leave a job in circumstances which one's employer can be persuaded or induced to regard as requiring some salving."[32]

On his last day at *Punch* he wrote in his diary: "For me it was now all over. I emptied my desk, which is so like emptying one's pockets. I removed the few traces of my five years' occupancy of the room, and made off, as so often before, down Bouverie Street, through the Inner Temple and along the Embankment; but this time not to return. There is a great joy in leaving a job, any job, a great joy in slipping away from anywhere or anyone. And yet, of course, mixed with the joy, a certain anguish. It is something over, a sanctuary lost."[33]

The BBC, where he now spent an increasing amount of time, could scarcely be said to be a sanctuary gained, more like a brothel where his vanity was caressed at the expense of his intellect; to be shamefacedly entered, the facilities exploited, and furtively left, hoping that few were watching.

His broadcasting career had begun in 1947 as a panel member of *The Critics*. From the beginning he was of two minds about it: "Agonizing to refuse the money but more agonizing to appear in the programme."[34] The idea was that each of the four critics saw a new film or play, listened to a program, read a book, went to an art exhibition, and then came together to talk about it. The programs were prerecorded, which was fortunate since, on his first one, Muggeridge was reprimanded by Donald Boyd because ". . . some of my remarks had had to be cut out because they were too strong."[35] More often the problem was tedium rather than controversy. At *Punch* he once attempted to produce a parody of *The Critics* to be called *The Pundits*, but a glance through old scripts convinced him it was hopeless. How could one satirize four grown men sitting about in a studio on a sunny afternoon analyzing a Third Program discussion between a Chinese philosopher and a Cumbrian shepherd?

Broadcasting House itself seemed to him unpleasant—the darkened, airless studios, troglodyte figures moving about soundlessly behind glass partitions, the ever-present cup with its always brackish water. It would be fitting, he thought, if everyone entering the building were required to put on a long white coat. "There is something peculiarly oppressive and depressing about the whole atmosphere of Broadcasting House. It is rather like a totalitarian state, full of uneasiness—very building somewhat prison-like. It reminded me of being in Russia."[36] Still there was also an undeniable fascination about the whole thing; early on, he wrote: "Rather intrigued by the idea of mastering broadcasting techniques, which is entirely different from journalism or public speaking."[37]

His first solo effort was a BBC radio broadcast on May 30, 1948, about the Webbs. A repeat broadcast, scheduled for June 21, was canceled when Lady Simon, wife of the then chairman of the BBC, objected to Muggeridge's astringent tone. So his broadcasting career began with a row, has been a series of more or less continual rows since, and must be considered likely to end with a row. The letter informing him of the cancellation of the Webb broadcast came from George Barnes, whose title—"Director of the Spoken Word"—matched his pomposity; while promising that his fee would be paid, he wrote that he was sure Muggeridge would agree that ". . . the overriding consideration must be to preserve sensibilities."[38] At that time the BBC still enjoyed an absolute monopoly on broadcasting, and those who wished to avail themselves of the airways could easily be induced to be compliant.

"Any who erred and strayed, failing to heed the sheepdog's admonitory bark, were just excluded from the flock."[99]

After *The Critics* came *The Brains Trust, Any Question?, Panorama, Let Me Speak, The Question Why,* and many other, often frivolous, programs. One consequence of this exposure, in fact massive overexposure, is that there are two quite distinct views of Muggeridge. Abroad, where he has seldom been seen on television, and then only in weightier programs like *A Third Testament* in which some pride could justifiably be taken, he is known almost exclusively as a writer and thinker. Mention of his name suggests, not a puckish image on a television screen, but articles and books. In England, by contrast, he is still thought of as a "telly man," a "talking head," even now when he seldom appears on television. As a result, it is in Canada, the United States, Australia, New Zealand, and South Africa, rather than in England, that his books sell best. It is abroad that he draws overflow audiences whenever he speaks and where he receives honorary degrees (mostly unwelcome). In England, he still carries, like an albatross, the old labels—"Telly Mugg," "the man you love to hate," the "pop Socrates," or "the poor man's Voltaire." Abroad he is appreciated as a consummate writer, the most influential lay exponent of Christianity since C. S. Lewis, and an authentic prophet of our confused time.

Throughout their long association, relations between Muggeridge and the BBC have been like those of a crumbling marriage, full of acrimonious bickering, infidelities and separations, yet somehow staggering on because of some mutual dependence. It is not difficult to understand the BBC's advantage. In Muggeridge they had discovered a congenial, witty talker capable of dealing intelligently with a serious subject and humorously with a silly one. Courteous but never sycophantic; controversial but seldom rude; absolutely never dull. A probing, skeptical interviewer unafraid to ask an Ursuline nun about her vow of chastity, a cardinal if there really was an afterlife, or to tell Bertrand Russell that his conception of human intelligence was a pipe dream.

So prodigious are Muggeridge's broadcasting talents that however much listeners affected to dislike him and his views, his presence on any program virtually guaranteed an increase in the ratings. The result of such exposure is celebrity, which is quite different from popularity or influence; one becomes famous simply for being seen—in the end becoming famous for being famous. Whether or not one's words have the desired effect, or indeed *any* effect, is quite another matter. As Dr. Johnson discovered (and who should know better than he?): "There is nothing by which a man exasperates most people more than by displaying a superior ability or brilliancy in conversation. They seem pleased at the time; but their envy makes them curse him in their hearts."

But what of Muggeridge? Why did he appear so much on a medium he affects to despise and whose influence he considers malign? He usually responds to this question by comparing his participation to a pianist in a brothel who occasionally includes "Abide With Me" in his repertoire, in the hope of consoling, if not actually reforming, the inmates. A less diverting, but truer, explanation is that he is a working journalist who earns his living by words, written and spoken. His free-lancing years taught him just how precarious such an existence can be and conditioned him, almost as a reflex, to say yes to whatever proposal is made to him. Even so, it must be admitted that he has spent an inordinate amount of time on frivolous programs that do little credit to his intellect. Even these he hardly regrets, just forgets, and marvels that people actually choose to spend time watching such nonsense. As far back as 1927, he said to Alec Vidler: ". . . it is possible to be attracted by what one despises."[40] However much he despises television, it also has an irresistible attraction for him. He readily concedes that most of his broadcasting falls into the category Dr. Johnson reserved for the plot of *Cymbeline*—"unresisting imbecility"—but nevertheless he goes on doing it, partly for income, partly because he likes showing off, partly to gratify a still ravening ego, and, occasionally, as in his religious broadcasts on Mother Teresa, Jean Vanier, and others, because he feels that there is something important to be said to people who will not be reached through any other medium. He once gave this explanation when the question was put to him directly: "I have tried to appear on TV as little as possible. You have to do a bit of it, of course, if you have a family to feed, and books to promote. You have to try to make a bargain with the people who have the money. You make a deal—a little unrighteousness for as much mammon as possible."[41]

Shortly before he left *Punch* he spent a fortnight in America. The editors of *The Saturday Evening Post* asked him then for a five-thousand-word feature article and, with little forethought or enthusiasm, he agreed. By the time it appeared in print, on October 19, 1957, Muggeridge had left *Punch* and quite forgotten the piece that essentially repeated some not very startling observations he had made two years before about the monarchy in a *New Statesman* piece called "Royal Soap Opera." The gist of it was that a materialist society is especially prone to hero worship and, having by and large ceased to believe in God, it pays increasing obeisance to a queen or royal family, making of a symbol ("no bad thing in itself") a kind of substitute or ersatz religion. A constitutional monarchy is desirable, he wrote, so long as its function was acknowledged to be purely ceremonial, granting baubles like knighthoods and peerages, and sitting atop the social pyramid in terms of class and social distinction. The Queen may reign so long as it is recognized that she does not rule. But when people begin to take it all seriously—as, for example, the BBC announcer who remarked in hushed tones at the coronation how all the burdens of an empire had now fallen on the Queen's frail shoulders—then it had become patently ridiculous; like saying that the burdens of Woolworth's rested on the frail, or not so frail, shoulders of Barbara Hutton.

It is unlikely that the article would have raised an eyebrow in the ordinary course of things; however, its publication happened to coincide with the beginning of a royal tour of Canada and the United States, and the British press, having got wind of it in advance from *The Saturday Evening Post,* smelled blood and pounced. The result was the most celebrated and acrimonious row in Muggeridge's turbulent career.

For sheer falsification and distortion, *The People,* followed closely by *The Sunday Express* (both papers engaged in a long-term vendetta with Muggeridge), led the pack. A week before the article ever appeared, *The People* ran a banner headline: "America Prints Amazing Royal Attack by English TV Idol"; the accompanying story described the, as yet unseen, article as: "ruthless, shocking, patronizing, gruesome, [and] a diatribe."[42] As one among many examples of distortion, Muggeridge was accused of having described the monarchy as ". . . a club for snobs and a drain on the British taxpayer." In fact, he never once referred to it as "a club for snobs," and what he actually wrote about the cost of the monarchy was this: "Those sour-faced journalists who specialize in being thought independent, but who are often, in relation to their employers, among the most sycophantic of men, are likely to write in such a vein. We just can't afford it, they suggest . . . Actually, compared to the cost of atomic submarines or guided missiles, the monarchy cannot be considered expensive."[43] Totally overlooked by Muggeridge's critics were sentences like this: "The British monarchy does fulfil an authentic purpose providing a symbolic head of state, transcending the politicians who go in and out of office, and proving extremely popular to the majority of people."

Public reaction to the article was immediate and hysterical. Muggeridge received abusive and threatening telephone calls. Letters arrived containing razor blades and human excrement. Some letters expressed pleasure at the recent death in a skiing accident of his son, Charles. "It means one Muggeridge less," wrote one enlightened scribe. Their house was vandalized, and their garage door and an adjacent barn (actually belonging to a neighbor) were sprayed with loyalist slogans for which the League of Empire Loyalists stepped forward to claim responsibility. The paint, Muggeridge noticed, was the same yellow color that had been used in Berlin in the late thirties to mark Jewish homes and shops. "Yellow must make a particular appeal to yahoos," he commented. Neighbors refused to allow him to take his customary walk along their hop fields. At a Unionist rally, Sir George Clark proclaimed that Muggeridge should be horsewhipped. The vicar of Chosley in Berkshire told a reporter: "He has a face it would be most satisfying to poke—the sort of face one just wishes to flatten out . . . . My study will be at Mr. Muggeridge's disposal and I will gladly provide a steak for his black eye." When this little homily was conveyed to Muggeridge, he replied: "Going to see the vicar would bore me. He is obviously a crackpot and I like talking to sane people."[44] In Brighton a man walking along the seafront came up to him and, without a word, spat in his face and walked on.

When Muggeridge went to Edinburgh to meet with the students who had nominated him to contest the rectorship of Edinburgh University, he required a police escort to leave the train at Waverly station. A press conference was disrupted by demonstrators who broke in chanting "God Save the Queen" and "No Mercy for Muggeridge." The day before the voting, his two principal student sponsors were kidnapped and left trussed up and gagged overnight in a deserted hostel. In the result, Muggeridge placed fifth in a field of eleven, polling 246 votes to the 1,003 of the winning candidate, James Robertson Justice.

The day the story broke in the British press, the BBC invited him to face his critics on *Panorama*. Two days later, five hours before the program was to take place, his appearance was canceled and the BBC issued the following press release: "We have come to the conclusion that we should not give further publicity to a matter which has already had enough."[45] The banning order came directly from Sir Ian Jacob, thenceforth to be known as "Sir Ban," but speculation was rife that it had in fact been ordered by Prime Minister Harold Macmillan. Muggeridge's reaction? "I am naturally distressed, but not, I confess, surprised. The BBC moves in mysterious ways its wonders to perform." Actually, it was a nice bit of fearful symmetry, although he may not have savored it at the time. He had become living vindication of his own arguments during the commercial television debate about the dangers of a government monopoly on broadcasting and, since he was then under exclusive contract to the BBC, he could not avail himself of the commercial network he had helped to bring about to make any reply.

So, with *The Saturday Evening Post* still not yet out, he flew to New York to be interviewed by Mike Wallace, "the Rocky Marciano of television," as Wallace was billed by CBS. The night before the program a senior CBS executive attempted to persuade Wallace to cancel the interview citing as his reason that "The Queen is the only bulwark against Communism." It was too much. Muggeridge went into fits of uncontrolled laughter, conjuring up pictures of Nikita Khrushchev holding his head in his hands in the Kremlin, stymied in his plans for world conquest by the English monarchy. To his credit, Wallace refused to be intimidated and went ahead with the interview. According to Alistair Cooke, who was there, Muggeridge reduced Wallace to ". . . a puppy eating out of his enemy's hand";[46] afterwards, Wallace conceded his "inability to shatter Mr. Muggeridge's aplomb."[47] The broadcast was blacked out in Washington to avoid giving possible offense to the royal party who were staying there.

On arrival back in England, Muggeridge discovered that *The Sunday Dispatch*, which only two weeks before had proudly announced their contract with "the most controversial writer in Britain today," had dumped him at the first sign of controversy. The BBC made it clear that he would never appear on television again. In fact when they used a film clip of an interview that he recorded with Augustus John before the monarchy row ever started, they had 150 letters and calls of protest from irate viewers. Ironically one of the few voices raised in his defense came from an old nemesis, *The Manchester Guardian*. In a leader on November 15, 1957, they wrote: "Anti-Muggeridgism has recently taken on the appearance of pre-war anti-semitism. Hysterical and obscene misrepresentations and misquotations have all been brought into the battle. It would be nice to say that they have all failed, but this would not be true. Muggeridge has been exposed to a campaign which the mildest supporter of Voltaire would have to oppose."[48]

At this point Muggeridge consulted a respected London barrister who, however, cautioned him against taking any action. True enough, the barrister said, the initial distorted newspaper accounts might well be considered libelous, but it would be virtually impossible to find an impartial judge and jury. "It was eerie and a little alarming to have the theory of 'people's justice', as administered in the Communist countries, thus expounded by this Dickensian figure—winged collar, dark suit, liability to press his fingertips together—in the antique quiet and tranquility of one of London's Inns of the Court."[49]

His only recourse was to file a complaint with the Press Council. In thirty years of journalism he wrote "I have tried to report events and express views as truthfully and vigorously as I could." After citing specific examples of misquotation and distortion by *The People* and *The Sunday Express*, he concluded: "A journalist's single asset is his reputation. To deprive him of this by distorting and falsifying his words is surely an infringement of the journalistic standards which it is the Press Council's statutory duty to uphold."[50]

After a long delay, the Press Council ruled against him, exonerating the papers in question, and concluding that Muggeridge was the author of his own misfortune. Needless to say, he replied pungently: "The so-called Press Council is a stuffed shirt. Its members come straight out of *Absalom and Achitophel*, recalling Doeg, who 'for almonds will cry whore to his own Mother.' When, from time to time they administer ponderous and self-righteous rebukes to individual journalists and newspapers, I am always reminded of how Mr. Winkle, having got involved in a fracas along with the rest of the Pickwick club, was seen to take off his coat and begin belabouring a small boy. It did not surprise me, therefore, that far from providing any redress when I found myself in the stocks, they joined the caterwaulers."[51]

In retrospect, the whole affair beggars belief. That (by his standards) so listless and pedestrian a piece in a family magazine in a foreign country should have touched off such a preposterous row with serious financial consequences for him, in a country ostensibly valuing free speech and fair play—who can account for it? Certainly the conduct of the BBC, *The People, The Sunday Dispatch*, and the popular press that ignited and kept the conflagration going was shameful. But what of the fabled commonsense of the ordinary British man who, even today, often associates the name Malcolm Muggeridge primarily with a row about the Queen? In one respect, of course, he was ahead of his time; two decades later a member of parliament could write a book calling for the abolition of the monarchy and scarcely an eyebrow was raised.

The monarchy row hurt him professionally, and undoubtedly contributed to the unwillingness of a segment of the British public to give serious attention to his writing and his views. Eventually, of course, it subsided, although it was still sufficiently alive in 1964 that Muggeridge had to resign his membership in the Garrick Club rather than submit to investigation by the club's executive of ". . . the propriety of a member of the Club speaking against the Monarchy."[52] And there was one final, and appropriately farcical, twist to the tale. In 1972 his friend Lord Longford became a Knight of the Garter and was presented to the Queen. Putting affection before discretion, Longford blurted out: "You know, Ma'am, Malcolm Muggeridge is really a very nice man." To which conversational gambit, Lord Longford's biographer records that the Queen made no audible reply but "looked thoughtful."[53]

·12·
A HUNGRY HEART

> . . . I am become a name;
> For always roaming with a hungry heart
> Much have I seen and known; cities of men
> And manners, climates, councils, governments.
>
> Alfred Tennyson, *Ulysses*

*   *   *

Banned from the BBC, with his only regular income from one article a week in *The Sunday Pictorial*, Muggeridge accepted an invitation to go to Australia for three months. Flying halfway around the world, dropping down from time to time in different climates and different lands, induced that numbing, trance-like state so peculiar to air travel. Incommodiously hurled across the sky, he could not but compare this to his first stately journey east aboard the S.S. *Moria* in 1924. Then the British Empire had seemed like an iron frame holding the area together; now there was no iron frame, and each country seemed more run-down, seedy, and confused than before. Even so, he rejoiced to find that those unaccountable flashes of illumination had not entirely deserted him: ". . . a sudden sense of serenity, clarity, like twiddling a radio set knob and getting confused sounds, and then suddenly it clarifies, a word, a meaning emerges."[1]

On the last leg of the flight, he was sandwiched between two unyielding talkers: One was a man who had started as a novice in a Franciscan order but given it up to become a script writer for television's *Flying Doctor* series; he filled Muggeridge's ear with how he tried to inject a bit of humor into the soap opera formula. In the other seat was the wife of the proprietor of *The Sydney Morning Herald* who meandered on about how marriage must be a relationship based on

203

perfect trust, mutual respect, etc.—"was not surprised to hear later in Sydney that she came back to a marital crisis."[2]

The plan was that he would move freely about the country, talking to Australians and writing on any topic that took his fancy. He began his assignment in Sydney, staying in a hotel catering to senior citizens, full of ". . . ancient ladies waiting to die—just the right place for me at the moment."[3] For his first story he sought out recent immigrants, questioning some aboard ship, others in transient reception centers, still others who had found private accommodations and a job and had begun to sink roots in their new country. Where had they come from, why, and what did they make of it? Their answers ran the gamut from the sublime—like the Hungarian who answered the question "Do you like it?": "Of course I like it. I like freedom"—to the contemptible, the latter mostly from British immigrants who complained at having to forego the elaborate social security arrangements back home. Of these, Muggeridge wrote: "The welfare state is a kind of zoo which provides its inmates with ease and comfort but unfits them for life in their natural habitat. Mangy and bleary-eyed, they grumble and growl as they walk up and down their cages wailing for slabs of welfare to be thrown to them at mealtime."[4]

Many immigrants, he discovered, came to Australia in search of one of the twentieth century's mythic gods, Equality. Australia was supposed to be free of class distinctions and the limiting traditions of the old country, a land of opportunity where everyone started with a fair chance. To check on this he visited Geelong Grammar School, "the Eton of the Antipodes," where the offspring of the wealthy patrician class were sent to be educated, and he spoke with its headmaster, Dr. Darling, and some of its graduates. Like their Etonian counterparts, Geelong graduates had a natural tendency to drift into the Foreign Office, that being thought a career worthy of their intellectual and social attainments, thus perhaps explaining an almost unbroken string of foreign policy reverses and failures. The graduates even looked alike, he noticed: ". . . of withdrawn face and sedate bearing . . . the funeral mutes who have followed the hearse of British policy from one disaster to another, without ever losing their breath, their composure or their infinite complacency."[5]

Controversy dogged his steps. "Australia is a rather remote and forlorn European outpost," he wrote, "10 million Europeans, mostly on the fringes of a vast continent, which geographically belongs to Asia." True enough, but not necessarily what the natives wanted to hear. In a nationwide broadcast, he told them: "Honesty compels me to admit that I have sometimes seen this country, even the great city of Sydney, as only a kind of temporary camp which no one has bothered to make permanent. It has seemed to me that a holocaust of history could sweep it away, not even leaving behind substantial ruins as the Romans did in the Middle East."[6] For such remarks, Muggeridge was branded a "prophet of doom," "a merchant of fear," or just the all-purpose stand-by "pessimist."

In the capital of Canberra, he was intrigued to discover that activity in the legislative chamber was signified by keeping a red light burning through the night. Parliamentary proceedings were broadcast, and from the gallery he watched how, as the peak listening hours approached, oratory grew more fervid, quips got sharper, and interjections became more spirited and frequent. Occasionally a member would use the opportunity to shout a personal message to some friend or relative back in his constituency, thereby hardly enhancing the esteem in which parliament was held.

He recorded a television series entitled *Malcolm Muggeridge Meets Australians* with leading politicians, most of whom retained an almost reverential awe for all things British and labored to recreate England's green and pleasant land on the fringe of Asia. The deputy government leader, Sir Arthur Fadden, for example, spoke of ". . . what I am still old-fashioned enough to call the British Empire." When Muggeridge pointed out to him that this was like calling a broken-down vintage Rolls Royce a coach and four, Sir Arthur took it amiss. When he followed this up with an article pointing out that there was no British Empire, no, nor even commonwealth, except in the sense of a holding company set up to dispose of the Empire's dwindling, residual assets, this was said to be provocative and inflammatory and called forth spirited defenses of the commonwealth from retired ex-captains of the Hampshire regiment with addresses in Melbourne and doughty school teachers residing in Brisbane.

But the highlight of his Australian wanderings was the remote, barren Northern Territory where a cattle station might be as large as England. This area was still governed by administrators from Canberra who descended from planes and ruled by fiat—". . . the only place left in the Commonwealth where the inhabitants have virtually no say in the conduct of their affairs."[7] It reminded Muggeridge of Simla, with Parkinson's Law likewise in effect and bureaucrats laboring mightily to make two files grow where only one grew before. But it was the outback itself, the remote country, that fascinated him.

One of the few places in the world which had escaped human habitation, which had neither past glories to regret nor future disasters to dread; where the debris of past civilizations has left no litter, and the promise of future ones to come raises no hullaballoo; where no troops have ever marched, no Fabian pamphlets have ever been printed, no Communist manifestoes ever proclaimed, no aspirins ever taken. A sweet, virginal empty piece of earth. Nature as it was before its subjection by human settlement—harsh and defiant and eerie and stupendous. [8]

In three months he finished sixteen major articles, plus book reviews, a television series, and countless public speeches, broadcasts, and interviews. When his tour ended, one syndicated Australian columnist summed up its impact in this way: "He is interested in everything and everybody. He writes to shake his readers out of their sunny hypocrisy, out of their placid habits and out of their horrible acceptance in having their thinking done for them. His name is on every lip and we think and talk about his wickedly witty words with varying degrees of warmth. He has slapped us awake."[9]

From Australia, he went to the Far East with stops in Japan, Indonesia, Thailand, Burma, Formosa, and Ceylon (Sri Lanka). His description of Hong Kong as ". . . a museum piece of old-fashioned colonialist government, capitalist economy and speculator's paradise"[10] stirred up another hornet's nest. From Hong Kong he journeyed by train to the frontier of China to begin a series touted in *The Sunday Pictorial* as ". . . Britain's most controversial writer in the world's most controversial country."[11] The train stopped about a quarter mile from the border, and the passengers got off and walked to a gap in the railway line where the immigration formalities took place. "The first thing I saw in Communist China was a poster showing some idealized workers looking at television. However, I thought, it's only a poster. They haven't actually got it."[12]

Although there were some inevitable restrictions, Muggeridge traveled extensively and relatively freely during his month in China, a country then shrouded in almost total secrecy. Virtually all his traveling was done by train, which suited him: "I have little interest in sightseeing, but I love looking out of a railway carriage window at a strange countryside and getting into conversations with strangers." The South China scenery was enchanting: ". . . exquisitely green—beautifully cultivated paddy fields, smooth as a billiard table. . . . The scene through the carriage window would have been the same before Julius Caesar came to Britain—the same soil tilled in the same way with the same patience." The people, too, he found agreeable: ". . . intent faces, a kind of youthful wisdom and innocence, eager, polite and infinitely charming."[13]

To his three female Chinese Foreign Office guides, each of whom appeared indistinguishable to him and all therefore collectively addressed as "Miss Chang," he explained that he knew nothing of science and could not distinguish between a conveyer belt and a blast furnace so might he, please, talk to some Chinese eggheads? Teachers, clergymen, poets, that sort? Though not wholly let off the conveyer belt tours, he did get to spend an afternoon in Shanghai at the "affluent but hideous" home of one of the last remaining Chinese capitalists who had read economics at Cambridge, spoke English, and purported to find the regime of Chairman Mao congenial. Most of the man's sentences began with "I don't mind telling you . . .," and what he had to say amounted to an extended *apologia* for his own former life and for his present masters. At one point he abruptly stopped the flow of talk to ask Muggeridge if he thought it was all an act he was putting on; "I said—of course not; and as a matter of fact I didn't think it was an act, just that he was a man demoralized . . . a truly woebegone figure."[14] Apparently he was satisfied for the flow resumed. Sitting thus in the fading sunlight, drinking tea, listening to a voluble, portly, wealthy man alternately denounce the capitalist system which had made him wealthy and praise workers' communes on which he would never work—was there some weird, inner dynamic to life, Muggeridge wondered, that inexorably ground out such fearful symmetry?

When he arrived in Peking, he was whisked off to a party at the British Embassy. "It was like a strange dream. We drove through a massive red gate into the large Embassy compound—a little bizarre world, all on its own, sealed and shut off. Our host was the counsellor with the inconceivably apt name of Maybe." The men were in white dinner jackets, the women elegant in evening gowns; with sedate music playing in the background ". . . it might have been a Noel Coward play, into whose idiom one instinctively slipped, the facetious retorts and anecdotes. . . ."

The only trouble with living in Peking, the wife of the Norwegian ambassador told him, was that you saw the same people over and over again at each embassy party, and inevitably the host wanted to show his home movies. Just as she said this, Mr. Maybe summoned the guests inside to see movies of his latest trip through Cambodia. "Obviously he had shown the films many times. His patter flowed on along a well-worn groove. . . . When the showing was over we all thanked him and took our departure. No image that I could have invented could have conveyed better than the embassy party did, what I conceive to be the present attitude of mind of the remnants of Western European bourgeois society. Had I invented the scene it would have seemed exaggerated."[15]

Before leaving China Muggeridge visited the Forbidden City: "It was exquisite—the gleaming roofs, the bizarre shapes, the bright colours, but too strange and outlandish to move me much. For buildings of any sort to make my heart stand still (as, for instance, Salisbury Cathedral and Chartres did), it has to be connected with what I understand and belong to. This was infinitely remote, infinitely strange. I wandered around, curious but not uplifted."[16]

In a widely syndicated article "Balance Sheet on China," he summed up the debits and credits of what he had seen. The debits were the coercive dictatorial government and, at least to Western eyes, the rigid and dreary conformity. On the credit side, the government commanded nearly universal respect and obedience; currency was stable; prostitution, opium smuggling, and corruption had been practically eliminated; there was no evidence of starvation; and, throughout the country, he detected ". . . an air of vigour and hopefulness."[17] The only predictions he made were that relations between China and her Communist ally, the Soviet Union, would become increasingly strained so that, in the end, China would look to America rather than Russia as an ally; and that China would achieve the kind of industrial revolution that Japan had undergone, but in half the time. Obviously he did not foresee the so-called Cultural Revolution; even so, it took Japan the better part of sixty years, so his prediction of China becoming an industrial giant in thirty years (that is, by 1988) may yet prove accurate. He also advocated immediate official recognition of China by both the United States and the United Nations: "The simple fact is that the Peking government rules all China and will continue to rule it in the foreseeable future."[18]

On June 27, 1958, he left Peking on board a Soviet jetliner bound for Moscow. Bad weather forced the plane to land at Sverdlov where he spent a night and most of the following day padding once again about Russian streets. "It is quite extraordinary to be back in this country after 25 years. I had never really expected to see it again and now there I was, walking about, looking."[19] His first impression was of incomparably greater affluence; gone were the pinched, wolf-like faces and glassy stares of starving peasants so indelibly burned into his memory from that other trip in the winter of 1932.

When he got to Moscow he went first to the massive mausoleum in the Kremlin wall where now two heroes of the Soviet Union were laid out instead of, as before, one. With the fascinating illogicality of life, the scornful denunciations of Stalin by Khrushchev and the party bosses had not yet led to Stalin's removal from this place of honor. In full marshal's regalia his ample corpse lay in a glass cage beside the more austere figure of Lenin. "I was older and the regime was older. An advantage of being older is that one hopes less and minds less. The brave new worlds which are promised, and do not come to pass,

A Hungry Heart

provide an occasion neither for excessive breast beating nor for excessive exultation."[20]

From Russia he journeyed to the Middle East, where he interviewed senior government officials and traveled extensively in Israel and the Arab countries. Talking to President Nasser's associates in Cairo, Muggeridge would occasionally glimpse a vaguely familiar face and wonder whether this one might have sat in the Zaffarian palace thirty years before stumbling over Keats's *Ode On a Grecian Urn*, or that one long ago have intended to be a doctor and carry his secrets in his bottom.

In the autumn, he was in New York to cover the deliberations of the United Nations: ". . . that huge symmetrical glass tombstone . . . whose occupants specialize in throwing stones."[21] Listening to the speeches, now ranting and threatening, now measured and sedate, all infinitely remote from the realities of life, he reflected how true an image the UN was of a loony bin in a world gone mad.

His next stop was Little Rock, Arkansas, where he interviewed Governor Orval Faubus who was refusing to allow black children to attend schools despite federal desegregation orders. When Muggeridge suggested to Faubus that he should yield, if not to justice then at least to the tides of history, Faubus just smiled benignly and pointed to his electoral majorities.

America seemed even more affluent and powerful than when he had been a correspondent in Washington; yet the sense of underlying doom he had felt then still remained with him. He sat up one night drinking and discussing this with Senator Hubert Humphrey whom Muggeridge found ". . . shrewd, talkative, audacious, energetic and extremely sympathetic";[22] decidedly more so than his political rival, John F. Kennedy, ". . . the easygoing, amorous, rather indolent and snobbish American patrician"[23] at whose hands Humphrey was shortly to suffer a humiliating defeat in the West Virginia primary.

Muggeridge finished up what had been a hectic year, even by his rather frenetic standards, standing on the border between the two sections of Berlin, then still unwalled, looking eastwards to the baroque Soviet architecture ". . . more cumbersome and grotesquely ugly than even the Victorians could achieve"[24] and beyond the facade a squalid, decaying slum; and then looking westwards to a city of glass and chrome built on what two decades before had been a heap of bombed rubble. Beyond he looked to the idiotic fantasies of hire purchase democracy, the consumer society, with advertising and eroticism at the ready to stiffen up appetites and desires that showed any signs of flagging. East and West, two different attempts to construct a kingdom of heaven on earth and between them only this dangerous, soon to be bricked-up, no man's land. Like Bunyan's pilgrim crying out "Whither shall I go?," except that no one appeared to point him the way by the wicket gate. Standing thus on the Berlin border, he wrote in his diary: "Resolved in all circumstances to live or die a free man. No tyranny, however odious, no warfare, however destructive, can prevent this. It is what I will do."[25]

His year abroad seems to have been regarded as a sort of atonement for the sin of writing about the monarchy. Newspapers once again became receptive to his articles, and even the BBC gradually and ever so cautiously lifted its ban, at first by the simple expedient of rebroadcasting several of Edward R. Murrow's *Small World* programs that Muggeridge had recorded in America. Any expectation that anyone may have entertained that he would return from the wilderness suitably chastened and contrite was quickly dashed. The BBC he called ". . . begotten by John Knox out of the Bank of England with the Fabian Society intervening," while its director-general, Sir Ian Jacob, ". . . had eclipsed the world record for apologizing formerly held by Uriah Heep."[26] Other ample rumps soon felt his gadfly sting: Clement Attlee was ". . . a sheep in sheep's clothing";[27] Lord Hailsham—". . .his attraction is that no one, least of all himself, ever knows quite what he is going to say";[28] Sir William Haley—". . . the pontifical siren of Printing House Square";[29] Richard Dimbleby—". . . Golden Microphone in Waiting";[30] John Foster Dulles—"Dull, duller, dulles."[31]

Occasionally he lashed out unfairly, as when he called Montgomery, whose only offense had been to befriend him, ". . . a cold, sharp, avidly egotistical little man with not much capacity for friendship or compassion."[32] When a reporter from *Reynold's News* rang up and read this to Monty, his laconic response was: "Good." But when the reporter read on: ". . . The converted mill in which he lives is already arranged as a museum, with all his trophies and portraits of himself on display. It is rather macabre, and even touching, to think of him thus living, an exhibit among exhibits . . . ," Monty snapped: "I don't want to hear any more. No comment" and hung up. It was a cruel end to a relationship Muggeridge had once called "benevolently unneutral."

In February 1959, he was again back in the Soviet Union, this time to cover the state visit of Prime Minister Harold Macmillan ("Macmothballs") at the invitation of Premier Khrushchev ("one of nature's blimps—a blimpsky"). As usual Muggeridge was skeptical of what was likely to be achieved by this kind of high level diplomatic gamboling, and he reminded readers how often in the past such journeys had actually given advantage to an enemy, as at Munich. Nor ought the British prime minister to delude himself into thinking that he might make some genuine impact on the average Soviet citizen; ". . . if Mr. Macmillan grasps the hands of occasional members of the public, they are quite likely to be coppers. In the Soviet Union they also watch who only stand and wait."[33]

Once the tour actually got under way, he and the other members of the press corps traipsed around after the two leaders; from the airport welcoming formalities to the Hall of Proceedings where the walls were lined with portraits of Russian leaders who had survived the purges, dominated by a giant picture of Stalin, looking on, Muggeridge wrote, ". . . with a somewhat quizzical expression at the spectacle of his successors in conclave with the British Prime Minister";[34] then it was off to the inevitable factory inspection, this one a nuclear power station at Dubra, and then to Moscow University where Macmillan stood beneath a huge red banner which proclaimed: "Welcome to the Glorious Red Army"—the Prime Minister ". . . looking so much like the chairman of the governors at a school speech-day that I fully expected him to ask for a day's holiday."[35]

Later, at a cocktail party and reception at the British Embassy, Muggeridge met Dr. Kapitza, a Cambridge science graduate of Russian origin who had been forcibly detained in the USSR while there on a visit. Kapitza pointed with evident disgust at the gaggle of diplomats crowding round the buffet table and remarked that cattle and diplomats were the only animals who ate standing up. He also told Muggeridge that he had learned a good rule in life, namely to keep as far away from the boss as possible and as near as possible to the kitchen, and when in doubt to go to sleep. Later, while Muggeridge was standing at the bar, Khrushchev was escorted over and introduced to him by Lady Reilly, the wife of the British ambassador to Moscow, and Muggeridge and Khrushchev began to talk through an interpreter about humor: "Khrushchev said he was not much amused by *Krokodil* (the Russian humour magazine) but said his grandchildren made him look at it and, what was worse, explain the jokes. I said that as a former editor of *Punch* I had recently been in this invidious situation. Nothing was more painful than explaining jokes, and anyway professional humorists were all melancholic. Khrushchev did not agree."

> "It's all right for you" I said "to be funny, as indeed you are. But just imagine having to do it for a living. And anyway life is funnier than anything you can think of. Take this reception, for instance . . ."
> "Life is good" Khrushchev said.
> I agreed that it was good but also funny.
> As he left, he said: "In your article write the truth."
> "Such" I replied "is my constant endeavour."[36]

In the middle of the state visit, with Macmillan off sightseeing, Khrushchev delivered a saber-rattling speech denouncing Western intransigence over Berlin. So enraged was the British delegation, Muggeridge reported, that some argued for packing up and going home immediately. As it turned out, they stayed and completed the itinerary, but from this point on the exuberant bonhomie of the early days gave way to frigid diplomatic formalities. In fact when his guests flew off to tour Kiev and Leningrad, Khrushchev remained behind in Moscow, indisposed, it was announced at the last moment, by a toothache. "A diplomatic toothache," Muggeridge called it, "which unlike the genuine variety does not hurt." He went on: "To me the thought of a Soviet dentist drilling away at one of Khrushchev's teeth is very diverting. This dentist must be a hero of the Soviet Union. I shall look when we get back to Moscow to see whether Khrushchev has a new gold filling to add to his already impressive array. I doubt, however, if I shall spot one."[37]

In Kiev, Macmillan was met at the airport by local Communist party dignitaries and proceeded to deliver a speech about how in the twelfth century an English monarch had married a Ukranian princess and ever since relations between these two great countries had been mutually beneficial and amiable. As he droned on, Muggeridge stole a look at the solid phalanx of Russian policemen in standard issue civilian suits to see what their reaction was to this historic linkup: ". . . in one or two I thought I detected a faint flickering of the eyelids expressive of surprise, wonder, and maybe an impulse to laugh." The speech concluded, the prime minister retired, only to reemerge later for a tour of a collective farm, dressed in plus fours, grouse moor tweeds and smoking a pipe, looking every inch a Conservative politician on his way to open a garden fete in the home counties. When, later that year, Muggeridge was invited by the editor of *Krokodil* to submit an account of the funniest thing he had ever seen (perhaps this was in fulfillment of the "expanded cultural exchanges" the final joint communique called for), he sent along an account of the British prime minister at Kiev. Needless to say, this was considered in bad taste, and *Krokodil* never printed it.

In Leningrad, the last stop on the tour, he watched as the leaders visited a polling booth set up for a municipal election. After Mr. Mikoyan voted, Macmillan was induced to go through the motions of casting a ballot. "I made (I fear somewhat eager) inquiries as to whether this act would legally deprive him of British citizenship. Apparently not."[38]

Summing up his impression of the visit, Muggeridge wrote that the Russian leaders were ". . . tough, calculating, astute men who had never been to Eton." The prime minister, looking as if he had just stepped from the pages of a tattered volume of *The Forsyte Saga,* was no match for them. "One minute they slap him on the back and drink his health, the next they pull his chair from under him as he sits down. They alternately bully and cajole him until the poor man scarcely knows where he is. It has been a tragi-comedy such as even our bizarre time has rarely produced."[39] By coincidence, Muggeridge and Macmillan crossed paths the following autumn in New York. Muggeridge was being driven to a lecture in a hired Rolls Royce. "Passing the Waldorf Astoria hotel, we got caught up in Harold Macmillan's cavalcade. At one point, his identical Rolls Royce drew level with mine, and I fancied that he peered in at me with distaste."[40]

On leaving Moscow, ". . . having crossed the great divide of our age," his exultation was real but short-lived. He landed at Copenhagen, in an all too familiar welfare state, where citizens enjoy plenty to eat and to wear, live in comfortable homes, drive new motor cars, and watch television. "It ought to produce universal happiness, or at any rate contentment. In fact, it has produced the highest suicide rate in Europe and a vast consumption of tranquilizers, pep pills and sedatives." Walking through Copenhagen's streets, eyeing its affluent, forlorn-looking citizenry, he kept asking himself Why? What innate law of contradiction required that the pursuit of collective virtue end in tyranny and that the pursuit of individual freedom end in the most desolate materialism? The only state worth living in, he eventually decided, must be one which aspires to the unattainable. What can be achieved ultimately becomes tedious and second-rate. The welfare state only aspires to what can be achieved—freedom from material want and an ever-rising gross national product. Once achieved, the result is boredom. For the West, only Christianity provided an alternative: "For 2000 years the Christian religion recommended to men a way of life which they could never hope to attain. They aspired after it, and, in aspiring, created a civilization of fabulous artistic, intellectual and material achievement."

The Communist countries likewise had an aspiration. Life there was hard and monotonous, but it had a purpose and a resolve, strove for an ideal, and was fortified by the belief that the inexorable flow of history was in its direction. In his last dispatch summing up the Russian tour, he wrote:

> The Russians sense some sort of destiny to make the world different—
> whether from your or my point of view better or worse is neither here nor
> there.
> When I was first in Russia twenty-five years ago, however much I
> loathed the régime and its intolerance and inhumanities, I never lost the

feeling that it was somehow the crucible of history. Each time I go back I have the same feeling. The future is being shaped there, not in the lush pastures of the welfare state.[41]

At least in terms of output, the sixties were Muggeridge's most productive journalistic years. He wrote regularly for a variety of papers, magazines, and journals at home and abroad. *The New Statesman,* founded by the Webbs as a mouthpiece for Fabian socialism, provided a forum for many of his articles and his *London Diary* column (written incidentally, not in London where he went as little as possible, but in Sussex). *"The New Statesman'*s great success as a propagandist," he wrote, "has been to establish the proposition that to be intelligent is to be Left whereas about the exact opposite is true."[42] As a voice in the enemy camp, he was as truculent and uncompromising as ever. When the self-styled "Anti-Jewish Pogrom Committee of the People's Liberation Army" at first issued a warning and then pronounced sentence of death on him for an article he wrote condemning antisemitism, he took no notice of it other than to write his next article on how Scotland Yard dealt with the lunatic fringe in British politics.

In his book reviewing (principally in *Esquire* and *The Observer*) he dealt with only what he chose to read and said exactly what he thought of it. The latest best seller, a much talked about novel, racy biographies, all were likely to be ignored in favor of a book on mysticism by an obscure fourteenth-century monk.

His book reviewing for *The Evening Standard,* a Beaverbrook paper, came to an abrupt end when he wrote an article for a Canadian magazine about Fredericton, New Brunswick, where Beaverbrook had spent his childhood and youth. With the Beaverbrook Hotel, the Beaverbrook Library and Art Gallery, the Beaverbrook Monument, the Beaverbrook Public Gardens and, in their center, the Beaverbrook Bird Bath, the town had become a shrine, he wrote, compared to which Shakespeare appeared forgotten in Stratford on Avon and Napoleon ignored in Corsica. Why not rename the town Beaverbrookton and have done with it, he asked? His employer was not pleased, and Muggeridge was informed by the *Standard'*s editor, Charles Wintour, that he had been sacked. He received the news "with relief," and replied: "My dear Charles, I have thoroughly enjoyed our association, and the fact that its ending is good news has nothing to do with you. Would you please convey to Lord Beaverbrook the contents of this letter. I am particularly anxious that he should know that, far from wanting to hang on in his employment, I only entered it reluctantly at your persuasion, and that I most urgently wanted to leave it the moment I sniffed a breath of displeasure coming from his direction."[43]

No one who wrote as much as Muggeridge did during this period could avoid saying things he would now as soon forget, much that is unmemorable, and occasionally sheer nonsense. Actually, this is truer of television than print; it is easier to be deceitful or fatuous in the spoken than the written word. The extraordinary thing in his case is how rare this is. True, he once said that Mrs. Eleanor Roosevelt was a threat to freedom compared to which Adolf Hitler paled into insignificance—but even here one sort of can see his point of view. After all, freedom did survive Hitler; it remains to be seen if it can survive the pernicious effects of New Deal liberalism. Likewise when he said that a savage bowing down before a painted stone deep in the jungle exhibits greater wisdom than the scientist in his laboratory; in acknowledging the unfathomable mystery at life's center the savage *is* in a sense wiser than the scientist who presumes to reduce human existence to measurable formulae.

Muggeridge's writing is least convincing when he writes of power. To regard power as intrinsically evil, as he does, is too facile an escape from having to shoulder the uncomfortable burden of action. However repugnant, power exists, it will go on existing, and it requires to be organized, exercised and, above all, controlled. Simply to give it up as a bad cause will not do, as Dietrich Bonhoeffer (a man Muggeridge admires) found out when, after much agonizing, he agreed to join in the plot on Hitler's life.

Muggeridge's writing is often guilty of hyperbole, malice, levity, and a distaste for allowing facts to get in the way of a good quip; but guilty seldom, if ever, of humbug, conscious deception, or inelegance. It is not easy to put one's finger on just what it is that gives his prose its distinctive quality. Colorful verbs, a preference for adverbs over adjectives, and a gift for the apt simile; all that, yes, but its compulsive readability is more than the sum of these techniques. Above all, he has something to say, and the means to say it appears to flow effortlessly from that. This, of course, is an illusion. He is a perfectionist who labors over his writing, one who accepts the dictum that hard writing makes easy reading. His sentences tend to be long, seemingly rambling, with subordinate clauses and interpolations and parentheses strewn about, then suddenly a strong verb at the end to pull the reader up short. His performance is like one of those circus clowns who rides about the ring at a furious gallop, always seeming to be just about to be thrown off, until one eventually realizes that this is a consummate rider in full control at all times.

His writing has changed remarkably little in half a century. What he wrote in his twenties may be slightly more florid and sentimental, inclined to priggishness, sometimes a shade imitative (particularly of

D. H. Lawrence and Anton Chekov), but it was unmistakably his. The technique has been refined not changed. Nor has he ever taken interest in the question of technique or writing style. His diaries and letters are as lucid and readable as what he wrote for publication. He believes writers are born not made and is skeptical about attempts to teach writing. When he agreed to spend two terms at a Canadian university, he insisted that, knowing nothing about what is called "creative writing," he not be asked to teach it. Incidentally, he also adopted the title "Old Hack in Residence" rather than the more portentous, professorial titles.

His television work in the sixties was varied. He wrote and narrated two acclaimed documentaries on the rise of Soviet and American power, *The Titans*, and made four one-hour documentaries about his own life. He appeared regularly on such apparently indestructible programs as *Any Questions, Panorama,* and *Meeting Point.* He interviewed such world leaders as Pandit Nehru, Ben-Gurion, Adenauer, and de Gaulle as well as a host of more interesting figures like Lord Reith, Billy Graham, Leonard Woolf, P. G. Wodehouse, and Bertrand Russell. Russell actually bet him twenty pounds that Joseph McCarthy would become president of the United States; Muggeridge exhibited no compunction about capitalizing on such certifiable paranoia and collected the bet. When he interviewed society hostess Elsa Maxwell and inquired sweetly: "Have you ever met any *unimportant* people, Miss Maxwell?" she replied: "Not until tonight." Another memorable interview was with Irish playwright Brendan Behan, whose play *The Quare Fellow* had just opened in London. Behan arrived for the interview "somewhat full" and proceeded to tank up further in the BBC hospitality room. Muggeridge saved the program from being canceled by arguing that this was what Behan was like and the audience would appreciate verisimilitude. By airtime Behan was utterly incoherent. At one point he took off his boots and muttered something about "having a leak." With the cameras rolling, Muggeridge put the questions, waited for Behan to grunt or mumble a little, and then imperturbably answered them himself. "It was the pleasantest and most rewarding evening I ever spent in Lime Grove."[44]

On a program called "Dr. Christian Barnard Faces His Critics," Muggeridge ventured to enquire whether the first heart transplant had been done in South Africa because the research, personnel, and surgical facilities were better there than anywhere else in the world, or because the vile doctrine of apartheid had so devalued human life that human beings could be seen as spare parts for experimentation? This caused a terrible row. The other "critics" on the program (mostly rather sycophantic British doctors) immediately disassociated themselves from Muggeridge's question and urged Dr. Barnard not to dignify it with an answer. When the program was relayed on Pretoria radio, the South African government revoked Muggeridge's passport so that a planned interview with the author Alan Paton had to be scrapped.

In addition to journalism and television, the sixties marked Muggeridge's screen debut when he played the part of a television interviewer in the Boulting Brothers film *I'm All Right, Jack*. He also made two extended American lecture tours, provided the text for a book of drawings of London (*London à la Mode*, with Paul Hogarth), wrote a play based on the obscenity prosecution of *Lady Chatterly's Lover* called *Too Much Venus*, and a novel, *Heavens Above*, intended originally as a film script for Peter Sellers. Muggeridge had a cameo role in the movie version, playing the part of a bishop resplendent in cassock and gaiters, perambulating around the cloisters as if to the cloth born. Unfortunately, the movie bore faint resemblance to his original plot, which had been about a country vicar, a very simple and honest man, who gets into endless ecclesiastical hot water because after years of unexceptional service to the church he suddenly finds himself believing in the truth of the gospels. Then he insists on saying so in the most inconvenient and unlikely places, like at synod meetings and even in the pulpit.

Running through all Muggeridge's activity in the sixties, like a strand of thread through a tapestry, one senses a profound feeling of dissatisfaction, not so much the melancholy to which he had previously been susceptible, but rather unworthiness, a sense of self-betrayal, what Shakespeare meant when he wrote of "goring mine own thoughts/ selling cheap what is most dear." What he did to earn a living, writing weekly journalism and appearing on television, had long since come to seem fatuous and derisory, unconnected with anything that was real and important in his life. Now he felt an increasingly painful awareness of lost opportunities to say or write something memorable, something which might shed some light amidst what he saw as evermore impenetrable darkness. The great majority of mankind are content with appearances as though they were realities and are more influenced by things that seem to be than by things that are. More and more he wanted to spend what remained of his life in pursuit of substance not appearances, reality not fantasy. When he was twenty-two, he had written to his father: "I am determined, sometime, to say my little say of truth."[45] There might not be much time left.

By the middle of the decade, religious themes had come to dominate his writing, and even television work; the notable programs from this period were his interviews with Cardinal Heenan, Bishop Huddleston, Archbishop Bloom, and his series on the life of Christ.

In 1966 a collection of his journalism appeared under the ghastly title

Tread Softly for You Tread on My Jokes (in the United States *The Most of Malcolm Muggeridge*). Thirty years before he had ridiculed such books as ". . . journalism dressed up to look like literature and literature in the habitments of journalism." Only the brave or foolhardy reprinted articles, he wrote then: "Most should be obliterated like a ship's wake. They belong to the moment and should perish with the moment."[46] In this case, it was sound advice. Although the subject matter in *Tread Softly* is recent and familiar, there is a leaden emptiness about it, or perhaps fadedness is a better word—like looking at dog-eared old photographs. Alone of all his books, *Tread Softly* is a chore to reread. The writing is accomplished, all the old technical skill and wit are on display, but compared to earlier works like *In A Valley* or *The Thirties*, it seems anemic, drained of zest and freshness.

Nevertheless, it enjoyed favorable notices. Turning these over now, it is interesting to note the writers with whom Muggeridge was most often compared: Swift (many times), Dr. Johnson (several times, although ". . . a thin Dr. Johnson" one reviewer insisted), Mencken, Blake, Hazlitt, Wilde, and most imaginatively (by J. W. Lambert in *The Sunday Times*) "a mealy-mouthed Thersites." One or two reviewers were perceptive enough to see that deep religious currents were churning beneath the smooth, acidulous surface. In *The Observer*, John Weightman said: "Somewhere inside him there is both a Puritan and a frustrated believer";[47] while in *The New Statesman*, Colin McInnes counseled Muggeridge to get off television ". . . retire to the hills, there to meditate and come up for us eventually with the consequences of his reflections. In other words, tell us no longer what he disbelieves, but where he thinks imaginative reality resides."[48] It was a challenge Muggeridge was to take up sooner, and with greater repercussions, than Mr. McInnes could have foreseen.

·13·

JESUS REDISCOVERED

The development of Mr. Malcolm Muggeridge from an intellectual gadfly into a seer seems to be accelerating.

The Times, April 22, 1968

* * *

The most common question now asked of Muggeridge is: When did he become a Christian? Put in this way, with an underlying assumption that one becomes a Christian with the same dramatic finality as one learns of a terminal illness, it defies any rational answer. Was Muggeridge a Christian when, as a schoolboy, he said that his ambition was to be a saint? Or as an undergraduate when his closest friend was a priest and he aspired to a similar vocation? When he was baptized, confirmed, and lived contentedly with an Anglo-Catholic religious community? Or was it later, at Travancore perhaps, when he wrote to his father: "I want God to play tunes through me. He plays, but I, the reed, am out of tune"?[1] Could it have been when he left Moscow, thirty years old and disillusioned by communism, wanting to have his children baptized and writing: "All he had ever seen or thought or felt or believed, sorted itself out. It was a vision of Good and Evil. Heaven and Hell. Life or Death. There were the two alternatives, and he had to choose. He chose."[2] Christopher Booker has advanced this as the decisive moment in what he called "the great Mugg riddle."[3] Or maybe it was later, in Calcutta in 1934, as he stood and watched almost enviously as a man fell down in the road, made a mark with a little stick he carried, got up, and stepped to that mark and fell over again, thus making a spiritual pilgrimage from Benares to Cape Comorin, his expression, Muggeridge noticed ". . . not in the least fanatical, but cheerful and normal,"[4] contrasting with his own bleak despair. Or later still, perhaps, in the middle of the war chasing the phantom shadows of

Intelligence when he wrote to Kitty: "To love is to know, as knowing God and loving God in the Bible are the same thing . . . All these things seem so clear, and all fear goes away because of this clarity. There is nothing to be afraid of—and then the light goes out—and one is left floundering in the darkness of the will again and full of dread again. So it goes on, and ever will, except that little by little, the vision stays longer and is clearer, until, I believe, there will be only vision for ever and ever."[5] Or in 1958 at the height of his television fame as a skeptic, an agnostic, a "cynical nihilist" as he was called, when he wrote in his diary: "Christianity, to me, is like a hopeless love affair. It is infinitely dear and infinitely unattainable. I carry its image with me always and look at it constantly with sick longing"?[6] Or not until a decade later, when *Jesus Rediscovered* appeared and, as Booker says, he came out with it at last?

Looked at in isolation, a convincing enough case could be made for any of these dates, or indeed many others, as the decisive turning point. But in the context of the man's whole life none is more or less significant than another, each one no more than a guidepost on an incomplete journey. The truth is that the whole of Muggeridge's life has been a restless quest for faith that has, even now, attained few certainties.

He knew what he disbelieved long before he knew what he believed. At least from the time he left Moscow, he disbelieved in collective solutions to the human predicament. Individual yearnings will not be assuaged by collective prescriptions. The kingdoms of the earth which the devil offered to Christ (noting that they were in his gift), an offer which Christ spurned, thenceforth seemed to him tawdry and derisory and he turned his attention to that kingdom which is not of this world. Along the way, there was no blinding revelation, no all-sufficing moment of illumination, no voice from on high speaking his name. His trek was to Emmaus, not Damascus, and only occasionally did he recognize the stranger who walked with him.

Faith, like loyalty, is seldom a cut and dried thing. It ebbs and flows, fluctuates with particular circumstances and with advancing age. Like a mountain it is seldom won by frontal assault, however spirited and determined; instead one clambers about the circumference, searching out a support here and a toehold there, occasionally pulling oneself up to a slightly more elevated plateau where the clouds are less dense and the summit less hidden, but no less often slipping back, clawing at loose shale in search of a grip, sometimes finding a stay and sometimes plunging into a chasm of doubt from which there seems no way back up.

Well before the publication of *Jesus Rediscovered* in 1969, there were observable changes in his personal life. He gave up smoking in 1964 during an American lecture tour. He was staying in a hotel in the Midwest, cooped up all day writing and lighting up cigarettes. When he got back that evening after his talk, the airconditioner had broken down, the room was stagnant, and the ashtrays were littered with the detritus of his habit. In a moment of nausea and self-disgust, he vowed not to smoke again and stuck to it. Nevertheless for years afterwards he continued to get letters from irate viewers accusing him of setting a bad example by smoking on televison. This illustrates one aspect of the pernicious influence of television: The viewer mostly sees in it what he expects to see. The medium begins in fantasy purporting to depict as reality what are only shadows and images set flickering by a complex of tubes and wires and circuitry, and it ends in fantasy. It relies for its effectiveness on tricks, not perceptiveness, complete with canned laughter, studio applause, special effects, and dawn for dusk—a medium fated never to get beneath the surface.

One example of this occurred in 1963 when Muggeridge recorded an interview with Archbishop Anthony Bloom of the Russian Orthodox church. The topic was suffering, and the discussion was low-key since both men were in agreement that suffering was an inevitable concomitant of man's free will and could sometimes be an enobling and creative experience. The next day a cabby said to Muggeridge: "I saw you on the telly last night with that bloke with the black beard. You knocked hell out of him."[7]

By the mid-sixties, he had also given up drinking and adopted a vegetarian diet. This new found asceticism confirmed the public impression that he had undergone some dramatic religious conversion. It also provided endless scope for his detractors to lampoon 3aliit Mugg," his latest incarnation as an aging ascetic wagging a reproving finger at those still enjoying pleasures that age had forced him to abandon. The bon vivant turned vegetarian, the drinker turned abstainer, the jaded *roué* who ceases to be a practitioner and becomes an excoriator of lechery, and so on. All good fun, no doubt, and certainly not unexpected.

In fact, though, Muggeridge's asceticism was based primarily on practical rather than puritanical motives. He has never believed that there is a virtue in self-denial for its own sake, or that one ought to forego pleasures simply because they are pleasurable, which is what puritanism means. Such an attitude he regards as foolish and potentially harmful. He once referred to minor vices, like smoking and drinking, as ". . . innoculations against the major vices,"[8] while his attitude to the Ten Commandments has always been to regard them as comparable to an examination paper—". . . eight only to be attempted."[9] He now chooses to practice a none too rigorous form of asceticism just because he prefers it. The practice of abstemiousness, he finds, sharpens the senses and allows one to distinguish between fantasy and reality with greater clarity and precision. Asceticism is like an arduous road, steeper and narrower than the main highway, taken not because of its arduousness but because the view is better, the vistas more enthralling, and the horizon more often within sight. Having made this discovery to refuse to put it into practice lest one be labeled a puritan would be as foolish as refusing to wear corrective lenses for fear of being called blind.

Nor is an ascetic way of life altogether new to him. In India he practiced a strict vegetarian diet. Gastronomy is one subject on which he is both totally ignorant and totally bored. He has always preferred plain, nourishing food to exotic gourmet dishes. Before he gave up meat altogether a typical dinner would have been eggs, bread, cheese, a slice of ham, and fruit; dropping the slice of ham can hardly be considered a morbid mortification of the flesh. Away from home, he often goes into a restaurant at mealtime, scans the menu, and leaves simply because he cannot be bothered by eating.

Through the ups and downs of his career, he has always lived frugally. Conspicuous consumption, profligate spending, and acquisition of luxuries make no appeal to him. Nor, on the other hand, has he been inclined to emulate the antics of a Tolstoy by striving to rid himself of property and possessions altogether.

There is another explanation for his latter-day asceticism. Rightly or wrongly, he believed that as he grew older abstemiousness was essential if he was to keep his mental faculties alert so as to go on working—". . . like a framework or scaffolding to hold up one's tottering life."[10] "When one reaches my age," he told an interviewer, "one must choose between suicide and sainthood. I have chosen sainthood."[11] Also, he was resolved that when he did make a profession of Christianity, his own personal life not discredit or embarrass it. Hugh Kingsmill used to say that no man can put more virtue into his words than he practices in his life. Since Muggeridge's words, from *Jesus Rediscovered* onwards, were to become more virtuous, he had first to clean up his personal life. "It would be very wicked of any man to say that he had completely achieved mastery of his fleshly appetites," he wrote, "but I felt able to declare myself a Christian when I was reasonably sure that a scrutiny of my life would not disgrace the inconceivably high standards that Christians I admire—like Tolstoy and Pascal—have set."[12]

Rereading his writing from the early sixties, one is conscious of a kind of emptiness in it. The words are wrapped around a hollow, skillfully served up but unnourishing, like candy floss at a circus.

Words proceeding from a void into a vacuum. The spark of his earlier books is missing. Prior to *Jesus Rediscovered*, he had become an apostle without a creed, a self-confessed "religious maniac without a religion,"[13] a writer with a gifted pen but little left to say. His writing told one what he was against, a useful but incomplete function, but not what he was for.

He was against the notion of progress, which he called ". . . the most pernicious delusion ever to take possession of the human mind." To believe in any sort of mechanical progress governing history by which men automatically improve and become more enlightened and humane *is* to confuse progress with change. Progressive materialism is the most foolish of all philosophies and requires the greatest credulity in those who hold it. But one next wants to know: Well, then, is progress ever possible? If not, is there any purpose in trying to improve life? It was this kind of question which, before *Jesus Rediscovered*, Muggeridge ignored. Actually, the closest he ever came to even attempting to formulate an answer was in his *Time and Tide* articles in the thirties as, for example, when he wrote: "That history, like each individual life, each moment of recorded time, makes a pattern is not to be denied; but a pattern whose key cannot be known to mortal men, only dimly glimpsed by them in rare moments. All we know or ever can know is that the pattern exists, and that each event great and small, each creature and each atom and each molecule, is necessary to it, and in being thus necessary has significance."[14]

Likewise he made clear his view that the pursuit of happiness, included along with life and liberty in the American Declaration of Independence as an "unalienable right" (added, incidentally, at the last moment in substitution for the more realistic defense of property clause) is both "fatuous" and ". . . responsible for a good part of the ills and miseries of the modern world."[15] Once when Dr. Johnson heard a woman proclaim in his presence that she was happy, he remarked in a loud, emphatic voice that if this was so her life gave the lie to every research of humanity for she was happy without health, without beauty, without money, and without understanding. Muggeridge would, as usual, side with Dr. Johnson and has, on occasion, been scarcely less astringent with contemporary pursuers of happiness. The difference between pursuing happiness and being content might be compared to the difference between a trapper and a birdwatcher: One tries unsuccessfully to snare an elusive quarry, to pin down that which by nature is meant to roam free and unconfined; the other seeks only sporadic glimpses and rejoices when unaccountably they come his way.

But if the pursuit of power, progress, and happiness are all fantasies, part of what Muggeridge calls "the legend," leading from nowhere to nowhere, where lies reality? By the mid-sixties people were growing tired of his demolition act. It was all very well to topple cherished icons and derisively kick away the pieces; but what, if anything, they wanted to know, could be built amid the rubble that remained?

Muggeridge's first tentative and qualified answer was in a book called *What I Believe* (Allen and Unwin), published in 1966, in which various authors were asked for a succinct statement of their personal credo. He wrote: "I should be proud and happy to call myself a Christian; to dare to measure myself against that sublimely high standard of human values and human behaviour. In this I take comfort from a saying of Pascal, thrown out like a lifeline to all skeptical minds throughout the ages—that whoever looks for God has found him."[16]

Typically, it was Christianity's essential pessimism about earthly circumstances that made an appeal to him. The concept of this world as a wilderness, a vale of tears through which one must make a solitary pilgrimage, accurately reflected what he had seen of most earthly circumstances. The contrary proposition—that earthly life can be satisfied within its own dimensions by satisfying the appetites—he had long since discarded, if indeed he ever believed it. In Christianity's beginnings, in what was to outward appearances abject failure—its leader humiliated and put to death, His ragtag band of followers dispersed and frightened—perhaps here was truth. He wrote that "Christianity, from Golgotha onwards, has been the sanctification of failure."[17] Artistically speaking, failure is considerably more interesting than success, and Muggeridge's approach to Christianity, indeed to all of life, is to see it in artistic not scientific or historical terms. In other words, that creating the universe and life itself was more analogous to Shakespeare's writing a play than to Einstein's conducting a laboratory experiment, that life's significance is less in the atoms, molecules, and gases by which it began than in the reason why it began.

If the pursuit of power and happiness inexorably led to fantasy and despair, then could it be that in Christ's earthly failure lay the seeds of reality and hope? "If Christ had been as successful as Billy Graham," Muggeridge once said, "we should never have heard of him."[18] Christianity's anti-Utopianism; its pragmatic view that "in this world ye shall have tribulation"; its insistence that now we see but through a glass darkly; that the flesh and the spirit are locked in perpetual conflict so that a person must die to the flesh to live in the spirit; that the kingdoms of earth are in the devil's gift; that man cannot live by bread alone but by the Word also; that treasure laid up on earth will be moth-eaten and rusted, and only treasure in heaven prove imperishable; that the wisdom of man is the foolishness of God—it was these

With Leonard Woolf, 1969

Malcolm and Kitty
at Park Cottage

Malcolm, Alec Vidler and Kitty on 'Australia' – a favourite walk

sentiments that made an appeal to him which finally proved irresistible. It could be said with justice that he backed reluctantly into Christianity. Instead of beginning with a belief in Christ's divinity and then coming to accept the doctrine built on that, he accepted the validity of the doctrine and then only gingerly and hesitantly came to consider the putative divinity of Christ. It was the barrenness and fraudulence of the alternatives, in other words, which drove him to Christianity. "I have found myself dislodged from one position after another; hauled out of each sanctuary; chased down Fleet Street, through Broadcasting House and the Television Centre, past Great Turnstile and Bouverie Street, Madison Avenue—from such cosy and easily accessible niches I am remorselessly driven. Where? To this symbol of our Christian faith which is also a gallows or scaffold—the Cross; to this foolishness of men which is also, we are told, the wisdom of God; to these two stark pieces of wood nailed together."[19] Muggeridge is the modern counterpart of Peter who, when Christ asked if he too would desert Him, replied (one imagines rather abjectly): "Lord, to whom else shall I turn?"

Before what he called his "hopeless love affair" with Christianity could be consummated, there remained like barred gates the two fundamental tenets of Christian dogma: the Incarnation and the Resurrection.

In the debate with Cardinal Heenan in 1959 Muggeridge acknowledged having ". . . a belief in a supreme being in a vague sort of way," but went on to say that it was "inconceivable" that such a being became man. In fact he suggested that the church should abandon such "unacceptable dogma" and concentrate all its efforts instead on ". . . teaching Christian values as an important corrective to the vicious trends in contemporary civilization."[20] In the context of a debate, this may have been devil's advocacy. In the context of much of the church's contemporary predicament—its Christianity drained of its transcendental meaning, its creed largely eviscerated, its preaching reduced to liberal platitudes and vaporous moralizing—he would now admit that such a prescription turned out to be devil's advocacy in a more literal sense.

As late as 1966, he wrote: "I don't believe in the resurrection of Christ, I don't believe that he was the son of God in a Christian sense, I don't believe that he was born of a virgin."[21] He did believe, he went on to say, that the Christian view of life contained "a profound and glowing truth," a proposition to which most agnostics, secularists, and humanists could assent. He was in an awkward position. "I find myself praising a position I cannot uphold, enchanted by a religion I cannot believe, putting all my hope in a faith I do not have."[22]

So what was it then, in the three years between 1966 and 1969, that changed his views about the Incarnation and Resurrection, that caused him to rediscover a Jesus whose deity he affirms and whom he called, in the title of a later book, *The Man Who Lives!*? As usual with him, there is no simple or obvious answer. The theory of a Damascus Road conversion is plainly mistaken, and yet there was a profound and observable crystalization of his beliefs and in the conviction with which he expounded them. Several things contributed to this.

In 1967, Dr. Alec Vidler retired as Dean of King's College, Cambridge, and returned to live close by the Muggeridges in Sussex. During the forties, fifties, and sixties, Vidler and Muggeridge had seen each other sporadically; now they were reunited as they had not been since their undergraduate days at Selwyn. Vidler's influence on Muggeridge is difficult to pin down but cannot be overlooked. It is less what he says than what he is. There is an imperturbable solidity to Vidler's faith, a kind of flinty, skeptical certainty that has proved irresistibly attractive not only to Muggeridge but to generations of inquiring students. Shortly after returning to Sussex, Vidler began a weekly Bible study group that originally met on alternate weeks in his home and the Muggeridges'. It now meets just at Vidler's house, but over the years the Muggeridges have been stalwart participants. To the extent that Muggeridge's views have developed along more orthodox theological lines, Vidler is primarily responsible. Indeed, Muggeridge acknowledged this in a tribute to Vidler with which he began their coauthored book on Saint Paul: "To you I owe my first true acquaintance with the Christian religion. What more fitting, then, than that half a century later I should be guided by you in coming seriously to grips with the founding father of Christendom?"[23] Vidler, incidentally, read *Jesus Rediscovered* in manuscript prior to publication and, in his journal, called it ". . . very moving . . . while no one can be altogether right, I think he is more right than anyone else uttering today. Of course, he's a prophetic type who doesn't make the qualifications dear to my academic heart. . . ."[24]

Even television, oddly enough, played a significant part in Muggeridge's spiritual odyssey. He spent the month of August 1967, at Sancta Maria Abbey in Nunraw, Scotland, for the purpose of making a BBC film about monasticism. He lived with the monks and observed their discipline; call at 4 A.M. (actually, only about an hour before he was accustomed to rise), mass at 4:30, then usually a walk on the moors above the abbey. "It was the lambing season, and as I looked at the young lambs frisking about, words I had just heard—*Agnus Dei*— echoed in my mind. What a terrific moment in history that was, I reflected, when men first saw their God in the likeness of the weakest, mildest and most defenceless of all living creatures."[25] After breakfast and an office, the monks went off to work in the fields while he puttered about gardening, chopping wood (a favorite pastime), walking, or reading. Afternoons were similarly ordered and uneventful, yet satisfying. The food was spartan—bread, fruit, vegetables, and cheese—but to him familiar. After Compline at 7:30 the monks retired to their dormitory beds. As a guest, he enjoyed the luxury of a room to himself. "I usually sat up for an extra hour or so, reading, thinking, or just looking out of my window. No heavenly visitations befell me, there was no Damascus Road grace; and yet, I know, life will never be quite the same after my three weeks with the Cistercians at Nunraw."[26]

Shortly after leaving Nunraw, he went to the Middle East to do a three-part television series on the life of Christ. Poking about the mostly fraudulent shrines, like Christ's exact birthplace in the Church of the Nativity in Bethlehem (where, by coincidence, another census was taking place), or wandering across hills dotted with sheep still tended by shepherds and dogs as they would have been in biblical times, or strolling in the cool of the evening by the lake of Galilee watching the fishing boats bring in their catch, he discovered that he was engaged in something more than a reconstruction of the life of one enigmatic and obscure historical teacher whom all sorts and conditions of men had ever since called Lord and Savior. What is less clear is the process by which this realization altered his own religious views. What is clearly documented is that by the time he came to deal with the Resurrection, his commentary went as follows: "Christ died on the cross as a man who had tried to show his fellowmen what life was about; he rose from the dead to be available to men for ever as an intermediary between man and God . . . What is not open to question is that today, two thousand years later, Christ is alive."[27] No longer did he find the Resurrection "inherently inconceivable"; thenceforth it was to be the cornerstone of his credo.

If these experiences served to rekindle a guttering faith, it was the Edinburgh University row that fired and galvanized it. Having been asked by a group of students in May 1966 to contest the rectorship, he agreed, and this time won handsomely against three other candidates (John Mackintosh, MP, Lord Dinsay, Chairman of the Scottish Land Court, and Quinton Hogg). "I agreed to run as a sort of joke," he wrote to his brother, Jack, "and now I'm landed with the job."[28] This was not entirely true, as he had previously contested the rectorship (1957).

The rector's term is three years, and his functions are a combination of the ceremonial and representative. For the latter purpose, the rector is assisted by an assessor, in Muggeridge's case, Alan Frazer, an

Edinburgh lawyer and friend. From the outset, Muggeridge made his position clear to the students; before assuming office he wrote to the president of the Students Representative Council.

> The Rector's job, as I understand it, is to work with you and your colleagues. If ever I felt for any reason that my relations with the S.R.C. precluded full cooperation I should at once resign. The purely ceremonial aspects of being Rector make less than no appeal to me, and if the job's usefulness as providing a liaison between you and the University authorities were to be limited or precluded I should resign.[29]

His investiture was on February 16, 1967. "Not since I gave a lecture in Pentonville Prison," he began his rectorial address, and just at this point his mortarboard fell off, "have I been so conscious as I am on this occasion of being wrongly cast, and on the wrong side of the fence." Education, the activity in which his audience of students, faculty, and administration were all ostensibly engaged, had become ". . . a sort of mumbo-jumbo or cure-all for the ills of a godless and decomposing society." He went on: "I have listened in my time to a great variety of bores—political bores without number, literary bores (Eliot, Leavis, Rowse—Oh God, Rowse!), scientific bores (some very fine specimens in that category too), the porno bore (a specialty of our time) and so on, but the educational bore in my experience stands alone, fit, like Lord Avon, to be given his international cap and to bore for Britain." The permissive society, the practice of sterility through contraception, drug taking, all these he condemned as manifestations of a society that had lost its bearings. He called on his audience to turn their attention instead to "the sublime truths of the Christian religion."[30] It was vintage Muggeridge, witty sentences barbed like a fishhook to catch the laugh in the hearer's throat, and plainly calculated to disconcert every segment of his audience: students, who thought they had elected an irreverent agnostic; faculty, with their smug sense of intellectual superiority; and administration, to whom the rector is in a way a rival authority. It would not have required much foresight to see that some fireworks lay ahead.

For most of his first year things went along smoothly, thanks largely to the diligence and tact of Alan Frazer who met privately with the S.R.C. executive to solicit their views before each meeting of the University Court. Then, in October, the magazine *Student* published an article advocating the use of the drug LSD in quantities demonstrably dangerous to health. The Discipline Committee of the university initially suspended Hugh Griffiths, the twenty-three-year-old editor of *Student*. Then, under pressure and in the face of accusations of censorship from the S.R.C., they yielded and reinstated Griffiths with a "reprimand." While this was going on, the student theater put on a play in which one of the male characters stripped naked and pranced about the stage uttering obscenities. More than forty years before, Muggeridge had written to Alec Vidler: "We may live to see nude actors in the theatre before we die";[31] he little suspected then that it would be at a reputable, nominally Christian, state-supported university of which he was rector. Fortunately, there was only one performance and controversy was avoided, but neither incident particularly endeared the students to their rector's heart.

After Griffith's reinstatement as editor, Muggeridge and Frazer were publicly criticized for not defending him at the time of the initial suspension. The criticism culminated in an S.R.C. motion, passed on November 14, 1967, declaring that the rector and assessor must express only S.R.C. views in all university councils, whatever their own opinions might be.

Muggeridge and Frazer independently notified the S.R.C. that such a policy was totally unacceptable to them and agreed to attend the next full S.R.C. meeting to discuss it. By the time that meeting occurred (December 7, 1967) there had been another S.R.C. motion that was to prove of great importance in the subsequent events; this one called on the university health authorities to provide birth control pills on request to all female students.

The S.R.C. meeting was stormy but orderly, and each side made its position unmistakably clear, as is evidenced by this exchange between Stephen Morrison, S.R.C. Director of Publications, and Muggeridge.

> *Morrison.* It is my view that the Rector's job is to represent students, represent their point of view no matter what his point of view may be. The Students Representative Council is the elected body of the students; if they put forward a view to the Rector, he must put this forward to the Court, no matter what his personal view may be. This is his job. He is our delegate, he is our representative; if he is not ready to fulfill this particular purpose . . . then he should not be there.
>
> *Muggeridge:* One thing I must say to Mr. Morrison—if he suggests that I, or my Assessor, would, under any circumstances, agree to represent his views, irrespective of our own opinions, he must think again. If that were the position, then without a moment's hesitation, I should resign . . . and I may or may not submit myself for re-election in order to find out whether it is indeed true that the suggestion that he has made, the views that he has put forward, represent the majority of the student population of this University. If they did, I should be most proud to be defeated, most proud.[32]

When term resumed after the Christmas break the first issue of *Student* had a cartoon depicting Muggeridge as half skull, half flesh, with worms crawling out of his nose. In an accompanying editorial entitled "Who Is Muggeridge?", it reminded readers of the rector's well-known opposition to the birth control pill and of the recent S.R.C. motion on the subject and threw down the gauntlet: "We ask you, our Rector, do you agree with the Student Council motion—or will you resign?"[33]

The students were not kept waiting for his answer. Three days later Muggeridge delivered his annual rectorial address from the High Kirk of St. Giles. It was broadcast by the BBC and had attracted a large press contingent. Taking as his text, "Blessed are the pure in heart for they shall see God," Muggeridge proceeded to excoriate the students for self-indulgence, sloth, insubordination, and escapism, all of which he said ". . . fills me not so much with disapproval as contempt. . . . All is prepared for a marvelous release of youthful creativity; we await the great works of art, the high spirited venturing into new fields of perception and understanding—and what do we get? The resort of any old slobbering *débauchée* anywhere in the world at any time—dope and bed." Then, in mid-address as it were, both he and Frazer resigned but not before booby-trapping the post for any potential successor: "It will be interesting to see what calibre of candidate will come forward to contest the Rectorship on the terms and conditions laid down by the present S.R.C. officers."[34]

His dramatic resignation had repercussions within and without the university. The principal (now Sir) Michael Swann accepted the resignations "with regret," adding: "It was the only course open to you and one that I too would, I hope, have taken."[35] In a subsequent written report of the events leading up to the resignation, Swann defended Muggeridge and Frazer and castigated the S.R.C. for "timidity" and the newspaper *Student* for "irresponsibility." At least some students, too, were chastened by the unexpected turn of events; a student union resolution: "That This House Supports Malcolm Muggeridge" passed by a vote of 479 to 416 two days after his St. Giles resignation address. The S.R.C. formally expressed regret at having provoked the confrontation and, in an artful piece of scapegoating, took temporary trusteeship over *Student*. For a time all editorials had to be vetted in advance by the S.R.C. executive, committed free-speechers all. A university committee set up to inquire into the whole question of student representation and publication eventually reported; like most academic documents, this one was long-winded, turgid, and shelved.

Alan Frazer resumed his disrupted law practice in Edinburgh. Despite a considerable number of letters and petitions from students and faculty, Muggeridge refused to recontest the rectorship and did not return to the university until ten years later when, at the joint invitation of the principal and S.R.C., he addressed a full university assembly and received a warm welcome.

More than anything else prior to *Jesus Rediscovered*, it was the extensive publicity given to his Edinburgh resignation speech that focused public attention on Muggeridge's alleged "conversion." The row actually influenced his Christian convictions (which were already deep) very little, but it did precipitate an unusually forceful and dogmatic public expression of them. Just as his opposition to the Bulganin-Khrushchev visit established his anti-Communist credentials in people's minds, so his resignation as rector established his Christian credentials. In both cases, it was not his own views that had changed so much as it was public perception of them. The man who wrote *Winter in Moscow* in 1933 only came to be thought of as an anti-Communist in 1956; the man who wrote *In A Valley of This Restless Mind* in 1938 only came to be thought of as a Christian in 1968.

When his publishers, Collins, pressed him for a collection of religious articles, he was initially dubious. When he looked over the proofs, all written at different times for different audiences, all random, imprecise and to some extent self-contradictory, he asked for time to revise and prune before publication. The publishers, and in particular Lady Collins, resisted; she contended that the strength of the book lay in its honest expression of doubt, its hesitance and uncertainty, and that to revise would be to falsify his own mental state. So, to fairly modest expectations on the part of author and publisher, the book appeared in 1969 as *Jesus Rediscovered*. It immediately became that rare phenomenon of publishing—a religious bestseller, running through (to date) fifteen reprintings and several hundred thousand copies.

"When a man writes a book to prove the existence of God, we know at once that he must seriously have doubted it, otherwise why should he trouble to write about it at all? Those things we know we never doubt."[36] So Muggeridge wrote at the age of twenty-three. *Jesus Rediscovered*, written in his sixties, did not conceal or minimize his lifelong doubts, but provided convincing evidence that they were finally subdued, if not entirely eradicated, and that thenceforth he saw his role essentially as a Christian propagandist. "I know that Christianity is true, I believe it. I would venture to put my own interpretation on some of its aspects, but essentially it's true. I propose through my remaining years to attempt to live by it and for it. In so far as I am able to communicate with my fellows, it is what I will communicate to them."[37] Muggeridge has stuck by this, although refusing to align himself with any particular denomination or church, thereby remaining true to Kingsmill's dictum that the kingdom of heaven must be sought and reached alone.

Whatever rejoicing may have been in heaven over a sinner who repents, there was none in the institutional church. In fact, the most withering criticism of *Jesus Rediscovered* came from ecclesiastical, not secular, quarters. "The Jesus he has rediscovered," one theologian sniffed, "is not one I want to follow."[38] Another claimed, with some justice, that ". . . the person who is rediscovered in this book is not Jesus of Nazareth but another side of Malcolm Muggeridge."[39] By now Muggeridge was pretty well inured to this sort of thing; when he resigned as rector of Edinburgh University, the Roman Catholic chaplain wrote to him; "The plain fact is that we do not find elderly journalists with a gift of invective useful allies in presenting Christian standards."

The antipathy was mutual. The institutional church, Muggeridge wrote, ". . . with its crazed clergy, empty churches and total doctrinal confusion"[40] was one of the major stumbling blocks he had to overcome, or more accurately ignore, when he came to declare his Christian allegiance. When he was young he had felt nothing but contempt for what he called "broadminded Bishops—their minds broad because all has gone into surface and none into depth."[41] And it was close contact with the institutional church and its emissaries in India that had initially turned him away from Christianity. With the church now in what he considered its final abject decrepitude, it held nothing to lure him back. It was over this matter that he and Alec Vidler differed; Vidler considered Muggeridge's attitude to the church ". . . rather silly—not that his sweeping dismissals have no warrant, but he never seems to have realized the need or possibility of a church reborn."[42]

Given his attitude to the church and clergy, it is amusing to read a news story every so often that Malcolm Muggeridge has just, or is just about to, join the church. The particular denomination varies with the story, but the Roman Catholic church seems to be most often favored. In the highly unlikely event he were ever to join, this might well be where he would wash up because of its internationalism, its appeal to very poor and simple people, and its valiant rearguard stand against modernity. If he did, parallels with G. K. Chesterton would undoubtedly be drawn, and that alone might keep him out. In any case, whatever inclination he may have had in the direction of Rome has been extinguished since Vatican II when, as he considers, the Roman Catholic church set itself upon the same disastrous course as the Protestant churches are pursuing and must inevitably finish up in the same way: "They'll have the same empty churches presided over by the same buffoons."[43]

It is not that he fails to appreciate the historic importance of the church in keeping Christianity alive; he once wrote ". . . a church is more important to society than the teachings of Christ. How silly, and how characteristic of the times, is the idea that truth is to be got by going back to, say, the Sermon on the Mount, or leaving out of account the historical fact of the Church, as though it were a sort of later parasitic growth."[44] But realizing its historical contribution to the survival of Christianity is one thing, joining it another. Temperamentally, Muggeridge is a nonjoiner, a freebooter who owes allegiance to no institution, ideology, party, or denomination. In any case, the church, like the society around it—indeed Western civilization itself—he considers moribund. Like Simone Weil (whose writings have influenced his views), it is safe to predict that he will remain outside, his destiny to be the bell which tolls to bring others to church. "I know perfectly well that, however much I may long for it to be otherwise, the bell does not ring for me."[45]

Few have tried harder to persuade him to modify his attitude to the church than Mother Teresa of Calcutta, who Muggeridge first met when he was asked to do a half-hour television interview with her shortly before *Jesus Rediscovered* appeared. Prior to this, he had never heard of her. The interview itself was unexceptional, so much so that there was some question whether it would be used. However, it was shown without fanfare on a Sunday night. The response was overwhelming. Although no appeal for funds had been made, letters containing cash, checks, money orders, even securities, poured in from all sorts and conditions of people, some letters with a single pound note, one containing three thousand pounds. Altogether some twenty-five thousand pounds found its way to Mother Teresa's work from this single interview. "All of the letters said approximately the same thing—this woman spoke to me as no one ever has, and I feel I must help her."[46]

This was no less Muggeridge's attitude, and a year later he arranged to take a BBC camera crew to Calcutta to make a film about her work. Various exigencies meant that they had only five days to shoot a one-hour film—an assignment to which six to twelve weeks would normally be allotted. Although initially dubious about it, Mother Teresa finally gave her full cooperation on the characteristic condition that filming must not be allowed to disrupt either the worship or work of the sisters.

When the crew came to film in the Home for Dying Destitute (formerly a temple to the Hindu god Kali), their cameraman, Ken Macmillan, felt that it was futile since the light from the two small windows high up in the walls was totally inadequate. In the end he was persuaded to have a go. By any natural explanation this part of the film should have been a failure; in fact, as anyone who has seen the film will attest, it is bathed in a beautiful, lambent illumination that is less light than a glow that seems (dare one say it?) not quite earthly. How to account for this? "Ken has all along insisted that, technically speaking, the result is impossible. To prove the point on his next filming expedition—to the Middle East—he used some of the same stock in a similarly poor light, with completely negative results. He offers no explanation, but just shrugs and agrees that it happened."[47] Never a man for understatement or qualification, Muggeridge calls it a miracle: "I am personally persuaded that Ken recorded the first authentic photographic miracle."[48] As for the producer, Peter Chafer (incidentally an agnostic), he will say only: "The whole of my television life with Muggeridge has been a series of miracles and bizarre, inconceivable happenings."[49]

With the filming completed, Muggeridge returned to England and shortly afterwards Mother Teresa wrote to him: "I can't tell you how big a sacrifice it was to accept the making of a film—but I am glad now that I did so because it has brought us all closer to God." He had not seen the as yet unedited and untitled film. "In your own way," her letter concluded, "try to make the world conscious that it is never too late to do something beautiful for God."[50]

The film and subsequent book *Something Beautiful for God* had an impact that is difficult to measure in purely quantitative terms. Prints of the film have been shown for fund raising and devotional purposes around the world. Sir Kenneth Clark, whose own *Civilization* series was to earn high acclaim, wrote that he considered the film ". . . the most moving and beautiful thing ever put on television."[51] Muggeridge donated all royalties from the sale of the book to Mother Teresa. A considerable number of novitiates now with the Missionaries of Charity first heard of the work through the film or book. As for the effect of Mother Teresa on Muggeridge, she demonstrated Christianity in practical application, seeing in every suffering man, woman, and child the image of her suffering Savior. He wrote of her: "It will be for posterity to decide whether she is a saint. I only say of her that in a dark time she is a burning and a shining light; in a cruel time, a living embodiment of Christ's gospel of love; in a Godless time, the Word dwelling among us, full of grace and truth. For this, all who have the inestimable privilege of knowing her, of knowing of her, must be eternally grateful."[52]

All of Muggeridge's books since *Jesus Rediscovered* have been on religious themes; with Alec Vidler he retraced the missionary journeys of Saint Paul (*Paul, Envoy Extraordinary*); he wrote what was, to some people's surprise, a highly orthodox account of the life of Christ (*Jesus, the Man Who Lives*); short studies of the saints and mystics who had most influenced his thinking—and an eclectic group they are: Saint Augustine, Pascal, Kirkegaard, William Blake, Tolstoy, and Bonhoeffer (*A Third Testament*); a baleful critique of television (*Christ and the Media*); and, in collaboration with Alan Thornhill, a play about euthanasia (which he calls ". . . the next great moral issue of our time") called *Sentences to Life*, which ran in 1978 at the Westminster Theatre in London. It is fair to say that each of these gives evidence of the sincerity of his faith, while managing to avoid the twin pitfalls of religious writing, unctuousness and spiritual exhibitionism.

With time everything and everyone has a tendency to become respectable. Today's runaway bride is tomorrow's pillar of the PTA. Although not yet in danger of any place on the Queen's Honours List, Muggeridge has become increasingly respectable, a process much accelerated of late by his fervent espousal of an evermore orthodox, even evangelical, brand of Christianity. In recent years his name has become associated with moralistic crusades like the Festival of Light, Pro-Life, and Lord Longford's inquiry into pornography. He is now often incongruously allied with religious groups who share his conclusions but are light years away from understanding the long and tortuous process by which he reached them; nor, in fact, do many of them have much real grasp of what he is driving at now. When he questions the possibility of communicating truth on television, they answer that there should be more Christians on it; when he contends that the decline and imminent collapse of Western civilization, what used to be called Christendom, is attributable to a death wish at the heart of liberalism, they promote liberal bromides as effective antidotes; when he talks of a civilization guttering out, they scurry for the Book of Revelation and look for the skys to unfurl like a scroll. It is his own fault. He has aligned himself with groups whose commitment is to collective action, which, as he knows, cannot remedy individual ills.

Even the pornography inquiry of his friend, Lord Longford, accomplished little to stem the tide of pornography but much to ridicule those engaged in it. There are few spectacles more intrinsically absurd than politicians whipping themselves into a lather over moral questions; and Lord Longford, though much else besides, *is* a politician. Admittedly, this was what Muggeridge would call "an imperfect sympathy" from the beginning, undertaken mainly out of friendship. In 1958 he wrote: "Pornography is a relatively simple and harmless importation. In a fatuous, infantile sort of way, it stirs up amiability—which exists abundantly anyway."[53] Of course pornography has become more explicit, perverse, and dehumanizing, to say nothing of more prevalent, since he wrote those words. Even so, as a lifelong opponent of censorship, his real objection to it was aesthetic rather than moral. And aesthetic considerations are an uncertain and dangerous foundation on which to advocate censorship. Muggeridge wrote the chapter on broadcasting in the Longford Report (and a confused, hyperbolic, and unusually ineffective piece of writing it is) and sounded all the expected notes of righteous indignation. It seems likely, though, that he was nearer the mark a few years earlier when he summed up such objection as he had to pornography in one droll sentence: "Its avowed purpose is to excite sexual desire which, I should have thought, is unnecessary in the case of the young, inconvenient in the case of the middle-aged, and unseemly in the case of the old."

In his sixties the manic-depressive moods of his early years, so inclined to melancholy and morbidity, finally yielded to an almost complacent serenity. His lifelong pilgrimage in quest of faith, the one thing he seems always to have needed, had found a sanctuary, if not a final destination. He could now take the world for granted, because he had learned to see beyond the world, inclined neither to rage with impotent fury at its injustice nor to delude himself with unrealizable hopes for its betterment. Like a gargoyle on a cathedral, he positioned himself where he could grin down on the antics of a world gone mad or gaze up to where the steeple pointed the way to God. It was the perch he had sought all his life.

·14·
A KIND of GENIUS

I write and write and write—I don't know quite why; and hope that someday something might come of it. I know there is a kind of genius in some of my work. Anyway I stand or fall by it. I mean there will be nothing else in my life besides.

Malcolm Muggeridge to Alec Vidler, January 30, 1928

* * *

If there is a single theme running through all of Muggeridge's writing, fiction and nonfiction, in early years and late, in moments of exultation and periods of despair, as evident in his private diaries and journals as in what he wrote for publication, it is the idea of living in the twilight of a spent civilization. In 1948 he put it this way: "Obviously we belong to a civilization that is guttering out, but we have the advantage of knowing that this has happened many times before and would inevitably happen many times again. It was just that by chance we were born at such an epoch. Question was whether life in the circumstances could give any satisfaction. In my opinion, unquestionably it could. Therefore undue despair was as mistaken an attitude as self-deception, though of course there was always a certain sadness in times of twilight."[1] Though often accused of incorrigible pessimism, self-evidently this statement is not pessimistic. He once summed up his outlook as "tactical pessimism and strategic optimism."[2]

Apocalyptic visions and dire prophecies are not uncommon symptoms of growing old, but in his case it was no latter-day development. This notion of living in a civilization nearing expiry can be found in his earliest letters and stories, although it became a predominant theme coloring his view of all issues—social, political, and religious—in the thirties.

The church, as he sees it, is not immune from this collapse; rather it is an important factor in it. By running with the tide, by transforming a transcendental faith into a charter on racial discrimination, poverty, better housing, and the United Nations, by bending the knee before the age's false gods—progress and the pursuit of happiness—the church hastens its own demise and Christendom's. "I have a pessimistic view of the future of the church," he wrote in *Jesus Rediscovered*, "because it seems to me that many of its leaders have, of their own accord, allied themselves with the forces of the world, and that is the one disastrous thing they can do."

Either one shares this view that Western civilization is terminally ill or one considers it ludicrous. There is very little middle ground. The odd thing is that both sides draw their conclusions from much the same evidence. Those of Pollyannic disposition derive comfort from precisely those developments that Muggeridge considers the most obvious external manifestations of the inner malaise, or death wish, eating away like a malignant cancer at the innards of Western civilization; such things as legalized contraception and abortion, drug taking, universal education, and the brave new world of genetic engineering. Trying to resolve this particular impasse by discussion or argument is as futile as a debate about the colors of a rainbow with someone who is color-blind. Some honestly see it one way, others another.

If Muggeridge is right about the collapse of Christendom, what lies ahead? On this question, he will not be drawn except to express a vague expectation that it will be some form of collectivized, authoritarian, and totally secular order. Whether of the right or left, and what precise ideological or political form it may take, he leaves to others to guess. Nor does he profess to know the imminence of a final collapse; in 1949 he wrote: "Western society is obviously in a state of dissolution, and it's just a question of how long the process will continue, and whether some chance development may affect its duration and course."[3]

What has happened since then has shortened the duration without altering the course. Writing in 1949, he did not foresee the kind of exponential increase in urban crime that would make people fear to leave their homes nor that essential public services like hospitals, schools, and fire protection would be paralyzed by what is called "industrial action," nor that small bands of anarchic terrorists would be permitted to hold states to ransom. On the international stage, he would not have guessed that in the final years of the seventies the West would stand by and watch Cuban troops invade Angola and Ethiopia, Communist coups occur in Afghanistan, South Yemen, and Cambodia, an ally unseated in Iran, and the mighty American army creep ignominiously out of South Vietnam under cover of rhetoric about "peace with honor," which made Munich seem honorable by comparison. The collapse he foresaw; the abject speed of it has surprised him.

It was for similarly gloomy reflections that the prophet Jeremiah got himself thrown down a well. While Muggeridge has so far been spared this fate (although he might be rather pleased if it happened), he has often been called a prophet, particularly in recent years. Cardinal Manning of Los Angeles referred to him as "the prophet of the twentieth century," while John Stott wrote: "I would like to suggest to you that we should regard Malcolm Muggeridge as a true prophet of the twentieth century. . . .While Christian civilization seems to be crumbling around us in the West, and there is an urgent need for Christian leadership, Malcolm Muggeridge is again and again a voice crying in the wilderness."[4] To both men Muggeridge replied in identical terms, adapting the words of Amos: "I was no prophet, neither was I a prophet's son; I was a journalist, a gatherer of news stories, and the Lord took me as I sat at my typewriter."

Is Muggeridge a major prophet or a minor bore? Those who incline to the latter view—and there are many, particularly in his own country—must somehow account for the reliability and veracity of his insights in the past: on the collapse of the British Empire in the twenties; on Soviet communism, the League of Nations, and the inevitability of war in the thirties; about a renaissance of Russian literature arising from the bowels of the Gulag Archipelago; about the schism between Russia and China, with China increasingly looking to the United States; about the decadence of materialism and the pernicious effects of television; and on and on. Muggeridge himself has never claimed to be any sort of prophet or seer; in fact, he wrote: "I dislike making prophecies; it is risky and may seem presumptuous."[5] Even so, it is against such a track record that one must ponder his most consistent prophecy, in a sense the one underlying all the others, that we are now living in the twilight of a spent civilization.

What is it about him that accounts for his prophetic instincts? First of all, a prophet must be detached to some degree, perhaps even alienated, from his time. Someone caught up in the web of events, in the shifting loyalties and enthusiasms of the moment, is unlikely to be able to see where it is all leading. Muggeridge's earliest recollection is of feeling a stranger in a strange land, of being an observer rather than a participant. Throughout his writing his favorite metaphors are those of the outsider: The man estranged from his time, the actor who has learned the wrong lines, the pilgrim, the castaway, the voyeur who peeps through the keyhole at the antics of the power maniacs. This quality of detachment makes him an unreliable recruit for any political cause, but a perceptive critic of the drift of events and their consequences.

Also a prophet must speak from a firm base, from a set of more or less absolute values to which he is committed. This gives his pronouncements a stridency, a shrill, sometimes grating intolerance but also the ring of conviction. All his life Muggeridge has had such values. What are they? A belief that life is creative, benignly intended and ultimately fulfills a purpose; that the only point in living is to strive to understand that purpose; that the nearest paradigm for understanding is through art, literature, and drama, not science; that the drama of life is played out in individual souls not in collectivities; that good and evil exist like positive and negative conductors, and the current of life flows between them; that fantasy, however alluring it may seem, in the end palls and sickens, and only reality satisfies; that, imprisoned in flesh and mortality, men may yet aspire to apprehend spirit and immortality, even though only dimly and fitfully.

A prophet must be willing to incur opprobrium and scorn, most often dropped from ivory towers on those who stand against what passes for being contemporary progressive thought. Academics vie with politicians in insisting that this is the most enlightened and humane century in history. What with equality, universal suffrage, women's liberation, artistic freedom, education, and an ever-expanding gross national product; what with this and that, on and on, and up and up. Has Mr. Muggeridge weighed this against that and, like a *Manchester Guardian* leader, found the truth in the grey area somewhere in between? No, he has not. He has said what he thought without regard for prevailing intellectual fashions. He is content to be called a clown by the scholar and a fool by the worldly wiseman. Actually, clowns and fools are more acutely observant than sociologists, and at least occasionally speak the truth.

Finally, a prophet needs a panoramic view, the ability to see interconnections between seemingly disparate events. He must be capable of discerning a pattern in what to other eyes may appear to be random occurrences, as a conductor brings out the harmony in otherwise random notes. Anyone can talk a lot about the collapse of civilization, but for most of us the exigencies of life require that we act on the assumption that tomorrow will be much like today. We are like the zealot who predicted the end of the world but took the precaution on the appointed day of leaving a note for the milkman: "Two quarts tomorrow, please." For the last two decades of his life, Muggeridge has been truly independent, owing allegiance to no employer, financier, ideology, political party, creed, or church. He has been free to sit back and assess the world's prospects without hope of advancement or fear of censure. He has tried to understand the *Zeitgeist*, the spirit of the age, what it is and where it is leading. He does not like what he sees, and he has had the courage and the ability to say so.

This does not make him dreary or gloomy. On the contrary, he overflows with witty talk and laughter; he is generous by disposition, a genial man with a tremendous, infectious enthusiasm for living, all of which belies his too frequent protestations about the joy that the prospect of death gives him. Anyway, he has gone on for so long about the imminence of his own death—without any evident diminution of his truculent vigor and energy—that this line has worn a bit thin. Auberon Waugh once began a mock obituary: "Many people will have been saddened to learn of the sudden death of Malcolm Muggeridge at the age of 150."[6]

His personal life follows a simple, disciplined routine. He rises between four and five A.M., makes tea, and reads a bit. Then he gets up, does a series of bending and stretching and deep breathing exercises, then goes for a walk or starts work. Out of the window or out walking, he watches the day begin as the first grey patches of cloud give way to sunrise. Then breakfast with Kitty about eight, a look over the papers, and he settles down to work about nine. If he works in his study there are usually interruptions; phone, mail, or callers who quite often turn up unannounced. In the summer months, when the tide of visitors reaches a peak, he usually works over in the Ark, built in 1971, and set a little way off from the house. The Ark has no phone and is entirely self-contained, with a tiny kitchen to make the ever present pot of tea, a fireplace at one end, a large oak writing desk in the center, and bookcases along one wall from the top of which peer down death masks of Blaise Pascal and William Blake. The other wall consists of double-glazed windows to catch the afternoon sun. After a light lunch of cheese, bread, and fruit, he will read, perhaps have a nap or work in the garden. By mid-afternoon he and Kitty are invariably off for a walk together, the length varying according to mood and the fickle Sussex climate; in foul weather, a short one, perhaps a mile or two; on a fair day any of several routes variously named "Australia," "Poppinghole Lane," "the long walk," etc. A particular favorite takes them across the hop fields and up the hillside where the sheep graze, over the rickety stile that leads into the apple orchard, along the crest of the hill to the dead oak tree struck by lightning, over another stile this one sturdy, and into Deadman's Wood where the path turns leisurely in the direction of home. Tea when they get back, then some gardening or more work. At dusk he is usually sitting by a window, looking out as the stillness descends. "It is a great joy to see each day's first and last light."[7] After dinner, about eight Kitty usually reads aloud from some perennial favorite like *Pilgrim's Progress, Don Quixote,* Boswell or Gibbon, or often Cranmer's *Book of Common Prayer.* Then he sets up a folding table and locks himself in the grim combat of patience. The concentration with which he plays the cards (with occasional mutterings—"It's not going to work out"—addressed to no one in particular), while Kitty dozes curled up on the sofa, makes an oddly poignant spectacle. They might listen to the evening news on Radio Four before retiring. They have no television; Malcolm tells people: "I've had my aerials removed; it's the moral equivalent of a prostate operation." Like all insomniacs, he keeps a small bedside library within reaching distance; not much, a set of biblical commentaries, Simone Weil, *The Cloud of Unknowing,* and Hugh Kingsmill's anthology of English literature *The High Hill of the Muses.*

He and Kitty are in their mid-seventies. They will be buried in Whatlington Cemetery in the graveyard just above the Mill House where they lived in the thirties. The plot they have chosen is next to H. T. Muggeridge's on a slope overlooking the rolling Sussex countryside. Tombstone? Inscription? "I leave that to others. I like to think one of our sons would put something pleasant up." If pressed about an epitaph, he will admit that "He used words well" would please him.

Assuming that there is a headstone and that the sleeper beneath does not suddenly stir, kick it over, and laugh and laugh, would this be an appropriate inscription? Does it fit? This is always a difficult question in respect to a living author. One cannot anticipate future books and one lacks much perspective on past ones. Also, literary assessments are notoriously subjective, and the prestige of an author is liable to rise and fall like a deranged barometer, particularly after his death. Even so, one or two objective factual points can be made. When *In A Valley of This Restless Mind* was reissued in 1978, it won greater acclaim and more than twenty times the number of readers as when it was first published in 1938. So that book (which may be his best) has stood up well and continues to be read forty years after it was written. *Winter in Moscow,* published in 1932, circulated for years in *samizdhat* in the Soviet Union and may, for all one knows, circulate there still. *The Thirties,* published in 1940, has scarcely been out of print since, and remains the most piquant and lively social history of that bizarre decade. And what of his memoirs *Chronicles of Wasted Time?* These volumes provide an inimitable account of the major events and personalities of our century, as well as a record of a questing, troubled mind. It is doubtful if they will ever be more than a minority taste, but for that minority they are likely to continue to be read.

But perhaps this is the wrong approach; perhaps the point is what effect, what impact, an author and his books have had? Did his writing change or influence people's lives? *Jesus Rediscovered* certainly did, as the thousands of letters he has received about it most movingly attest. His writings about the Soviet Union—not just *Winter in Moscow* but also the articles for which he was called a reactionary and a liar—opened eyes not immutably blinded by ideology to the truth about Stalinism. *Something Beautiful for God* made Mother Teresa and her work known around the world.

In fact, though, it is neither the number of readers, nor the actual effect of books, that determines an author's literary reputation. Instead, it is the judgment of a relatively small clique of critics and dons whose cardinal precept usually seems to be: What did he say about my books? This is what led Dr. Johnson to remark, "The reciprocal civility of authors is one of the most risible scenes in the farce of life." Here Muggeridge's reputation is in trouble for he has not played the game, or, as his friend in the thirties put it, he has not licked the right boots. He has been a lone wolf snarling and snapping at those whose favors make or break literary reputations. It would be in error, in fact ludicrous, to convey the impression that he regrets or worries about this. Muggeridge has always cared little enough for the opinions of critics. He wants to be remembered as one who used words well, but he is prepared to look beyond the pages of the *Times Literary Supplement* and the English department syllabus, beyond the critical matadors he has so often gored, to a larger audience of readers, readers of journalism as well as of books, and take his chances on posterity.

Honesty, courage, and humor are the sources of his kind of genius, and these qualities have a way of surviving when much that is thought to be solid or avant garde has been forgotten or is remembered only as foolishness. At the age of twenty-three, he wrote to his father. "I will fight out the struggles of life on paper, and whether the world cares a button about reading the words in which I struggle doesn't worry me in the slightest. If my words are sincere, true words, hot from my soul, they will live; if not it is best that they should die. All that matters is that one have tried."[8]

NOTES

CHAPTER 1.

1. Malcolm Muggeridge, *Chronicles of Wasted Time: The Green Stick* (London: Collins, 1972), p. 51.
2. Henry Thomas Muggeridge to Alec R. Vidler, November 11, 1926.
3. Muggeridge, *The Green Stick*, p. 32.
4. Canon T. E. Edmond to M. Muggeridge, November 9, 1970.
5. M. Muggeridge to Vidler, March 15, 1921.
6. Alwaye Union Christian College Magazine (March 1926).
7. Muggeridge, *The Green Stick*, p. 16.
8. *Time* Magazine, January 6, 1967.
9. *The Spectator*, May 13, 1960.
10. *Woman's Mirror*, February 19, 1966.
11. "A Socialist Childhood," *BBC 1*, October 13, 1966.
12. Muggeridge, *The Green Stick*, p. 12.
13. Ibid., pp. 13–14.
14. Diary of Malcolm Muggeridge, December 13, 1936.
15. *The New Statesman*, August 27, 1955.
16. Muggeridge, *The Green Stick*, p. 58.
17. Papers of Henry Thomas Muggeridge.
18. Muggeridge, *The Green Stick*, p. 73.
19. M. Muggeridge to Vidler, July 1921.
20. Muggeridge, *The Green Stick*, p. 74.

CHAPTER 2.

1. M. Muggeridge to Vidler, August 22, 1922.
2. "An Elderly Schoolteacher," *The New Statesman*, December 1, 1928.
3. Malcolm Muggeridge, *A Twentieth Century Testimony* (Nashville: Thomas Nelson; London: Collins, 1978).
4. M. Muggeridge to Vidler, July 1921.
5. Alec R. Vidler, *Scenes From A Clerical Life* (London: Collins, 1978), p.39.
6. Ibid., p. 39.

7. M. Muggeridge to Vidler, August 1921.
8. M. Muggeridge to Vidler, September 21, 1925.
9. M. Muggeridge to Vidler, November 1922.
10. M. Muggeridge to H. T. Muggeridge, October 19, 1925.
11. M. Muggeridge to Vidler, November 5, 1923.
12. M. Muggeridge to H. T. Muggeridge, October 19, 1925.
13. M. Muggeridge to Vidler, December 19, 1923.
14. Muggeridge, *The Green Stick*, p. 79.
15. Diary, undated.
16. M. Muggeridge to Vidler, May 23, 1924.
17. Vidler to M. Muggeridge, June 12, 1924.
18. Muggeridge, *The Green Stick*, p. 93.

CHAPTER 3.

1. M. Muggeridge to Vidler, December 1924.
2. M. Muggeridge to Vidler, April 27, 1925.
3. M. Muggeridge to Vidler, January 22, 1925.
4. M. Muggeridge to Vidler, March 4, 1924.
5. Editorial, Alwaye Union Christian College Magazine (August 1925).
6. Ibid.
7. Alwaye Union Christian College Magazine (March 1926).
8. Diary, undated.
9. M. Muggeridge to H. T. Muggeridge, undated.
10. Bernard Levin, *Pendulum Years: Britain in the Sixties* (London: Cape, 1970); in the United States, *Run It Down The Flagpole: Britain In The Sixties* (New York: Atheneum, 1971), p. 98.
11. Alwaye Union Christian College Magazine (August 1925).
12. "Why I am not a Pacifist," *Time and Tide*, November 28, 1936.
13. Muggeridge, *The Green Stick*, p. 111.
14. *Calcutta Guardian*, November 4, 1926.
15. M. Muggeridge to Vidler, February 21, 1925.
16. Papers of Malcolm Muggeridge.
17. M. Muggeridge to H. T. Muggeridge, October 6, 1925.
18. Diary.
19. M. Muggeridge to Vidler, December 20, 1925.
20. M. Muggeridge to H. T. Muggeridge, August 25, 1925.
21. M. Muggeridge to H. T. Muggeridge, September 19, 1925.
22. M. Muggeridge to Vidler, February 2, 1926.
23. M. Muggeridge to H. T. Muggeridge, October 10, 1926.
24. Diary.
25. H. T. Muggeridge to Vidler, November 4, 1926.

CHAPTER 4.

1. "A Socialist Father," papers of M. Muggeridge.
2. M. Muggeridge to Vidler, March 14, 1927.
3. Papers of M. Muggeridge.

4. Malcolm Muggeridge, *Something Beautiful for God* (London: Collins, 1971), p. 138.
5. Muggeridge, *The Green Stick*, p. 135.
6. M. Muggeridge to Vidler, November 14, 1925.
7. Muggeridge, *The Green Stick*, p. 140.
8. Ibid., p. 142.
9. Malcolm Muggeridge, "The Bewildered Soul," introductory memoir, unpublished.
10. M. Muggeridge to Vidler, October 27, 1927.
11. M. Muggeridge to Vidler, January 5, 1928,
12. Ibid.
13. "Subject Peoples," *Young Men of India* (October 1928).
14. M. Muggeridge to Vidler, April 13, 1928.
15. Muggeridge, *The Green Stick*, p. 153.
16. "Egypt Then and Now," BBC Interview, September 7, 1966.
17. M. Muggeridge to Vidler, November 13, 1928.
18. Muggeridge, *The Green Stick*, p. 161.
19. Ibid., p. 162.
20. "A Socialist Father," papers of M. Muggeridge.
21. Kingsley Martin, *Editor* (London: Hutchinson, 1968), p. 2.
22. *Hansard*, vol. 237, no. 110, March 26, 1930, p. 556.
23. Diary, November 9, 1934.
24. Muggeridge, *The Green Stick*, p. 202.
25. Malcolm Muggeridge and Hesketh Pearson, *About Kingsmill* (London: Methuen, 1951), pp. 2-4.
26. *The Evening Standard*, November 26, 1931.
27. Muggeridge, *The Green Stick*, p. 177.
28. David Ayerest, *The Guardian: Biography of a Newspaper* (London: Collins, 1971), p. 471.
29. Malcolm Muggeridge, "Picture Palace" (1934, unpublished), p. 170.

CHAPTER 5.

1. Diary, September 16, 1932.
2. Dispatch, March 27, 1933.
3. Diary, October 14, 1932.
4. Muggeridge, *The Green Stick*, p. 230.
5. "Many Winters Ago In Moscow," *Encounter* (March 1958), p. 35.
6. *The Daily Telegraph*, April 17, 1933.
7. M. Muggeridge to H. T. Muggeridge, August 10, 1926.
8. Conversation with Alec R. Vidler, September 12, 1978.
9. *The Listener*, October 3, 1968.
10. Malcolm Muggeridge, *Winter In Moscow* (London: Eyre and Spottiswoode, 1934), p. 207.
11. *The Listener*, October 3, 1968.
12. *The New Statesman*, July 2, 1965.
13. Muggeridge, *The Green Stick*, p. 256.
14. Ibid., p. 257.
15. Muggeridge, *Winter In Moscow*, pp. 244-45.
16. Muggeridge, *The Green Stick*, p. 258.

17. *The Manchester Guardian,* January 1, 1933, and *The Economist,* January 5, 1933.
18. *The Manchester Guardian,* February 1933.
19. *The Manchester Guardian,* February 26, 1933.
20. *The Manchester Guardian,* March 28, 1933.
21. *Encounter* (May 1974), pp. 84–85.
22. Ayerest, *The Guardian,* p. 512.
23. Muggeridge, *Winter In Moscow,* pp. 248-49.
24. M. Muggeridge to W. P. Crozier, quoted in Ayerest, *The Guardian,* p. 513.
25. *The Morning Post,* June 6, 1933.
26. Martin, *Editor,* p. 73.
27. Kitty Muggeridge and Ruth Adam, *Beatrice Webb, A Life* (London: Secker and Warburg, 1967), p. 243.
28. R. Ellis Roberts in *Time and Tide.*
29. "To Friends of The Soviet Union," *English Review* (January 1934).
30. "Winter In Moscow," BBC Script.
31. Malcolm Muggeridge, *Things Past,* Ian Hunter, ed. (London: Collins and New York: William Morrow, 1978), p. 249.
32. Diary, November 17, 1934.
33. "Men and Books," *Time and Tide,* July 17, 1937.

CHAPTER 6.

1. Diary, August 18, 1933.
2. Diary, August 19, 1933.
3. M. Muggeridge to H. T. Muggeridge, October 31, 1925.
4. Diary, September 20, 1933; and October 10, 1933.
5. Diary, October 10, 1933.
6. Diary, September 21, 1933.
7. Muggeridge, "Picture Palace," p. 29
8. *Time and Tide,* January 14, 1939.
9. Diary, October 10 and 11, 1933.
10. Diary, October 13, 1933.
11. Diary, December 2, 1933.
12. Diary, December 4, 1933.
13. Muggeridge and Pearson, *About Kingsmill,* p. 29.
14. *Nineteenth Century and After* (1934).
15. Diary, February 2, 1934.
16. Diary, September 25, 1934.
17. M. Muggeridge to Vidler, September 30, 1934.
18. Malcolm Muggeridge, *Chronicles of Wasted Time: The Infernal Grove* (London: Collins, 1973), p. 20.
19. Diary, November 21, 1934.
20. Diary, November 28, 1934.
21. Diary, October 3, 1934.
22. Diary, October 13, 1934.
23. Ibid.
24. Diary, October 15, 1934.
25. Diary, October 19, 1934.

26. Diary, October 13, 1934.
27. Muggeridge, *The Infernal Grove*, p. 27.
28. Diary, October 17, 1934.
29. Diary, October 19, 1934.
30. Diary, October 8, 1934.
31. Muggeridge, "Picture Palace," p. 91.
32. Diary, November 19, 1934.
33. "The Literature of India," *Adam International Review* (1971), p. 11.
34. Diary, October 20, 1934.
35. Diary, January 1, 1935.
36. Diary, February 14, 1935.
37. Diary, February 23, 1935.
38. Diary, March 20, 1935.
39. Diary, March 15, 1935.
40. Muggeridge, *The Infernal Grove*, pp. 41–42.
41. Diary, April 15, 1935.
42. Diary, May 6, 1935.
43. Muggeridge, *The Infernal Grove*, p. 44.
44. Hesketh Pearson to M. Muggeridge, November 6, 1935.
45. Hugh Kingsmill to M. Muggeridge, December 18, 1935.
46. *The Listener*, September 23, 1936.
47. *The Earnest Atheist: A Study of Samuel Butler* (London: Eyre and Spottis-woode, 1936), introduction.
48. George Orwell to M. Muggeridge, December 4, 1948.
49. H. T. Muggeridge to M. Muggeridge, August 27, 1936.
50. Diary, May 6, 1935.
51. Diary, June 10, 1936.

CHAPTER 7.

1. M. Muggeridge to H. T. Muggeridge, August 10, 1926.
2. Diary, September 29, 1935.
3. Muggeridge, *The Infernal Grove*, p. 60.
4. Diary, January 1936.
5. Diary, January 1, 1936.
6. Diary, January 4, 1936.
7. Diary, January 6, 1936.
8. Alec Waugh, *My Brother Evelyn and Other Portraits* (London: Cassell and New York: Farrar, Straus, Giroux, 1967), pp. 94–95.
9. Diary, February 1, 1949.
10. Michael Holroyd, *Hugh Kingsmill: A Critical Biography* (London: The Unicorn Press, 1964), introduction by Malcolm Muggeridge.
11. Diary, January 13, 1936.
12. Muggeridge and Pearson, *About Kingsmill*, pp. 42–44.
13. Muggeridge, *The Infernal Grove*, p. 62.
14. Diary, September 23, 1949.
15. *Time and Tide*, November 28, 1936; July 10 and 17, 1936.
16. *Time and Tide*, November 30, 1935.
17. *Time and Tide*, December 19, 1935.
18. *Time and Tide*, November 30, 1935.

19. Diary, February 3, 1936,
20. *Night and Day,* December 9, 1937.
21. Muggeridge and Pearson, *About Kingsmill,* pp. 71-72.
22. Muggeridge, *The Infernal Grove,* p. 65.
23. Kingsmill to M. Muggeridge, July 3, 1938.
24. Diary, March 11, 1938.
25. Diary, August 23, 1936.
26. Diary, August 30, 1936.
27. Diary, September 29, 1936.
28. Diary, November 26, 1936.
29. *Time and Tide,* February 4, 1939.
30. Diary, December 16, 1936; *Time and Tide,* April 24, 1937.
31. Diary, January 24, 1937.
32. Diary, January 18, 1937.
33. Diary, May 5, 1937.
34. Diary, May 10, 1937.
35. Douglas Jerrold to M. Muggeridge, September 10, 1937.
36. Rupert Hart-Davis to M. Muggeridge, October 25, 1937.
37. Hart-Davis to M. Muggeridge, October 29, 1937.
38. *The Spectator,* May 20, 1938.
39. *Books and Bookmen* (October 1978).
40. Martin Tindall in *Time and Tide.*
41. E. S. Osborne in *The Daily Telegraph.*
42. Beatrice Webb to R. Dobbs, June 14, 1938.
43. Pearson to M. Muggeridge, May 29, 1938.
44. *Forward,* April 30, 1938.
45. *Time and Tide,* May 14, 1938.
46. *Time and Tide,* June 4, 1938.
47. M. Muggeridge to Kitty Muggeridge, October 19, 1943.
48. *Time and Tide,* September 24, 1938.

CHAPTER 8.

1. *Time and Tide,* October 3, 1938.
2. *Time and Tide,* November 28, 1936.
3. *Time and Tide,* October 22, 1938.
4. Diary, September 5, 1939.
5. Diary, September 5, 1939.
6. Muggeridge, *The Infernal Grove,* p. 81.
7. *Newspaper World,* December 9, 1939.
8. *The Observer,* January 29, 1967.
9. *The Daily Telegraph,* September 18, 1947.
10. M. Muggeridge to Kingsmill, November 20, 1940.
11. Muggeridge, *The Infernal Grove,* pp. 91–92.
12. Diary, October 3, 1940.
13. Diary, September 16, 1940.
14. Diary, September 19, 1940.
15. Diary, September 16, 1940.
16. Diary, October 3, 1940.
17. Pasted in diary, January 18, 1950.

18. M. Muggeridge to Field Marshal Montgomery, July 24, 1941.
19. Muggeridge, *The Infernal Grove*, p. 116.
20. M. Muggeridge to K. Muggeridge, undated.
21. M. Muggeridge to K. Muggeridge, undated.
22. M. Muggeridge to K. Muggeridge, May 16, 1941.
23. M. Muggeridge to K. Muggeridge, May 2, 1941.
24. Muggeridge, *The Infernal Grove*, p. 121.
25. M. Muggeridge to K. Muggeridge, April 11, 1942.
26. M. Muggeridge to Kingsmill, May 6, 1942.
27. M. Muggeridge to K. Muggeridge, May 20, 1942.
28. M. Muggeridge to K. Muggeridge, May 23, 1942.
29. M. Muggeridge to K. Muggeridge, July 4, 1942.
30. M. Muggeridge to K. Muggeridge, August 21, 1942.
31. Muggeridge, *The Infernal Grove* p. 154.
32. M. Muggeridge to K. Muggeridge, March 21, 1943.
33. Muggeridge, *The Infernal Grove*, pp. 183–85.
34. Muggeridge, "Picture Palace," pp. 231–32.
35. *The Daily Sketch*, April 14, 1966.
36. Muggeridge, *Infernal Grove*, p. 186.
37. M. Muggeridge to K. Muggeridge, October 7, 1943.
38. M. Muggeridge to K. Muggeridge, November 5, 1943.
39. M. Muggeridge to K. Muggeridge, December 25, 1943.
40. M. Muggeridge to K. Muggeridge, undated.
41. *The New Statesman*, December 10, 1965.
42. Muggeridge, *The Infernal Grove*, p. 211.
43. M. Muggeridge to K. Muggeridge, November 15, 1944.
44. Diary, December 15, 1948.
45. Muggeridge, *The Infernal Grove*, p. 257.
46. Ibid., pp. 288–89.

CHAPTER 9.

1. Diary, April 28, 1945.
2. Diary, May 5, 1945.
3. Diary, May 8, 1945.
4. Diary, May 18, 1945.
5. Diary, June 1, 1945.
6. Diary, undated.
7. Muggeridge, *The Infernal Grove*, pp. 261–62.
8. Malcolm Muggeridge, ed., *Ciano's Diary* (London: William Heinemann, 1947), p. xiii.
9. Malcolm Muggeridge, ed., *Ciano's Diplomatic Papers* (London: Odham's Press, 1948); and *Ciano's Diary 1937–38* (London: Methuen, 1952).
10. Muggeridge, *Ciano's Diplomatic Papers*, introduction, n. 9.
11. M. Muggeridge to K. Muggeridge, April 3, 1946.
12. Ibid.
13. M. Muggeridge to K. Muggeridge, April 10, 1946.
14. M. Muggeridge to K. Muggeridge, April 16, 1946.
15. M. Muggeridge to K. Muggeridge, June 4, 1946.
16. M. Muggeridge to K. Muggeridge, April 21, 1946.

17. M. Muggeridge to Kingsmill, May 12, 1946.
18. Ibid.
19. M. Muggeridge to K. Muggeridge, July 7, 1946.
20. M. Muggeridge to K. Muggeridge, April 24, 1946.
21. M. Muggeridge to K. Muggeridge, July 7, 1946.
22. "Our Own Correspondent," papers of M. Muggeridge.
23. M. Muggeridge to K. Muggeridge, May 21, 1946.
24. "News to Newzak," *Washington Sunday Star*, April 18, 1971.
25. M. Muggeridge to K. Muggeridge, July 1, 1946 and September 30, 1946.
26. Interview with M. Muggeridge.
27. Muggeridge, "News To Newzak."
28. M. Muggeridge to K. Muggeridge, August 3, 1946.
29. M. Muggeridge to K. Muggeridge, September 15, 1946.
30. *Daily Telegraph*, June 11, 1946.
31. Diary, November 2, 1947.
32. Diary, November 12, 1947.
33. Diary, November 12, 1947.
34. Diary, November 13, 1947.
35. Diary, November 18, 1947.
36. *Daily Telegraph*, December 24, 1947.
37. Diary, November 30, 1947.
38. Diary, November 11, 1948.
39. Muggeridge, *The Infernal Grove*, p. 264.
40. Diary, March 25, 1948.
41. Malcolm Muggeridge, *Affairs of the Heart* (London: Hamish Hamilton, 1949), p. 201.
42. *The Tablet*, February 4, 1950.
43. *The Sunday Times*, December 8, 1949.
44. *The Daily Mail*, January 7, 1950.
45. Muggeridge, *Affairs of the Heart*, p. 6.
46. Diary, February 9 and 18, 1948.
47. Diary, March 12, 1948.
48. Diary, February 11, 1948.
49. Diary, February 21, 1948.
50. Diary, November 9, 1948.
51. Diary, March 8, 1948.
52. Diary, August 23, 1950.
53. Diary, July 15, 1950.
54. Diary, July 12, 1950.
55. Diary, July 13, 1950.
56. Diary, December 8, 1950.
57. Diary, July 17, 1950.
58. Diary, July 21, 1950.
59. Diary, August 2, 1950.
60. Diary, July 7, 1950.

CHAPTER 10.

1. Diary, July 23, 1949.
2. Diary, June 17, 1950.

3. Diary, March 23, 1948.
4. Diary, February 25, 1948.
5. Diary, October 11, 1949.
6. Diary, July 6, 1948.
7. Diary, April 17, 1948.
8. Diary, May 12, 1948.
9. Diary, January 20, 1949.
10. Diary, May 7, 1949.
11. Muggeridge and Pearson, *About Kingsmill,* p. 172.
12. M. Muggeride, Introduction to Holroyd, *Hugh Kingsmill,* p. 20.
13. *New English Review* (June 1949), pp. 407-08.
14. Diary, March 26, 1957.
15. Diary, June 15, 1950.
16. Hugh Kingsmill, *The Poisoned Crown* (London: Eyre and Spottiswoode, 1944).
17. Holroyd, *Hugh Kingsmill,* p. 13.
18. Conversation with M. Muggeridge.
19. "George Orwell" in *The English Review,* (March 1950), p. 218.
20. "Orwell: A Reminiscence," *The London Magazine* (September 1963), pp. 41–42.
21. Diary, July 6, 1945.
22. Papers of M. Muggeridge.
23. "Orwell," *World Review* (June 1950), p. 47.
24. Symons, "Orwell: A Reminiscence," pp. 41–42.
25. Orwell to M. Muggeridge, December 4, 1948.
26. Diary, February 19, 1949.
27. Orwell to M. Muggeridge, undated.
28. Diary, December 25, 1949.
29. Diary, January 19, 1950.
30. Diary, January 21, 1950.
31. Malcolm Muggeridge, "The Knight of the Woeful Countenance," in *The World of George Orwell,* ed. Miriam Gross (London: Weidenfeld and Nicholson, 1971), p. 174.
32. Hesketh Pearson, *Hesketh Pearson By Himself* (London: Heinemann's, 1965), p. 314.
33. Pearson to M. Muggeridge, January 16, 1939.
34. Diary, March 15, 1950.
35. Muggeridge and Pearson, *About Kingsmill,* p. 120.
36. Introduction to reissue of Hesketh Pearson, *Gilbert and Sullivan* (London: Macdonald and Janes, 1975).
37. Joyce Pearson to M. Muggeridge, March 9, 1964.
38. Prologue to Memorial Service (written by M. Muggeridge). Papers of M. Muggeridge.
39. *The Times,* April 13, 1964.

CHAPTER 11.

1. Diary, January 1, 1953.
2. Letter of Alan Agnew, November 28, 1952; Papers of M. Muggeridge.
3. Diary, January 1, 1953.

Notes

4. Diary, January 6, 1953.
5. *Newsweek*, April 25, 1956.
6. Interview with Leslie Illingworth, January 10, 1979.
7. Claud Cockburn, *I, Claud* (Harmondsworth: Penguin, 1967), pp. 358-60.
8. Malcolm Muggeridge, *Tread Softly For You Tread on My Jokes* (London: Collins and New York: Simon and Schuster, 1966), p. 15.
9. Diary, February 4, 1953.
10. *Time,* September 14, 1953.
11. *Punch,* August 19, 1953.
12. R.G.G. Price, *A History of Punch* (London: Collins, 1958), p. 319.
13. *Punch,* February 3, 1954.
14. Cockburn, *I, Claud,* p. 366.
15. "Boring for England," in Muggeridge, *Tread Softly,* p. 150.
16. *The New Zealand Herald,* July 15, 1954.
17. M. Muggeridge to Dr. Geoffrey Fisher, February 29, 1956.
18. "In Defence of Bad Taste," *McLean's Magazine,* August 3, 1957.
19. *Time,* October 20, 1953.
20. Overseas Press Club Dinner, May 12, 1953.
21. "My Life With the BBC," *New Statesman,* February 14, 1959.
22. *Time,* November 2, 1953.
23. *Truth,* March 29, 1956.
24. *The Times,* March 27, 1956.
25. John Thompson in *Truth,* March 29, 1956.
26. *The News Chronicle,* April 13, 1956.
27. *The Manchester Guardian,* March 29, 1956.
28. *The Daily Worker,* March 28, 1956.
29. Cockburn, *I, Claud,* pp. 372-73.
30. Diary, April 13, 1957.
31. *The Manchester Guardian,* July 28, 1957.
32. Diary, undated.
33. Diary, undated.
34. Diary, May 12, 1949.
35. Diary, April 1, 1948.
36. Diary, April 1, 1948.
37. Diary, April 4, 1948.
38. George Barnes to M. Muggeridge, June 18, 1948.
39. "My Life With the BBC," *New Statesman,* February 14, 1959.
40. M. Muggeridge to Vidler, February 1, 1927.
41. *Toronto Star,* November 4, 1972.
42. *The People,* October 13, 1957.
43. "Does England Really Need A Queen?" *Saturday Evening Post,* October 19, 1957.
44. *Railway Review,* November 15, 1957.
45. *The Evening Dispatch,* October 10, 1957.
46. *The Manchester Guardian,* October 21, 1957.
47. *World Press News,* December 15, 1957.
48. *The Manchester Guardian,* November 15, 1957.
49. "The Queen and I," *Encounter* (June 1961).
50. M. Muggeridge to Press Council, November 7, 1957.
51. Muggeridge, "The Queen and I."
52. *The Sunday Telegraph,* April 12, 1964.

53. Mary Craig, *Lord Longford* (London: Hodder and Stoughton, 1978), p. 178.

CHAPTER 12.

1. Diary, March 5, 1958.
2. Ibid.
3. Diary, March 6, 1958.
4. Broadcast; Australian Broadcasting Commission, May 4, 1958.
5. *The West Australian*, May 10, 1958.
6. Broadcast; Australian Broadcasting Commission, May 4, 1958.
7. *The West Australian*, May 10, 1958.
8. *The West Australian*, April 21, 1958.
9. *The West Australian*, May 12, 1958.
10. *The South China Morning Post*, June 9, 1958.
11. *The Sunday Pictorial*, June 15, 1958.
12. Diary, June 1, 1958.
13. Diary, June 2 and 3, 1958.
14. Diary, undated
15. Diary, June 1958.
16. Diary, undated.
17. *Toronto Telegram*, July 15, 1958.
18. *The West Australian*, July 30, 1958.
19. Diary, June 28, 1958.
20. *The Sunday Pictorial*, July 13, 1958.
21. *The Sunday Pictorial*, November 11, 1958.
22. *The Sydney Sun Herald*, March 22, 1959.
23. Muggeridge, *Tread Softly*, pp. 133–34.
24. *The Sunday Pictorial*, December 16, 1958.
25. Diary, undated.
26. *The Sunday Pictorial*, June 24, 1959.
27. *The Sunday Pictorial*, January 18, 1959.
28. *The Sunday Pictorial*, March 19, 1960.
29. *The Sunday Pictorial*, May 10, 1959.
30. *The Sunday Pictorial*, February 4, 1958.
31. *The Sunday Pictorial*, April 26, 1959.
32. *The New Statesman*, May 10, 1958.
33. *The Sunday Pictorial*, February 22, 1959.
34. *The Daily Mirror*, February 24, 1959.
35. *The New Statesman*, March 14, 1959.
36. *The Daily Mirror*, February 25, 1959.
37. *The Daily Mirror*, February 27, 1959.
38. *The Daily Mirror*, March 2, 1959.
39. *The Daily Mirror*, March 3, 1959.
40. Diary, October 7, 1960.
41. *The Sunday Pictorial*, March 8, 1959.
42. Diary, April 25, 1950.
43. M. Muggeridge to Charles Wintour, May 4, 1964.
44. Muggeridge, *Tread Softly*, p. 308.
45. M. Muggeridge to H. T. Muggeridge, November 14, 1925.

46. *Time and Tide*, September 12, 1936.
47. *The Observer*, September 4, 1966.
48. *The New Statesman*, September 9, 1966.

CHAPTER 13.

1. M. Muggeridge to H. T. Muggeridge, August 1925.
2. Muggeridge, *Winter In Moscow*, pp. 225–26.
3. *The New Statesman*, March 24, 1978.
4. Diary, November 13, 1934.
5. M. Muggeridge to K. Muggeridge, December 13, 1943.
6. Diary, 1958.
7. Malcolm Muggeridge, *Muggeridge Through The Microphone* (London: BBC Publications, 1967), p. 143.
8. M. Muggeridge to H. T. Muggeridge, October 10, 1925.
9. Muggeridge, *Muggeridge Through The Microphone*, p. 129.
10. M. Muggeridge to K. Muggeridge, June 16, 1946.
11. *The New Republic*, May 6, 1978.
12. Malcolm Muggeridge, *Jesus Rediscovered* (London: Fontana, 1969), p. 169.
13. *The Daily Telegraph*, January 28, 1966.
14. *Time and Tide*, November 19, 1938.
15. BBC Broadcast, October 5, 1965.
16. *What I Believe* (London: Allen and Unwin, 1966), p. 143.
17. *The Observer*, December 19, 1971.
18. *The Daily Herald*, January 11, 1962.
19. Sermon in Great St. Mary's, Cambridge, May 31, 1970.
20. *The New Statesman*, November 11, 1959.
21. Muggeridge, *Muggeridge Through The Microphone*, p. 31.
22. *British Weekly*, September 16, 1965.
23. Malcolm Muggeridge and Alec Vidler, *Paul: Envoy Extraordinary* (London: Collins, 1972), p. 20.
24. Journal of Alec Vidler, February 16, 1969.
25. *The Observer*, August 20, 1967.
26. Ibid.
27. Muggeridge, *Jesus Rediscovered*, p. 88.
28. M. Muggeridge to Jack Muggeridge, November 13, 1966.
29. M. Muggeridge to Brian McClelland, December 7, 1966.
30. Rectorial Address, February 16, 1967.
31. M. Muggeridge to Vidler, December 10, 1925.
32. S.R.C. minutes, December 7, 1967.
33. *Student*, January 11, 1968.
34. Muggeridge, *Jesus Rediscovered*, p. 91.
35. Michael Swann to M. Muggeridge, January 15, 1968.
36. Editorial, Union Christian College Magazine (March 1926).
37. Muggeridge, *Jesus Rediscovered*, p. 177.
38. Harvey Cox in *Saturday Review*, August 30, 1969.
39. Dr. John Gibbs in *The Minneapolis Tribune*, October 19, 1969.
40. Muggeridge, *Jesus Rediscovered*, p. 9.
41. M. Muggeridge to H. T. Muggeridge, June 12, 1926.

42. Journal of Vidler, February 16, 1969.
43. *Man Alive*, CBC Television, January 1, 1970.
44. Diary, November 16, 1934.
45. Muggeridge, *Something Beautiful For God*, p. 56.
46. Ibid., p. 31.
47. Ibid., p. 41.
48. Ibid., p. 44.
49. Interview with Peter Chafer.
50. Mother Teresa to M. Muggeridge, undated.
51. Sir Kenneth Clark to M. Muggeridge, May 5, 1971.
52. Muggeridge, *Something Beautiful for God*, p. 144.
53. *The West Australian*, May 5, 1958.

CHAPTER 14.

1. Diary, April 18, 1948.
2. Diary, April 11, 1959.
3. Diary, January 1, 1949.
4. Malcolm Muggeridge, *Christ and The Media* (London: Hodder and Stoughton, 1977), pp. 121–22.
5. *The Sunday Pictorial*, February 8, 1959.
6. *The Daily Mirror*, May 9, 1960.
7. Diary, April 6, 1961.
8. M. Muggeridge to H. T. Muggeridge, July 19, 1926.

BIBLIOGRAPHY

Muggeridge, Malcolm. *Three Flats*. London: G. P. Putnam's Sons, 1931.
————*Autumnal Face*. London: Putnam, 1931.
————*Winter in Moscow*. London: Eyre and Spottiswoode, 1934.
————*"Picture Palace"* London: Eyre and Spottiswoode, 1934, withdrawn.
————*The Earnest Atheist: A Study of Samuel Butler*. London: Eyre and Spottiswoode, 1936.
————*Brave Old World* (with Hugh Kingsmill). London: Eyre and Spottiswoode, 1936.
————*Next Year's News* (with Hugh Kingsmill). London: Eyre and Spottiswoode, 1938.
————*In A Valley of This Restless Mind*. London: George Routledge and Son, 1938. Reissued London and Cleveland: Collins, 1978.
————*The Thirties*. London: Hamish Hamilton, 1940; reissued London: Collins, 1967.
————*Affairs of the Heart*. London: Hamish Hamilton, 1949.
————*About Kingsmill* (with Hesketh Pearson). London: Methuen, 1951.
————*Tread Softly For You Tread on My Jokes*. London: Collins, 1966; in United States, *The Most of Malcolm Muggeridge*. New York: Simon and Shuster, 1966.
————*London A La Mode* (with Paul Hogarth). London: Studio Vista, 1966.
————*Muggeridge Through the Microphone*. London: BBC Publications, 1967; London: Fontana, 1969.
————*Jesus Rediscovered*. London: Fontana, 1969.
————*Something Beautiful for God*. London: Collins, 1971.
————*Paul: Envoy Extraordinary* (with Alec Vidler). London: Collins, 1972.
————*Chronicles of Wasted Time: volume 1 The Green Stick*. London: Collins, 1972; volume 2 *The Infernal Grove*. London: Collins, 1973.
————*Jesus: The Man Who Lives*. London: Collins, 1975.
————*A Third Testament*. London: Little Brown and Co., 1976.
————*Christ and the Media*. London: Hodder and Stoughton, 1976.
————*Things Past*. London: Collins, 1978.

Bibliography

Malcolm Muggeridge as Editor

————*Ciano's Diary*. London: Heinemann, 1947.
————*Ciano's Diplomatic Papers*. London: Odhams Press, 1948.
————*Ciano's Hidden Diary*. London: E. P. Dutton, 1953.

Additional Biographical Sources

Cockburn, Claud. *I, Claud*. London: Penguin, 1967.
Holroyd, Michael. *Hugh Kingsmill: A Critical Biography*. London: Unicorn Press, 1964.
Ingrams, Richard. *God's Apology: A Chronicle of Three Friends*. London: Andre Deutsch, 1977.
Vidler, Alec. *Scenes From A Clerical Life*. London: Collins, 1977.

INDEX